Work, Consumption and Capitalism

Work, Consumption and Capitalism

Work, Consumption and Capitalism

LYNNE PETTINGER

First published 2016 by
PALGRAVE

Palgrave in the UK is an imprint of Macmillan Publishers Limited, registered in England, company number 785998, of 4 Crinan Street, London, N1 9XW.

Palgrave Macmillan in the US is a division of St Martin's Press LLC, 175 Fifth Avenue, New York, NY 10010.

Palgrave is a global imprint of the above companies and is represented throughout the world.

Palgrave® and Macmillan® are registered trademarks in the United States, the United Kingdom, Europe and other countries.

ISBN 978–1–137–34280–5 hardback
ISBN 978–1–137–34277–5 paperback

This book is printed on paper suitable for recycling and made from fully managed and sustained forest sources. Logging, pulping and manufacturing processes are expected to conform to the environmental regulations of the country of origin.

A catalogue record for this book is available from the British Library.

A catalog record for this book is available from the Library of Congress.

Printed in China

Brian and Carol Pettinger, with thanks.
Gina Duffy, in memory.

Contents

Acknowledgements

Thanks to:
Andrew Goffey
Dawn Lyon
Ewen, Una, Comhnall, Liam and Eoghan Speed
Brian and Carol Pettinger
Gail Pettinger and Stephen Wells
Tejvan Pettinger
Rowena Macauley
Keith and Jackie Hargreaves
Matt Hill

Friends and colleagues at Essex University, especially
Miriam Glucksmann
Mark Harvey
Linsey McGoey
Darren Thiel
Jackie Turton
Robin West
Michael Halewood
Michele Hall
Melissa Tyler

Friends and colleagues at Warwick University, especially
Amy Hinterberger
Maria do Mar Pereira
John Solomos
Carol Wolkowitz

For miscellaneous help, which they may or may not have realised they
    offered
Maria Adamson
Ben Fincham
Tracey Potts and Jane Treglown
Kirsten Forkert
Rebecca Taylor
Tracey Warren
Mark Banks
David Hesmondhalgh
James Scott

List of Tables and Abbreviations

Tables

Abbreviations

ANT	actor-network theory
BGR	branded garment retailer
BRIC	Brazil, Russia, India and China
CCT	consumer culture theory
Cedefop	European Centre for the Development of Vocational Training
CSR	corporate social responsibility
EPOS	electronic point of sale
EU	European Union
FDI	foreign direct investment
FMCG	fast-moving consumer goods
ICT	information and communications technology
ISCO	International Standard Classification of Occupations
ISIC	International Standard Industrial Classification of All Economic Activities
ISW	interactive service work
JIT	just-in-time production
NGO	non-governmental organisation
OECD	Organization for Economic Cooperation and Development
STS	science and technology studies
UN	United Nations
VET	vocational and educational training
ASEAN	Association of Southeast Asian Nations
CAD	computer-aided design
CRM	customer relationship management

HCT	human capital theory
HE	higher education
ILO	International Labour Organization
IMF	International Monetary Fund
LPT	labour process theory
NAFTA	North American Free Trade Agreement
NES	new economic sociology

Chapter 1

Introduction

The production of consumption

This book considers the work of designing, marketing and selling consumer goods, services and experiences and considers how these products are made desirable. I wanted to write this book for a number of reasons. One of the most important ones was to contribute to a comprehensive, extensive and imaginative understanding of work. I believe that work – what it is like for those who do it, how it is organised by employers and how it interacts with other significant dimensions of social life – to be one of the most important topics for study by social scientists. Work affects life chances, is a source of inequality, is a source of pleasure and provides a sense of who we are as people. I consider it impossible to study work as though it existed outside of society, outside of social relations, other economic relations, the sensory and natural world and our understandings of what's right and what's wrong (Pettinger et al., 2006; Strangleman and Warren, 2008: 4). In this book I focus on certain kinds of entwinings, some relationships, as it is not possible to cover all without being superficial. I focus specifically on those which concern consumers, consumption and consumerism (terms that I'll explain in Chapter 3), as we should notice the work that makes consumption, as this helps us to understand both what work is like, and what consumption is like, and provides an insight into how global capitalism operates.

A great deal of the work that produces consumption involves branding: branded goods like a bottle of *Evian*, branded outlets like

1

Subway or a supermarket chain, or branded places like theme parks or even cities (think of New York, 'the city that never sleeps'). Branding is central to how selling occurs; it is the phenomenon that links design to marketing to sales, and so this book will pay a lot of attention to how branding is put into place (whilst recognising that not all consumer products are branded). All the workers, occupations and activities considered in this book are included because they contribute tangibly to the saleability of a consumer product, by adding value, encouraging us, the consumers, to buy or by signalling something about the product that we're interested in.

Different kinds of work are involved in getting a product into our lives, but not all of those forms of work are of interest here. I've followed two principles in deciding what to consider. The first is to distinguish between goods and services made for ordinary consumption and other kinds of goods and services. The market in intermediate goods, goods predominantly bought by states, corporations or financial services, is not considered here. The second is to focus on the forms of work that contribute to sales by adding symbolic value, in particular on those forms of work where the individual has a strong impact on the outcome. Substituting one advertising creative for another means a campaign will change, but substituting one logistics company for another won't influence how desirable a product is, as long as the product arrives in time. It is the specificity of a worker's involvement in the consumption process that makes them of such interest. Table 1.1 is my list of the kinds of occupations and activities that count.

At first glance, these occupations seem diverse. It's easy to guess what some of them involve; others are not so obvious. All of them are real and have been gleaned from published research. Some are highly paid; others are not. What they share is that they make an obvious and explicit contribution to the production of consumption, to selling, to making consumer capitalism happen, and to generating a particular experience of being a consumer. It is this shared engagement in the production of consumption that brings them together in this book under the heading 'commercial work'. Contemporary service-based economies have substantial numbers employed in these occupations, facilitating the consumption of goods, services and leisure experiences of others. In some instances it is possible to find many of these occupations within the same organisation, as in the case of large experience-led corporations like *Disney*. In other cases, specialist organisations (such as branding agencies) provide services for a range of client companies who employ customer-facing staff.

Table 1.1 Commercial occupations

Advertising creative	Advertising director	Bartender
Brand builder	Brand designer	Brand manager
Brand consultant	Brand essence creator	Brand explorer
Brand positioner	Brand president	Brand refresher
Buyer	Call-centre operative	Casting director
Clerk	Communications director	Content developer
Cool hunter	Copywriter	Creative director
Customer experience manager	Customer relations manager	Designer
Dreamweaver	Fashion buyer	Flavourist
Kitchen salesman	Leisure manager	Marketing strategist
Media director	Merchandiser	Model agent
Place marketer	Product designer	Publicity manager
Sales assistant	Sales person	Shopkeeper
Stylist	Ticket agent	Tour guide
Trendspotter	Waiter	Window dresser

Five questions about consumption

Are you wearing denim? There's a strong chance you are: half the population wears denim on any given day (Miller and Woodward, 2011). Thinking through how it is that you came to be wearing the jeans you're wearing is an ideal way to introduce the key themes of *Work, Consumption and Capitalism*, as it reveals the complex and interlinked forms of work that make consumption possible. I have five questions to ask you about your jeans, as a way to introduce the key themes of this book.

Do you have a favourite pair of jeans?

They're yours, you own them and you've shaped them as you've worn them. Perhaps the knees are a little bit baggy and there are a few paler

patches. Consumption refers not just to the act of buying a standardised product like jeans, but to the more personalised practice of
using the product. Denim companies and their brand agencies have
worked hard to teach us that the personalisation of a well-worn pair
of jeans is something worth having. You have a sensory encounter with
these jeans (Candy, 2005): they feel comfortable, not too tight, but
warm. They help you fit in, as they did for Kerry who had been mocked
by schoolmates for wearing a purple jumpsuit. Kerry distanced herself
from being the 'purple image girl' by wearing ordinary blue jeans,
white t-shirt and black blazer (Nenga, 2003: 179).

The symbolic value of jeans matters here. Symbolic values are the
immaterial associations that something has: jeans signal conformity,
but carry the memory of earlier associations with youth rebellion.
How are our personal experiences of consuming goods and services
affected by social position? What work do we do on the things we
own? In Chapter 3, we will ask questions about consumer behaviour,
feeling and experience to understand how individual consumption is
influenced by the networks of relationships that surround us, the social
and cultural milieu in which consumption happens, and the economic
organisation of consumption. In Chapters 6 and 7, we will explicitly
address how commercial work affects individual consumption.

Are your jeans fashionable?

Vintage flares, bootcut, skinny, low-hanging so your underwear shows,
loose and relaxed: at different times these styles count as fashionable
or unfashionable. You may not be bothered about being fashionable
yourself, but you can see the impact of the fashion system on the
consumption practices of those around you, or perhaps you have
watched the film *The Devil Wears Prada* and recall a scene where
fashion magazine editor Miranda explains how the specific colour of
fashion refusenik Andy's cheap cerulean blue jumper originated in
the colour decisions made by high-status fashion designers. What
counts as fashionable emerges through a complex and ongoing mediation process, whereby some styles and items become fashionable and
others lose that status. At some point, someone decides that what was
once a 'cool' denim jacket at the start of the season is not so appealing any more, and puts it on the sale rack (Entwistle, 2006: 318).

Clothing buyers look through, and try on, possible denim ranges in
order to decide which should be stocked in their stores, and where in
the shop they belong – are they 'cult' high fashion jeans, or mainstream ones? The aesthetics of the jeans are central to this judgement

process, with 'the main qualities of selection being their fit on the body and detailing in the fabric – for example, "distressing", "whiskers" (tiny lines around the crotch and knee) and wash – all of which cannot be reproduced faithfully in two-dimensional form' (Entwistle, 2006: 712). Fashion writing in traditional magazines and blogs mediates 'what's cool', tells potential consumers about a new cult brand or style. Design work, marketing, advertising and other kinds of promotion are also involved in mediating what counts as fashionable. How are these decisions made about what should be sold, and on what criteria? Buyers are just one of the occupations that mediate production and consumption and influence what is fashionable, and we will consider their relationship to other occupational groups (Chapter 4), assess the skills and knowledge of comparable workers (Chapter 5) and explore how emotions and aesthetics affect fashion (Chapters 6 and 7). We will see how the many categories of commercial workers are interconnected.

Are your jeans branded?

Branding is one of the most important dimensions of the promotional work aimed at making a product like denim appealing. Whilst much of the denim we wear is a 'nondescript' (Miller, 2009: 34), standardised product bought in a supermarket or other mass-market store, branded denim is common. *Levi Strauss* defines its jeans as 'workwear'; *Wrangler* references the history of denim as the clothing for cowboys and outsiders, and it's likely that people reading this book, like many other global consumers, have heard of at least one of these brands. They are 'global' brands, marketed as culturally American. New, expensive denim brands (*Acne, 7 For All Mankind*) can be two or three times as expensive to buy, reflecting how denim has been repositioned as a high-status product.

Your jeans might come from a 'branded garment retailer' (BGR), selling to a specific consumer segment of people like you (according to age, class and gender). Or they might be jeans bought to signal your attachment to a subcultural group. Brand owners do a lot of work to find out who buys different brands and styles, and how they use and feel about them. *Levi Strauss* does not just sell jeans, but shirts, jackets and other items too. Not all are made from denim, but all have been carefully assessed as being compatible with the core brand values (Holloway, 1999: 71, cited in Lury, 2009: 75). This brand signals something to you as a customer (which it hopes is distinct from competitor brands), and has a set of attributes that make it attractive to some groups of customers and hence valuable. How are brand values developed in a global marketplace? Brands, and the work that generates brand attributes and brand value, are central to contemporary promotional culture and to the production of consumption. We will build a picture of the work that builds brands, especially in Chapters 3, 5, 6 and 7).

Why did you buy your jeans?

The range of sales strategies used to make goods alluring, including advertising, viral marketing, promotional discounts and active selling, are critical activities in a global capitalism that depends on consumer markets for goods and services. Your jeans, whether bought from a highly branded 'experience' outlet like *Original Levis*, from a global or regional BGR like *Gap*, from a department store that stocks a range of different brands, from a supermarket, market stall or second-hand retailer, have been worked on to make them more attractive to you and consumers like you.

Levi Strauss was a 'market leader' with shrink-to-fit jeans in the 1980s until 'hip-hop came from nowhere to loosen all jeans' (Molotch, 2003: 208). Since then, it has worked to develop a new 'brand image', represented by a recent (2010) advertising campaign under the slogan 'we are all workers'. *Levi Strauss* is represented in this campaign as the clothing of ordinary people, struggling in the face of economic recession. An actual town, Braddock in Pennsylvania USA, is reconfigured as a 'brand community', and citizens of Braddock model *Levi* jeans (Banet-Weiser, 2012: 142–3). The campaign is designed to have a distinctive emotional appeal, as emotion, like aesthetics, is central to contemporary consumption. Perhaps you were attracted by this campaign, or one like it.

Alternatively, it's feasible that you were shopping with friends and decided to try some jeans on. Market researchers say that the proportion of men who try jeans on and go on to buy them is far higher than the proportion of women who do the same (Underhill, 2000: 17). Market researchers also know that people behave differently when they're on their own or with others. Young people browse with their friends but buy with their parents (Underhill, 2000: 152). There's a 'science' to selling you things, and a group of workers encouraged to sell to you. Here's how one sales worker felt when selling jeans:

> When I first started, it was, 'Have you heard how great our jeans fit?' Because we were really pushing denim. Who really wants to say that? Nobody. I really hated saying the tag line. It's the most embarrassing thing. (Williams and Connell, 2010: 358)

This extract (from a qualitative interview) suggests that retail workers are trained and managed by their employers to sell the brand's products. Sales work is a big employer, and plays an important role in encouraging and managing the exchanges of consumer goods and services. How are consumer goods made saleable? This is the biggest of the questions, around which the others are organised. Answering it means exploring links between knowledge work and body work (Chapter 5), the feelings associated with things (Chapters 6 and 7), and the rights and wrongs of persuasion (Chapters 3 and 8).

Where did your jeans come from?

It's very unlikely that the company that sold you the jeans was also the company that made them. The production of consumer goods is often organised through a series of subcontracted companies; so that the retailer adds symbolic meaning to the jeans but someone else organises the stitching and dyeing. The common use of subcontracting produces global 'supply chains' and is one of the key reasons why we cannot understand consumption without also thinking about how production is organised. Interlinked firms, distributional networks, 20 million tonnes of cotton, technological infrastructures and knowledge are all important to how your denim ended up in your wardrobe.

However you got your denim, many people from different places, employed by different organisations and with different job titles have done quite a lot of thinking about who you are and why you chose the jeans you did. They've thought about the design and manufacture, paid attention to current fashions, considered who you are, what you're likely to wear those jeans with, what kind of jeans you might buy next ... and even what kind of jeans you might be buying in ten years' time, when you're older, perhaps a bit plumper, perhaps a bit richer and perhaps a bit less cool. They've thought also about how they could sell to someone similar to you but from a different country, and how to sell to people who don't currently know anything of their product. Capitalism searches for new markets, and understanding how an ordinary good such as denim has come to be so common in our lives involves unpacking some complex economic, social and cultural processes that are central to the operation of global capitalism. The work that produces consumption is spread over the globe, is remunerated differently, and involves different kinds of skills. We need to link the themes of Chapter 2, on global capitalism, with those of subsequent chapters to see how individual consumers are thought of as part of similar or different lifestyle groups, and then to consider the ethical implications of global consumer capitalism (Chapter 8).

This book explores the work that produces consumption. It considers the design, marketing and selling of consumer products: goods, services and experiences. It focuses on those who work in these fields and explores how they create desirable products. It makes three assumptions. Firstly, that it is helpful to understand consumption's role in global capitalism if we think of it as something that is worked on. Secondly, that exploring what workers in different occupations contribute to encouraging consumption helps us understand consumption as a whole, even when (as we will see) the occupations that make up work in consumer capitalism differ in other respects. Thirdly, and most importantly, it assumes that capitalism operates under the skin and in the bones of daily life; abstract processes have a real impact on social life, and on our bodies.

Approaches to global consumer capitalism

If you are to understand any claim to knowledge, then you must understand something about where the ideas and evidence come from. To understand this book, you must recognise that it was written by a sociologist drawing on insights from other disciplines, and by someone based in the UK trying to think globally.

Thinking across disciplines

Too often, scholars and students from different disciplines don't get a chance to hear what others think. Even new disciplines that developed by bringing together ideas from older disciplines tend to set up boundaries around what distinguishes their approach from others. For example, management and organisation studies, where some of you may be based, draws on economics, sociology and psychology. This is an inevitable process of developing a new and specific way of thinking. Within sociology, my own current discipline, there are those who study work, those who study consumption and those who study the production of commercial cultures, and conversations between sub-disciplines are fairly unusual. Sometimes too, the benefits of intra-disciplinarity, let alone inter-disciplinarity, are not recognised by those working within an established trope of how to research a topic. In this book, I bring together literatures from quite distinct fields of study, as well as those which are really quite similar, if only they knew it. You'll see references to marketing, sociology, anthropology, cultural studies, history, economics and political theory. Sometimes it will be important for you to know the history of an idea or thinker, and I'll give you some clues. At other times you will need to do a bit of detective work yourself (for example, to look at where research was published) to understand it in more detail. Questioning of sources and knowledge claims is at the heart of being a university student, and is a skill worth honing. A good question to have in your mind is: 'On what grounds is this claim being made?' You might consider the disciplinary background of the author and the research methodology used to interrogate the social world in assessing any claim. You might also think about how your own intellectual biography makes you predisposed towards the insights of some disciplines rather than others. This kind of work is absolutely central to becoming a critical thinker, which is what your university studies are all about.

An exchange in the journal *Consumption, Markets and Culture* between marketing scholar expert Morris Holbrook and the historian of consumption Colin Campbell (Campbell, 1997; Holbrook, 1997) nicely illustrates the benefits and challenges of inter-disciplinarity. They agree that reading across disciplines is fruitful for providing alternative and complimentary insights. But whilst Holbrook suggests Campbell would benefit from reading the marketing research literature, Campbell suggests that Holbrook is promising insights that this literature is not able to deliver. Different methodological positions, different historical foci and – underdeveloped in this exchange – differences between economies and culture are all challenges for inter-disciplinary work, which has to sacrifice depth for a broad perspective.

Thinking globally

I am a British academic who works in a British university. It would be easy to assume that British, or at least European, examples provide 'good enough' instances of the phenomena we're studying here to stand in for other places, or at least those that are at a similar level of economic development, that are geographically close or speak the same language and so on. However, it's important to be wary of such a claim to universalism. Whilst the concepts and theories I use tend to have been developed in the 'West' or 'Global North', I've searched for examples from elsewhere, and have asked you to think of others. One of the notable features of global consumer capitalism is the way similar experiences (going to a *McDonald's*, to use the most common example) sit alongside remarkable global differences in the kinds of goods, services and experiences, the feel of consumption or how

people behave in consumer spaces. By the end of the book, you will
be able to make your own argument as to what these similarities and
differences are, and whether it's important to maintain differences.
Challenging and questioning the intellectual dominance of written
English, and the perspective of the developed West when looking to
understand consumer capitalism, relies on being able to understand
how scholars make tacit assumptions about how general an experience might be. This is another area where you will develop your
critical skills in the course of reading this book, by asking the question,
'How well would this idea fit in a different setting?' That setting might
be your own home town or region or those of your classmates or even
a place you've visited as a tourist.

In the case of consumer capitalism, it's particularly important to consider how well an idea extends beyond an intellectual tradition because
of how 'global' the phenomenon itself is. The story of denim makes clear
that production and consumption are linked: the jeans you're wearing
might have been made in Turkish factories subcontracted by an international brand like *Wrangler* or *Levi Strauss* and sold in your local
department store. Or they might have been sewn in China for a branded
garment retailer that sells throughout Asia. There are also significant
interconnections in the production of consumption, as when American
advertising agencies design campaigns for African products, or when
European clothing brands open stores in Singapore, or when Indian
food products are exported and marketed as enabling the customer –
wherever they are – to produce authentic curries. We need to ensure
that we register and understand these interconnections both for what
they tell us about the operation of global capitalism, and for what they
make us feel about the world: what it is like to *imagine* what will make
a product sell in Ghana, to *sense* the difference within the familiar retail
outlet, to *feel* that you've made a tasty and sophisticated dinner for your
family. Part of the operation of global consumer capitalism lies in the
production of feelings, sensory experiences and aesthetic judgements,
and we must pay attention to how these are created and worked on.

The plan of the book

Global capitalism

This chapter explains what global capitalism is, what its history is and
how it works. It shows how production and consumption are
interdependent. You will learn about different theoretical approaches to

understanding global capitalism. In this chapter, we see what lies behind individualised, personalised and meaningful consumption. We will see that consumer goods, services and experiences are produced through the operation of a complex capitalist system, that markets for things are made rather than natural and that the consumption of ordinary items relies on globally interconnected networks or chains of firms and workers. The tools and ideas we have available to make sense of this complex and important process are contested. In this chapter, we introduce approaches to understanding markets derived from different disciplinary perspectives, and consider the value-laden assumptions each entails, so that you will be able to understand how these standpoints might influence the kind of arguments you will assess in later chapters.

Consumption

The role of consumption in global capitalism is the topic of this chapter. You will see what consumption means to individuals, and how 'consumer capitalism' is produced through the many forms of marketing in use today. We need to understand consumption if we are to be able to understand the work that produces it. We use historical evidence to explore how consumption changes, so as to understand the infrastructural, organisational and demographic influences on contemporary consumption, and to explore differences in consumption between places. We will also discuss how consumption is not simply the act of a freely choosing individual. Not only are individuals constrained (for example, by income, by what's available to them), but there are multiple influences on how individuals consume. Age, lifestyle, gender, nationality, ethnicity, family circumstances and values are some of the factors that influence consumption; marketing, advertising, branding and fashion industries pay attention to these.

Commercial work

This chapter looks at the kinds of work that are important to making consumption possible, and explores different ways of thinking about this work: as part of a service sector, and as engaging in the production of culture. It looks at definitions of 'service' and considers how commercial work includes different kinds of 'service'. In order to explore more specifically *how* commercial work produces consumption, you will consider the concepts of culture work and cultural intermediation as useful for understanding how symbolic value is produced. This chapter will provide you with an understanding of how commercial work is organised and experienced in contemporary capitalism as flexible work. It also considers how paid workers are not the only influences on the production of symbolic values, and asks what 'work' consumers do.

Doing work

Skill, craft, knowledge and body work are the key themes of this chapter, which compares the different occupations involved in the production of consumption. We unpick the competencies and skills of commercial workers. Skill, knowledge and craft abilities are at the basis of commercial workers' different claims to be effective in producing consumption. Understanding how they work gives us important insights into both their experience of work and their effectiveness in producing consumption.

Emotion

In this chapter, we consider how important emotion is to the workings of global capitalism, considering how marketing uses emotion to sell and exploring the effects of this on those working in consumer capitalism. We explicitly relate the questions of how commercial workers operate to one dimension of consumer culture: the production and management of emotion. We explore the relationship between the science of emotion and attempts to manage customer emotions, and we consider the power of feeling for brands, goods and experiences that comprise consumer capitalism.

Aesthetics

This chapter looks at the production of aesthetic experiences in global consumer capitalism, and considers how sensory experiences of consumption are produced. It develops themes from Chapter 6, but this time foregrounds the aesthetic and the sensory. In doing so, it discusses explicitly how branding, fashion and design workers contribute to consumer capitalism by generating the small differences between products: a new colour or a refinement to the shape of a thing that gives it a new kind of value and appeal.

The ethics of global capitalism

This chapter pulls together the threads of the discussion of ethics that has woven through the earlier chapters to consider the rights and wrongs of global consumer capitalism. It returns to the 'rival views' typology of Chapter 2 to see how different disciplinary positions lead to different kinds of ethical judgement, and considers how we may assess such competing ideas given subsequent discussion of the production of consumption. It also considers the ethical implications of our understanding of key themes in the book: consumption, work and global capitalism. What makes 'good' work for commercial workers? How might we assess the rights and wrongs of promotional culture? What impact on the world does consumption have?

Taking seriously the production of consumption

We conclude with some reflections on the project. What does answering the five questions introduced here tell us about the production of consumption? The conclusion summarises key arguments made in the book, and reflects on the different kinds of knowledges referred to in the earlier chapters. It makes suggestions for the kinds of research projects students could carry out to investigate some of the themes in the book in a setting they are familiar with.

Research and discussion tasks

At the end of each chapter of this book you will find a series of suggested tasks to help you develop your understanding of the issues that we have been exploring. The research and discussion activities are designed to make it easier for you to develop your own understanding of a topic. There are two kinds of activity.

Research tasks have been devised on the basis that one of the best ways for anyone to understand complex arguments is to try to apply them to the world for themselves. Researching the world that is being described on these pages is a good way both to check your understanding of the claims that have been made here as well as to help you in developing your own critical perspective. Exploring these research tasks can be a useful way of gathering useful material for written assessments that you might have to do as part of your studies. And you might want to consider using these tasks as a way to investigate your own place of origin, or to develop a specialist knowledge of another region of the world.

Discussion questions are provided for each chapter as a way to start conversations about the material it contains. Verbalising your thoughts about the material, in conversation with other people – friends, classmates – is a really good way of learning how to develop your own position on the issues in question and to think through the implications that they raise.

Research task

Take a consumer item currently in your possession and write a short response to each of the five questions. This will involve you being reflective about your own life. Think not just about describing what you do as a consumer, but how your practices link to broader phenomena. Consider comparing yourself to other consumers: who are you similar to?

Discussion questions

1. Consider Table 1.1.
   a. Can you think of other occupations that you would add to the list?
   b. How could you group the occupations listed in the table? What are their similarities and differences?
2. What effect does your place of origin or country of residence have on your experiences of consumption?

Chapter 2

Global Capitalism

'Capitalism' is the name of the system through which production and consumption are organised. There are multiple, often competing, theories that have been used to explain what capitalism is, its global operation and what it feels like to live with. These draw attention to different dimensions of the workings of capitalism and differ in the ethical implications of their reasoning. Such differences are significant not just because of how they influence how we develop an account that feels 'true', or 'valid', but also because ideas do not just reflect the world; they shape it (they are *performative*). In addition to theorising capitalism, this chapter suggests that it is worth looking at historical change and geographical variations in order to make sense of how consumption operates. We will consider the global phenomenon of capitalism, focusing on trade and exchange in consumer goods and services, that is, on consumer capitalism.

The chapter is divided into three main sections. The first section, 'Global capitalism', defines capitalism and then considers how global trade became 'global capitalism'. It explores the development of consumer goods like silks and spices, and considers the global power relations that affect the shape and nature of capitalism at different times and places by considering ideas of globalisation. 'Production and consumption' looks at ways of thinking about how production and consumption operate within global capitalism and theorises the interconnections and interdependencies between these. 'Theorising capitalism's values' introduces some of the theories of capitalism that have been especially influential and that need to be understood to make sense of the discussion in subsequent chapters. It considers how different theories of markets and capitalism reflect and produce different moral claims about the impact of capitalist production and consumption.

Global capitalism

What is capitalism? Before we can really make claims about 'global' and 'consumer' capitalism, we must say what we mean by capitalism. That is the topic of the first part of this section. We then consider global trade and show that it has a long history prior to its emergence as global capitalism, supported by institutional governance structures. We also consider economic globalisation as a key dimension to contemporary global consumer capitalism in order to contextualise the themes of consumerism and the commercial work that are the main focus of *Work, Consumption and Capitalism*.

Defining capitalism

'Capitalism' refers to both an (always evolving) history and a theory of how economic life is organised and entwined in social life. Capitalism relies on markets, defined as arenas of social interaction in which property rights for goods and services are exchanged for money, under conditions of competition (Fligstein, 2001). The three key dimensions are:

Private property Capitalism relies on the existence of a social and legal system that defends the existence of property rights and the private ownership of property. Private property includes ownership of goods and services, workers' ownership of their own labour power, which they exchange for a wage, and private ownership of land, factories, sites of production, machines and so on (referred to by Karl Marx as the means of production, to be considered in 'Destructive markets'), as well as ownership of shares and financial products. The institution of private property means that others are excluded from accessing what you or I own, and a significant motivation for you to engage in economic activity is the benefit that you will accrue.

The pursuit of profit Profit (rather than wealth) is central to the dynamic of capitalism, a dynamic characterised by Weber as 'the pursuit of profit, and forever *renewed* profit' (Weber, 1976: 17); we will discuss more of Weber's thought in 'Feeble markets'). Changes to what is produced, and to how it is produced, contribute to generating profit. Capitalism uses markets to arrange the exchange of goods and to determine the price of goods. Making the same products more cheaply or finding new markets (for example, new groups of consumers or new commodities such as 'free' video games that invite players to buy more 'lives' or 'bonuses') are at the heart of capitalism. Profit is made at the meeting point of production and consumption – the marketplace – where buyers (consumers) pay more than it cost the sellers (producers) to make the goods or services, hence production and consumption are closely related.

Competition   Competition between market actors is fundamental to capitalism (even if in practice not all markets are competitive). Markets allocate goods and services by providing the mechanisms through which buyers can 'meet' sellers, sometimes face to face (as when you negotiate with a salesman over the price of a car), but often via distancing technologies (as in online retailing where buyers can easily compare prices). Competition means that prices are not fixed once and for all, and that other producers may be keen to enter a market if they think they can make some profit. There is a key role here for the work that produces consumption: it draws attention to and assigns value to markets for goods, services and experiences. Advertising and marketing are key mechanisms through which buyers are informed of what sellers have on offer and which sellers hope will be persuasive.

These three principles should be understood as operating in specific social, legal, cultural and economic contexts. The government of a nation state may intervene to protect private property rights, to set taxes or to maintain competitive markets by preventing a monopoly. It may limit imports of consumer goods, or run campaigns to persuade citizens to buy local products (although consumers may resist these kinds of campaigns, as in Ghana, where consumers resisted protectionism in favour of better quality goods from elsewhere (Saffu and Walker, 2006)). Civil society organisations such as trade unions and consumer rights bodies may seek to intervene in the markets for labour and for goods to limit exploitation, as seen in campaigns in China against selling tainted food (Cheng, 2012). Further, social and cultural understandings of what markets are 'really' like, and judgements as to whether different kinds of activity are acceptable or worthwhile, all matter to understanding how capitalism operates, as they affect what people expect the state to provide and what they expect to buy themselves.

Let's now consider capitalism as a global entity and begin to address its geographical and historical variation.

From global trade to global consumer capitalism

Centeno and Cohen define global capitalism as 'a historically created social system: a structure of relationships between organisations and individuals that has evolved over time in response to challenges and promises' (2010: 3). This system is institutionalised and embedded in daily practices. Accounts of the 'Silk Road' from China through Central Asia tell us that people, ideas and cultures migrated with trade goods (Liu, 2010) for hundreds of years prior to the emergence of industrial and post-industrial global capitalism. Historians tell us about the trade in specific goods and the circuits of commerce, and it is useful for us to think about their (different) accounts.

Werner Sombart (1863–1941), influenced by both Marx and Weber, anticipated the interests and approaches of many contemporary writers in his book *Luxury and Capitalism* ([1913] 1922). He looked to Italy in the 14th century and to Germany and the Netherlands in the 16th century to see traces of a new kind of society where capital was accumulated through trade, especially trade with colonies, and where new luxury commodities appeared. New markets in spices, perfumes, silk, tea, coffee and chocolate emerged as European traders and colonisers went to what they called 'new worlds'. The goods brought back counted as luxuries in Europe and were part of a different kind of 'modern' courtly life that privileged luxury, material pleasures, sensuality and manners. Trading in luxuries required a different mode of economic organisation. Credit markets and banking institutions to enable capitalisation and capital accumulation developed.

Sombart suggests that the luxury status of the commodities affected their consumption and production. Greater access to luxury goods sat alongside further rationalisation of production and a new dynamics of fashion, affecting everyday consumption. The importance of luxury goods to cultural life is shown by Wolfgang Schivelbusch (1992), whose accessible history of 'spices, stimulants and intoxicants' draws on Sombart's ideas. The 16th-century European fondness for 'exotic' spices in food gave way to a preference for the newly imported – and more stimulating – drinks of coffee and tea, which were consumed in new kinds of public spaces and seemed to herald a shift in social values. Not only was coffee imported, but so was a coffee culture: those public spaces new to Europe were echoes of the much longer (from the mid-16th century) history of café culture earlier in the Ottoman

Empire (Karababa and Ger, 2011). Sombart suggested that economic culture developed a more rationalist orientation to production, and consumption (for the wealthy) was more conscious and considered in the 17th and 18th centuries. Luxury goods, for example, could be counted as decent – moral and legitimate – when configured as part of a system of accumulation rather than as 'wasteful' consumption. In this he provides a counterbalance to Weber's arguments about the importance of Protestantism in the culture of production.

Unlike Sombart, Fernand Braudel (1902–1985), a French historian with a specific interest in long-term historical changes, does not find the pursuit of 'luxury' useful to explain emergent global trade. In *Civilization and Capitalism, Vol. II* he explores commerce and describes circuits of intercontinental trade from the 15th to 18th centuries (Braudel, 1992: 138–54). Commercial networks then relied on cooperation and communication between near and distant places, on trade links being as secure as possible, and on a lingua franca. Ordinary entrepreneurs matter more when understanding commerce than aristocrats and their desires, says Braudel.

Trade pre-dated the emergence and dominance of industrial capitalism in the 19th century, and was essential to its development. This is especially obvious when we consider the relationships between European colonial powers and the places they subjected. The 'triangle' of slaves, cotton and sugar, and manufactured goods of the late 16th to 19th centuries (Mintz, 1985), and the Dutch and British East India Companies' influence on trading and political relationships between Europe and India (Chaudhuri, 2006) are important examples of these global links and show how trade is closely related to political power and exploitation. For writers in the 19th century like Marx and Engels, concerned with industrialisation in Europe, the cotton mills of England looked like the heart of the industrial revolution. But they were reliant on cotton imports and competed with the fashionable patterns and cheaply produced Indian cottons. In turn, cotton manufacturers in India were bound and constrained by the political power of the British colonisers. Thus, global trade, production and consumption were, and still are, entwined with politics and domination.

A capitalist world system?

The development of global trade into global capitalism has been conceptualised using world-systems theory. World-systems theorists say that we cannot understand capitalism by studying nation states. Domestic (national) economies do not engage in global capitalism as equals, but are marked and affected by their position in a hierarchy of 'core' and 'periphery'. The most important world-systems theorist, Immanuel Wallerstein (1974, 2004, 2011), suggested that global capitalism emerged in the 17th century, as a result of the colonial and imperialist expansion strategies of Europe from the 16th and 17th centuries. Following the logic of capital's desire to expand its reach and its profit-making power, imperial expansion brought new regions into global capitalism. According to this theory, Northern Europe in the 16th century was the origin of the capitalist mode of production. Individual European countries had quite different political structures and none was a dominant power alone. But they shared a similar economic system: capitalism marked by specialised agriculture, an emergent proletariat (wage labourers) distinct from those capitalists who own the means of production and enforceable private property relations. Capitalism's search for new sites of production and new sources of profit stimulated Northern Europe's expansion into (and political domination of) other parts of the world. The world system changed in subsequent centuries, but followed a comparable model.

The theory suggests that three regions exist in the current global world system. The dominant core was originally Northern Europe and now includes North America, much of the rest of Europe, Japan and – perhaps – other parts of East Asia. Core regions are noted for how advanced production and consumption are, for their financial and producer services sectors and for their comparative technological sophistication. They contrast notably with peripheral regions, which provide raw materials and some foods, sometimes through indenture and slavery as much as wage labour. Semi-peripheral regions may be 'transitional' economies undergoing development, intermediary economies with specialised political structures (such as communist or ex-communist states) or states that are reliant on one valuable natural resource for their wealth (oil-producing states). Countries exchange with each other in ways that maintain these hierarchical positions. Those at the core have close relationships that manage risks and instability, and greater control over what happens within their own borders. Peripheral countries may be less trusted when making transactions with the core regions, and may be dominated economically, politically and/or militarily.

World-systems theory recognises that 'global interconnections' are often based on relations of difference and inequality and have the logic of capitalist accumulation at their heart. It also provides insights into why some places appear to be 'winners' and others 'losers' in the 'global race'; it is difficult for peripheral countries to break away from the longstanding relationship with core countries keen to maintain advantage. When making this kind of argument, it is worth bearing in mind a key criticism of this theory: its focus on 'the West and the rest'. The world-systems model makes a distinction between developed countries of the West and the rest of the world. Because it starts from what happened in Europe in the 16th century, it inevitably finds that Europe (and later other Western states) is the 'core'. Different historical starting points produce different outcomes: at many other periods in history (including our own), China and other parts of East Asia might well look like the core (Frank, 1998).

Where a nation state might fit in this typology of core, semi-periphery and periphery is a complex and politically loaded question; consider the advanced BRIC (Brazil, Russia, India and China) economies, characterised by recent development but high levels of poverty in rural, subsistence regions. This indicates how the regions described as 'core', 'semi-periphery' and 'periphery' are not internally homogeneous. For example, the coastal cities in China, especially Shanghai and the free-trade zones that focus on production of consumer goods for export, look quite different to inland, rural areas. Further, the theory can explain production in factories in 'middle-income' export-led countries for consumption in the US, Europe and other service-dominated economies. But it doesn't explain the emergent middle classes in these countries who do not work in factories and are active consumers; it downplays differences within local areas.

Macro-historical accounts like world-systems theory have been criticised for being 'grand narratives'. Grand narratives are over-arching theories that seek to provide full and complete explanations. In making grand claims to the truth of an account, nuance, complexity and specificity are omitted (Kumar, 2005: 156). Further, the importance of culture or ideology is ignored.

Building contemporary global capitalism

Contemporary global capitalism was shaped in the 20th century by upheavals of war, the introduction of new global and regional governance mechanisms, technological innovations in goods, production and consumption, changing income levels, discourses of right and wrong in economic management and so on. Global, regional and national institutions of governance support and may set limits on how global capital can act. Many emerged after the Second World War. The World Bank (founded in 1944) intervenes in the making of national policies (for example, in how it allocates support packages for struggling economies). The UN and its associated agencies and regional political organisations (such as NAFTA, the EU, ASEAN) seek to influence the operations of global capitalism, whether by setting limits on trade (EU farming subsidies), by encouraging 'export-led' growth or by taxing (or not taxing) global and local corporations. These are specific examples of the social, legal, cultural and economic contexts within which capitalism operates, discussed in 'Defining capitalism'. National governments set up economic plans to encourage manufacturing or services, to attract investment from overseas corporations or to encourage entrepreneurial development by their own citizens. Political interest in the development of global capitalism and an awareness of different countries' and regions' places within the global capitalist order are significant.

Despite pressures from global institutions to make nation states follow specific economic policies as a condition for other assistance, and despite the apparent hegemony of US-style capitalism, there is great differentiation as to what capitalism looks like in different places, as economic and social policy, including 'welfare state' provision, varies. So although we might describe the 21st century as an era of global capitalism, there is no one monolithic version of capitalism; there is a world of difference between Russia's new energy markets, 'capitalism with Chinese characteristics' (Huang, 2008), the US model of rationalisation embodied in global brands like McDonald's and Starbucks, and the way labour is protected in Sweden. With this in mind, let us now consider the way globalisation affects and is affected by capitalism.

Globalisation and capitalism

Contemporary global capitalism is characterised by interdependency and complexity. Interdependency is encouraged by the governance institutions described above and facilitated by information and communications technology (ICT). This interdependency is facilitated by the discursive triumph of capitalism and the power of neoliberal arguments (defined in 'Doux commerce') within the global institutions that seek to influence world trade. So far, our discussion has focused explicitly on economic practices. What, though, of global culture? Globalisation theorists have long been asking whether the world is increasingly interconnected, increasingly similar, and whether that similarity (homogenisation) is akin to Americanisation. 'Globalisation' has been defined in so many competing ways, and often with an implicit or explicit moral agenda that sees it as negative (e.g. Ritzer, 2004) or very positive (Ohmae, 1995). A globalised world is qualitatively different to what preceded it, marked by the deep integration of people and places. Nation states are supposed to matter less in the globalised world, and time and space seem to be compressed (Harvey, 1990). Castells, writing in the 1990s, suggests that the global economy is distinctively new and interdependent. It is 'an economy with the capacity to work as a unit in real time on a planetary scale' (1996: 92). This economy has an advanced ICT infrastructure, which supports a global trade. Global financial trading and transnational corporations are two of the key indicators of globalisation.

Strong arguments for there having been a radical change in the 1980s and 1990s are challenged by other scholars. Many suggest that Castells overstates the importance of ICT and the size of global trade. Hirst and Thompson (1999) take a sceptical view, arguing that the current era is not a radical shift but part of a longstanding trend towards internationalisation. Held et al. (1999) argue that global relationships and global integration vary across time. The current moment of 'thick' globalisation is marked by multiple, close transnational connections. We might well note that, despite the apparent benefits of these connections, such interdependencies of ICT and finance can generate vulnerabilities, for example when computer viruses travel beyond national borders, when damage to infrastructures (such as electricity production, internet cables) in one specific place have a knock-on effect elsewhere (Graham, 2011) and when participating in a global market means being vulnerable to its shifts, as when the repercussions of the 2008 financial crisis were felt.

Economic globalisation is not identical to political and cultural globalisation, although it overlaps with these. Key processes that contribute to and indicate a globalised world are: trade, financial and investment flows, the (new) international division of labour, global marketing and branding (and hence global corporations) and new forms of marketisation. These interweave, as when Taiwanese businesses invest in Southeast Asian factory production to make branded consumer products that will be marketed to wealthy consumers all over the world using regionally specific marketing strategies (as in Sri Lanka, where advertisers look to present overseas brands in ways 'near enough to be recognisable, distant enough to be worthy of desire' (Kemper, 2003: 50)). Globalisation is not an abstract logic, but involves agents, institutions, networks and regulations; it involves informal informational exchanges between consumers as well as institutionalised policies and strategies that have unforeseeable consequences. It also involves complex and multi-faceted processes through which consumption is made possible.

More recent work assessing the nature of cultural globalisation considers the potentials of cosmopolitanism (Tomlinson, 2013), as flows of symbols and products around the world do not inevitably produce cultural homogeneity. Local cultures persist, may be protected and may have very different encounters with the wider world (Ahmad, 2013). They may be commercialised and sold elsewhere as 'exotic' or 'authentic' representations, or they may exist outside of the hubbub of commercialisation. In other instances, the meanings embedded in specific cultures are changed through commercialisation. Well-known 'classic' Italian dishes like pizza margherita or pasta al pomodoro that might be sold in Italian restaurants or as authentic Italian products in supermarkets are fairly recent inventions, not emerging until the 19th century, 300 years after the tomato was first brought to Italy (Gentilcore, 2010). These dishes were then recreated by Italian migrants elsewhere, and new versions emerged, such as frozen pizzas with different kinds of toppings. Their associations, however, are as real peasant food with a long history.

Production and consumption

In 'Global capitalism', we considered capitalism as a system and looked at some of the macro-level dimensions of its operation, including the involvement of nation states and others in its governance. In our discussion of globalisation, however, we began to consider more specific details of the production and consumption of goods and services. The next section develops that discussion. It considers how production and consumption in different historical moments of capitalism have been organised and explores the relationship between production and consumption. At the heart of industrial capitalism is the idea of mass production and mass consumption. A simple story that is often told (and we should always be wary of simple stories) states that most consumption in developed countries in the 20th century was of standardised goods produced for homogenous consumers. This is known as Fordism. Contemporary global capitalism, however, does not seem to be marked by this mass system but by differentiation between geographical areas and between consumers with different lifestyles. How can we explain the regular turnover of fashionable things, cool brands and valued experiences?

Fordism

Fordism, named after the Ford Motor Company, is used as shorthand for a system of economic production and consumption marked by standardisation that emerged in the early years of the 20th century. Henry Ford's (1863–1947) famous saying, 'You can have any colour as long as it's black', typifies Fordism. Ford cars were made on a production line (to keep costs low) by workers paid comparatively good wages for the time (to reduce labour turnover) who might become the kind of people able to afford a Ford car for the first time. Goods were produced using assembly lines that meant identical products could be made comparatively cheaply, because they were standardised and so craft work was not necessary. We'll discuss this further in Chapter 5, 'Craft'.

The links between production and consumption are clear. Production is organised to make goods more cheaply, and production workers become a new group of consumers (an example of how expansion into new markets is a central feature of capitalism; see 'Defining capitalism'). The Ford Motor Company was also significant for how it enshrined into US law the idea that companies should be run to maximise shareholder profit (in Dodge Brothers vs Ford, 1919), an important moment in the development of US capitalism. In the post-war years, mass production and mass consumption persisted. However, social and technological change from the late 1960s contributed to fragmentation of the mass system. This is often referred to as post-Fordism.

Post-Fordism

Scholars who observed how companies responded to the overproduction of unpopular products (such as maxi skirts) in the 1970s started to think about the end of mass production and mass consumption. As consumers seemed increasingly individualised, they preferred differentiated products. Post-Fordism, marked by short-run production, flexible technology that can be manipulated to make new versions of products and innovations in design, could respond to differentiated demand. Post-Fordism relies on an effective marketing infrastructure that informs potential consumers what is available, and on market technologies that inform producers what is popular and how fashions are changing. Specialised goods can be targeted to people with particular lifestyles and can be differentiated and constantly updated (think of how many kinds of phone each mobile phone brand offers).

Here we see the importance of the contemporary focus on branding. The differentiation of target markets, often via branding, is a key dimension of contemporary promotional and marketing culture and hence central to the themes of this book. Selling to multiple defined and redefinable markets requires more effort than selling to simple, fairly homogeneous markets where consumers are motivated by conformity, not difference. This lies behind the efforts at promotion by commercial workers, and it rests on important theoretical ideas about the relationship between production and consumption, and between culture and economy. Branding and marketing influence the meanings of consumer goods, and hence we see production affecting consumption. However, the inverse is also important: consumption affects production, as when consumer activities affect the meanings that goods have. The logic of branding in post-Fordist production draws on, develops and is affected by the relationships between consumers, brands and the social world.

For some post-Fordist writers, the shift from mass to differentiated consumption was matched by a move to differentiated production by firms engaged in flexible specialisation, a 'craft' alternative to mass production that stresses innovation (Piore and Sabel, 1984: 17). This requires markets where consumers are willing to pay a premium for differentiated goods (Hirst and Zeitlin, 1991: 7). Large-scale production of differentiated goods in response to market demand is made possible because of technology that enables 'just in time' (JIT) delivery, instead of production in advance of demand. Minor differences can be achieved cheaply by re-tooling machines. More commonly, mass firms differentiate consumption within standardised mass production. Clothes washing powder is a good example, as many mainstream brands are owned by large, global corporations such as Unilever or Procter & Gamble but appear to consumers as distinctive niche goods; post-Fordism here describes production that gives the impression of differentiation (Hirst and Zeitlin, 1991: 10). The operation of post-Fordism relies on the flow of information and communication facilitated by technologies, including flows of finance and communication about consumption. Post-Fordism gives us a theory of how production and consumption might be organised; other descriptions of contemporary global capitalism as informational, cognitive and communicative make comparable points, with different stresses (Fuchs, 2010; Moulier Boutang, 2012; Dean, 2009). But how is 21st-century production organised in a global capitalism where production is differentiated and consumerism is increasing?

Chains, networks and global production

How goods and services are produced for consumption is a critical dimension of global capitalism. Global capitalism relies on and produces links between places, as when a global or regional chain retailer provides a recognisably similar product or service in different parts of the globe, or when a global corporation sells a product made from parts sourced from multiple points of origin. Transactions, objects and relationships are often mobile, and move more rapidly than was possible at earlier points in history. This speed affects all facets of life, from newly normal consumption (as when teenagers download songs, Courtois et al., 2012) to abstract finance, to production itself (Gereffi and Korzeniewicz, 1994); it has led some commentators to suggest that time and space are compressed in global capitalism (Harvey, 1990).

Many consumer goods are produced through a 'commodity chain' or 'supply chain' (although 'chain' sounds very linear and perhaps the interconnections might be better described as spiders' webs). The goods you are currently using have travelled further than you have yourself; the pen you make notes with, the clothes you wear, the chair you sit on, all probably have components manufactured in several places and assembled in another, to be sold to you near your home, or as a memento of your holiday. Studying commodity chains gives us insights into the key features of global capitalism: trade and investment flows, the international division of labour and global marketing.

Global commodity chains link raw materials and finished products sold in one or many countries via networks of intermediary products and the chain relationship is marked by an unequal distribution of wealth and power. Take coffee as an example: growing and processing beans may happen in Colombia or Ethiopia, comparatively poor countries. These are roasted, ground and packaged in an array of ways by big global brands and smaller regional ones, in places where coffee cultures are long established, or in places like Japan where it is a new 'foreign' and 'niche' product (Grinshpun, 2013). The work of developing a Fairtrade soy piccolo or a grande latte with cinnamon syrup as a new product for sale in a global chain like Starbucks happens in the US (Talbot, 2004), and these standardised coffee drinks are made and sold in the chain's outlets in an increasing number of places. Global consumer capitalism draws on this kind of product design, branding and marketing of goods and services.

Garment production is another good example, and typically involves asymmetric power relations with branded retailers. That is to say that the brand retailers – sometimes called manufacturers without factories – dominate their suppliers (Gereffi, 1994, 2005). For example, a typical pattern is for a brand retailer to have a relationship with several suppliers, each of whom is dependent on the retailer for work, meaning that suppliers are comparatively vulnerable. This way of organising production can easily be read in line with world-systems theory.

Branded garment retailers are often based in or near to fashion capitals like New York, London, Paris and Milan, in 'core' countries, and suppliers in 'peripheral' regions. However, Aspers (2009) suggests that something new has emerged recently. Firms in countries that have mainly manufactured but not designed garments have learned from the retailers they worked with and have developed new skills in design and tailoring. The Turkish firms Sarrar and Erak have both moved from manufacture alone to design, branding and retail (Tokatli, 2003). The 'Mavi' brand, made by Erak, is now sold globally. These companies have learned how to make clothes; they have also learned how to understand the consumer in order to make clothes that are desirable (Tokatli, 2003). Understanding and knowing consumers is important to global consumer capitalism. The emergence of new consumers with disposable income, the growth of new production and the always shifting interconnections between global and local production and consumption, and the institutional embedding of production and consumption, means that global capitalism cannot be understood using a 'West versus rest' model.

Comparable interconnections are visible when we consider very different kinds of consumer good. Film makes a good case through which to see the complex workings of the commercial production of cultural products. A film is a product produced by workers with wide-ranging skills, from location scouts to set designers to make-up artists to directors and actors, to say nothing of the computer programmers making CGI, musical directors trying to ensure harmony between action and score (Dickinson, 2008), screenwriters (Conor, 2014) and other workers (Dawson and Holmes, 2012). All kinds of 'mundane' work are fundamental to the success of a film set: caterers, truck drivers and the like. There is also a complex financing arrangement, and production companies from different countries may be involved. Cultural symbols and capital flow in order to make a film.

The film will have a marketing campaign. Its target global or regional audience was probably considered before filming began, as a condition of financing. It may have its origins in another cultural product, as in the case of the 'Harry Potter' books and films which use 'perpetual marketing' to tease customers and build their excitement (Gunelius, 2008). It is possible that all kinds of extras are produced: memorabilia and marketing tie-ins with fast-food chains. The film may be cut into different versions for different regions. Distributors are needed, as are cinemas to show the film. Often, these cinemas will be local, national or international chains, with a whole array of branded snack foods on offer for filmgoers (see Athique and Hill, 2010 for a great discussion of multiplexes in India). The shadow economy is also present, if a bootleg copy of film is downloaded for free, or if fake versions of the branded toys are bought and sold. Cultural production can be a complex global collaboration.

In this section, we've discussed how consumer products are simultaneously global and differentiated, and considered how their production is organised within the context of global capitalism. In the course of doing this, we have made a few references to quite different ways of thinking about capitalism (when we've used the term 'neoliberal', or have referred to Weber and Marx). It's time to look in more detail at more abstract theories about capitalism.

Theorising capitalism's values

So many of the thinkers who have tried to explain capitalism have a strong sense of its rights and wrongs, and it's hard to understand what they argue without also thinking about the values and ethics that their different interpretations rely on. Max Weber (1864–1920) argued that social science investigators want to study problems that are 'value relevant' to them, that is, problems that they think are worth studying (1949). Weber also says that we should leave our values at the door and not bring them to our desk. That is, how we study the world should be value neutral, and we should not impose our preferences and presumptions on the data. The question of 'value neutrality' relates also to a longstanding philosophical argument as to the difference between facts and values. Facts tell us 'what is'. Values are statements about what ought to be. In Weber's rather austere version of social science, values should only matter at some moments and should be carefully excluded from consideration during the course of research and interpretation.

Extensive critiques of this position have argued that a value-free science is impossible, whether they point out the importance of emotion for scientists, consider how implicit worldviews have shaped 'scientific' claims or consider whether researchers should take an explicit stance about what is right and wrong with the world. In the course of your studies you might read material where it's easy to tell what the writer thinks of the world they are studying, and other times when it's not as obvious. It is worth interrogating material you read with this in mind. It also matters to think about values because an education in the workings of the social world inevitably shapes who you are, and is affected by your sense of wrongs and rights – a sense which will evolve as you learn. Given that global capitalism has such an impact on our daily lives, it's hard to avoid judging its effects and asking, 'Is our world fair?' In this section, we present a typology of different ways of conceiving of capitalism that draws attention to the values and ethics embedded in the work of different scholars. In later sections of the book you will see these writers, and those inspired by them, discussed.

Rival views of market society

Albert Hirschman ([1986]1992) distinguished between three 'rival views of market society', and his thesis was updated by Fourcade and Healy (2007) to recognise how recent scholars' work has refined these positions. The first view, 'doux commerce', suggests that markets have civilising effects. The second view is named the 'self-destruction' thesis by Hirschman, and is referred to as 'destructive markets' by Fourcade and Healy. It suggests that capitalism carries 'the seed of its own destruction' (in Marx's words), as it corrodes social values. The 'feudal shackles thesis', updated to 'feeble markets' suggests that capitalism might have reached an ideal state of peace and harmony had not special interests got in the way of it working properly, that is, had the bourgeoisie adequately moved away from the constraints imposed by the feudal lords of the pre-capitalist era. It is concerned to consider how best to regulate markets and capitalism. Fourcade and Healy (2007) add a fourth view, 'markets as moral projects', which considers that market practices and discourses do not only reflect the social world, but form it, including by shaping its values. You'll notice that I've started to use the term 'markets' as well as capitalism. These are not equivalent concepts, but how scholars have understood markets to operate influences what other scholars have to say about capitalism, so we must look into what is said about both. We'll consider thinkers who fit into each category in turn, exploring historical and contemporary writings.

Doux commerce

Adam Smith (1723–1790) is the most famous of the names associated with the 'doux commerce' point of view, and is most known for his ideas about the 'invisible hand of the market' as the key to mobilising human activity for beneficial development (see *The Wealth of Nations*, 1796[1999]). In the time Smith was writing, many thinkers advocated the idea that commerce is gentle and may pacify a human nature that – many feared – was naturally rough and violent, so that 'the market and capitalism were going to create a moral environment in which society as well the market itself were bound to flourish' (Hirschman, 1992: 135). Commerce operates as a moralising force, encouraging some behaviours like hard work and integrity, and discouraging unpunctuality, dishonesty and wastefulness (Hirschman, 1992: 109). Smith's ideas influenced later generations of economists, and the ideas of 'doux commerce' are implicit in historical and contemporary economic thought and practices, including understandings of how consumers behave.

From classical to neoclassical economics   In the course of the 19th century, economists like Marshall, Jevons, Walras and others began to develop abstract models about how markets and economies worked that could be tested. Instead of thinking of markets as concrete, realistic and situated places (Smith used the idea of a pin factory that made real pins), markets were theorised as a way to determine prices and to allocate resources (see Vaggi and Groenewegen, 2003 for a nice introduction to the history of economic thought). The simple theory of how markets work is as follows. A perfect market allocates resources efficiently. It works when there is perfect information and perfect competition. Perfect information means that all participants, buyers and sellers, know what's happening elsewhere in the market (and so no one can price gouge: charge high prices because of consumers' ignorance). Perfect competition means that buyers and sellers are free to enter and leave the market at will, with no barriers to entry or interventions from elsewhere. Walras suggests that the world is comprised of a set of interconnected markets, an idea that tells us a lot about how economists understand the world.

   This kind of economics is known as 'neoclassical'. It appears simple at first sight. Markets work because at some price, willingness to supply a good will equal demand for that good. If I bake some cakes to sell, I want to make sure the price is low enough for you to be willing to buy them, but not so low that I don't cover my costs and make a bit of profit. All kinds of imperfections might get in the way of this perfect market hypothesis. For example, if I can rely on you not knowing the price of cakes for sale just down the road, then I can set my price higher and trust that you'll think it's a fair price. You might also be willing to buy more expensive cake when you're particularly hungry or feeling like you deserve a treat, so I'll set my stall just outside the swimming pool. If I can market my cakes well and give them a cool brand identity, you might even be willing to pay more.

   The textbook vision doesn't bear much resemblance to actual markets, which are far more complex. Think about what I need to ensure my cakes are baked: a whole supply chain for the ingredients, a hot oven that relies on an electricity or gas grid; think about the multiple possible suppliers of cake and substitutable goods; and consider what influences demand for cake. Economists do recognise that the world is more complex, and try to model this complexity, as we will see.

From neoclassical to neoliberal economics   The simple understanding of micro-level markets is important, though, as it encapsulates what many economists take for granted about how markets work (and is also central to the claims that some make about how economies should work at macro level). Economics has a dominant paradigm, that is, a scientific approach to studying the world. Neoclassical ideas are at the heart of this. Two key groups developed neoclassical economics in influential directions. The Austrian School, a group of liberal thinkers who include Hayek and von Mises, suggests that markets will allocate effectively as long as property rights are provided and protected, and the few institutions necessary for markets to work are effective. Notably, 'markets' are not things, but processes, spontaneous results of individual human action. This view has been politically popular, especially in the US, and is often referred to as 'neoliberalism'. Neoliberal economists are also associated with the second significant group, the Chicago School, who advocated the importance of information to understanding how markets work (recall the neoclassical view that the best market is one with perfect information), and who argued that individuals made rational decisions (sociologists should note that this is a different Chicago school to the one you have studied with its interest in the micro-complexities of everyday life). The Chicago School of economics took on board many of the Austrian School ideas and has been politically influential. A nation state or global institution that supports the neoliberal project will remove regulations, provide tax breaks to investors, privatise national assets and legislate for flexible labour markets, as this is thought to ease the accumulation of capital. As we will see in later chapters, the lived experience of work is affected by how economies are organised and markets regulated, and being on the receiving end of a flexible labour market is pretty tough.

In the simplest explanation we can give (and once again, recall the dangers of oversimplification), much of what is now taken for granted by the managers of firms and by national and regional economic policymakers in some places adheres to the precepts of neoclassical economics, and to the moral codes that are attached to this (Sandel,

2012). We can see the neoliberal project in the policies of the World Bank and International Monetary Fund (IMF), as well as – in different forms – in some national governments. The precepts are: that market mechanisms will produce the best allocation of scarce resources; that a market that runs without interference is most efficient; that consuming individuals will make rational, utility-maximising decisions.

Challenging rationality and perfection   From within the discipline of economics, a number of challenges to the simple models have been made by behavioural economists and by heterodox economists. Behavioural economists show how the assumptions that we are all rational and make satisficing decisions are problematic (although did anyone other than economists ever believe we are rational?). Using insights from psychologists, they point out that people deviate from rationality quite often, and are interested in explaining why (McFadden, 1999). These ideas have been popularised (e.g. Ariely, 2009), although they maintain many of the assumptions of mainstream economics (Berg and Gigerenzer, 2010). Heterodox economists, of whom there are many kinds, tend to be keen to recognise the role of structures and institutions of different types. For example, they might say that consumer markets are operated by the visible hand of the multinational corporation rather than the invisible hand of the market (Chandler, cited in Harvey, 2006: 99–100).

Destructive markets

The critique of neoclassical models from within economics is significant. However, critiques from outside economics are more productive for generating the kind of complex theories that will help us account for the operations of work and consumption in global capitalism. Of the many arguments made to show the damaging and destructive nature of market actions, most refer to capitalism rather than follow the economists' focus on markets.

Marx and Marxisms   Most famously, Karl Marx (1818–1883) and thinkers influenced by him provide a strong critique of the negative effects of the spread of markets and their particular manifestation in industrial capitalism. Marx was one of the many European scholars and activists who observed the industrialisation of Europe, the growth of towns and cities, of manufacturing industries and of new kinds of consumption, and were moved to analyse and criticise what was going on. Marx combines a carefully built theory as to how capitalism works with a strong moral argument about its damaging effects. Newcomers to Marxian analysis may feel uncomfortable: don't the abuses that we know took place within communist societies and the downfall of most of these societies mean that Marxism is discredited? It's important to realise that the political project of communism, as applied under Mao and Stalin, looked quite different to the theories developed by Marx and Engels. Furthermore, so many of the tools we have to analyse contemporary economies bear the influence of Marxian ideas that it would be impossible for us not to think about, and with, Marx.

In Marxian analysis, understanding the mode of production is central to understanding the material world and social life. Culture, social institutions and so on are a 'superstructure' to the economic 'base'. Societies change as the economic system changes, driven by conflicts between social groups and, in capitalism, by competition and profit. The capitalist mode of production emerged from feudalism, and provided some benefits initially, but the drive to accumulate capital through competition makes owners of the means of production (capitalists) want to reduce costs, especially wage costs. In capitalism, those who own the means of production – factories, machines and so on – are a distinct group from those who produce things. This division is the source of class differences and inequality. Those who sell labour in capitalism, the proletariat, have little wealth, power or privilege, live and work in poor conditions and sustain life on low wages. Marx argues that profit derives from the exploitation of wage labour by capitalists who appropriate the value created by the workers. In this theory, economic value is derived from labour time and profits are the 'surplus value' produced by workers over and above their wages.

In *Capital*, Marx says that human needs are shaped to the needs of production: desires are induced in wage labourers to keep the system of production flowing and provide profit for the owners of the means of production (1976). Consumption beyond the minimal level needed to meet physical needs for food, clothing and shelter involves 'commodity fetishes'. Commodity fetishism means that wage labourers do not recognise the products of their own efforts and social relations and values are hidden. The wage system and the way commodities are valued by price mean that people value things in monetary terms and do not notice the work that goes into these products. Marx theorises this by contrasting two sources of value: use and exchange. Use value is that part of a commodity which satisfies needs, reflecting the relationship between a person and an object, the need and its satisfaction. Exchange value refers to the rate and ratio that a commodity can be exchanged with another: its equivalence to other commodities, mediated by money. Marx saw commodity consumption as being inseparable from production, but production was the driver of social change. Consumption is a palliative offered in return for hard work and cannot address the real problem faced by wage labourers: that they are alienated from their own productive work because of the wage-labour system. 'Animal functions' (Marx, 1997: 66) such as dressing well are 'needs' entirely induced by capitalism, and serve to hide the real value of goods: the labour that made them. Marx's analysis suggested that capitalist markets were destructive because they corrupt human life. Wage labourers are alienated, commodities are fetishised and those who own the means of production (capital goods) exploit those who are forced to sell their labour.

Polanyi and embeddedness   Karl Polanyi (1886–1964) certainly read and was influenced by Marx's writing, but he argued against the 'economy first' position shared by the thinkers discussed previously. Instead, he showed how the relationship between economy and society affected social cohesion. He also showed us the value of a historical perspective on the transformation into capitalism. Polanyi's approach was 'substantivist', based on historical analysis of markets (unlike the 'formalist' position of the ideas discussed in the section 'Doux commerce' where abstract theories about demand and supply in markets are built and tested).

Polanyi reflected on the 19th century from the perspective of the middle of the 20th century, and was keen to understand his own times of world war and fascism through historical analysis. In *The Great Transformation* (1957[1944]), he explored how, in the early years of the 19th century, England became the first industrialised nation dominated by markets. When market society arrived, traditions and communities that had previously 'embedded' markets in society were broken and lost (for example, when people migrated to cities to sell' their labour), leaving an economy that was 'disembedded'. Markets emerged for labour, land and goods. Private property, competition and the calculations and self-interest of individuals and firms were supposed to self-regulate the market, but cold capitalist markets carried few of the means to make community.

Polanyi's work suggests that it is false to see market trading as a natural part of human societies, or that markets are the best way of organising societies (see also Gibson-Graham, 1996). Economic activity is destructive and dehumanising when it is disembedded and not governed or constrained by non-economic spheres. A 'human economy is embedded and enmeshed in institutions, economic and non-economic' (Polanyi et al., 1957: 250). Markets work through institutions that order and constrain, as when state legislation protects consumers from the untrue claims made by advertising companies. That is, economies work through an instituted process. Without 'the protective covering of cultural institutions' (Polanyi, 1957: 73), life is horrid for those near the bottom. Whilst the coming of market society involved a 'double movement' that both promoted market society and also tried to ameliorate some of the damages of the new market reforms, Polanyi suggests these did not work well at protecting social interests. The damage to social relations caused by capitalism was great, and left a legacy of inequality and oppression that provided fertile ground for the seeds of the fascism that was visible in Polanyi's day.

Feeble markets

One of the important criticisms that has been made of the ideas we've seen so far in this section is that society and culture do not seem to have much power: either markets exist without reference to culture or they dominate culture. The next way of thinking, 'feeble markets' takes a different view.

Weber   Max Weber (1864–1920) is well known for his work on the influence of culture, in the form of religion, on economic life. His work provides an excellent way of thinking about the relationship between economy and society. In *The Protestant Ethic and the Spirit of Capitalism*, Weber discusses Northern European economic growth in the 19th century, and suggests that it reflects a distinct 'spirit' that explains the comparable economic success of Northern Europe in contrast to the Catholic countries of Southern Europe. Protestantism, the dominant religion in Northern European countries from the 16th century reformation of the Church, stressed the promise of a good afterlife in heaven if a believer chose diligence and denial in their earthly life. Saving (both saving souls and saving money) is set in opposition to wasteful, hedonistic excesses of consumption:

> the old leisurely and comfortable attitude towards life gave way to a hard frugality in which some participated and came to the top, because they did not wish to consume but to earn, while others who wished to keep on with the old ways were forced to curtail their consumption. (Weber, 1976: 68)

Culture, in the form of religion, plays an important role in economic life. The 'spirit of capitalism' values instrumental rationality, a rationality that makes it desirable to act in ways that lead to increased profit. In other spheres, other values and other rationalities might be important. Making money is not directed at producing wealth but done in order to invest in new profit-making pursuits, as the individual's duty is to build capital (Weber, 1976). Weber argues that Northern European individuals internalised this spirit and instrumental rationality. The values of Protestantism made the pursuit of profit virtuous. Living a good life meant working well; a worker with a vocation, willing to work long hours in a steady way, was a lucky man indeed, and a man would work hard because religion promised him rewards. Whilst many now suggest that this thesis is overstated (e.g. Swedberg, 2003), nonetheless, it is important to indicate how values – religious or otherwise – may have a strong, constitutive relationship to economic life, that economic life is part of the social world. We'll develop the idea of 'ethics' and capitalism in Chapter 3, when we look explicitly at consumption, and consider rationality and its relation to emotions in Chapter 6. Weber says comparatively little about consumption, although in a market society where rationality dominates, consumer goods may be used instrumentally, for example, as indicators of social status in market societies (Weber, 1946, cited in Zukin and Smith Maguire, 2004).

The new economic sociology   Although no longer very new, the 'new economic sociology' (NES) project adapts Polanyi's ideas about the embedding of markets in the social to suggest that economic action happens through all kinds of institutions and structures. When new economic sociologists use the term 'embeddedness', they mean something a little different to Polanyi. Rather than there having been a historical shift from markets being embedded to being disembedded, they see markets as always embedded in some way, and the task of the economic sociologist is to unpick how this embedding works. For Granovetter, the 'ongoing structures of social relations' (1985: 481) permeate economic action. Markets are embedded through social networks and organisations (Granovetter, 1985; White, 2002), as well as through culture and politics (Zelizer, 1985; Fligstein, 1996, 2001). In this view, neither the economists who assume that we make rational, individualised decisions that maximise our self-interest nor the sociologists who see how social structures and institutions constrain action are right. Non-market factors such as networks, institutions and understanding shape markets and affect the limits of market influences. Economy is not independent of human society, but enmeshed within it.

The idea of embedding markets in the social is very helpful to making sense of commerce. It allows us to understand in greater depth the sorts of behaviour that drive individual economic actors. It also reveals elements that dominant economics cannot, namely how markets come to be structured, why they differ between places, times and according to what is being bought and sold. This matters very much, as it shows that the patterns of commerce in one place and time are not universal and that market society is not monolithic: many transactions occur outside the headline-grabbing industrialised consumption of the supermarket, shopping mall, branded leisure complex and so on.

The NES project has been criticised because it seems to collapse everything into the social. Sociology thereby becomes an all-powerful explanatory discipline (Fraser, 2009). By privileging human action, NES forgets how technology, infrastructure and science influence how economic action occurs. These criticisms are made particularly by researchers working in a fourth category of the typology presented by Fourcade and Healy (2007) (and not on Hirschman's radar), those who understand markets as scientific and moral *projects*.

Markets as moral projects

So far, we've seen economists putting economic activity at the heart of social life, and sociologists bringing economy under the umbrella of social life. Science and technology studies (STS) scholars, influenced by 'actor-network theory' (ANT) have a different ontology (understanding of what exists in the world) and a different politics. ANT seeks to recognise the power and reach of non-human actors, both large scale and small and mundane, as when Latour talks about 'a wall hole, often called a *door,* which although common enough has always struck me as a miracle of technology' (1992: 228). Now some people find the idea of exploring the agency of so simple an artefact as a door fairly comic. Others find the idea that non-human actors have an influence on how people can possibly live usefully provocative.

STS writers suggest that the relationship between economy and society should be rethought by considering the technical operations of economic life, and that techniques, technologies and discourses of economic action do not passively reflect the world but constitute it. As Çalışkan and Callon suggest, 'What would an economy be without commodities and their physical properties and materialities?' (2009: 384). In the context of consumer capitalism, Cochoy (2007) considers also the 'market-thing', the shopping trolley, which is so important to supermarket retail: who would shop at a supermarket without something to put their goods in? We might consider also how consumer products are brokered by computer algorithms that make recommendations to us based on previous purchases as an important 'marketthing'. Comparatively little STS work considers consumer markets (rather than financial markets).

Two themes of STS research are particularly important. The first is the performativity of economic activities, theorising and ideas. Many STS theorists have explored how the 'science' that is economic theory makes markets (Callon, 1998), and this work criticises the 'doux commerce' view of markets by indicating how markets are made, not given: economic theory produces 'homo economicus' (economic man), 'formatted, framed and equipped with prostheses' (Callon, 1998: 51). In the case of consumer markets, branding is the key means through which theories of how markets work are performative of that market, both in how markets are framed by branding discourses and practices, and by how consumption is legitimated by such actions. Lury (2004) describes the performativity of branding and marketing as structuring the relationships between producers and consumers. Branding is not merely calculative, but creates affective responses (see Chapter 7). It develops knowledge about objects, consumers (and competitors) and then translates that into marketing practices. Elsewhere, Lury (2009) suggests that brands model the world, rather than represent it: brands assemble culture. Araujo (2007) and Azimont and Araujo (2007) go further in considering how the science and activity of marketing make markets through how they understand categories of goods, or categories of consumers. Customer relationship management (CRM) technologies reflect but also constitute ideas about consumer practices, albeit in ways full of error (Knox et al., 2010). How do ordinary economic practices like developing a branding strategy or reviewing a service on a website create, stabilise or destabilise markets?

The second is noticing and understanding the technical infrastructures that make markets happen and so make consumption possible. When Knox et al. (2010) look at CRM technologies, they indicate the ways that these technological devices are active agents in constituting the world they seem to reflect. Cochoy (2007) describes what is taken for granted by supermarket retailing, that is, the 'assemblage' of the supermarket: the reliance on cars, acceptance of behavioural norms about how to consume, temporal rhythms of work and consumption, the discrete yet constant presence of distribution, fixed prices, and 'market-things' like trolleys and tills. Far from the

individual buyer and seller meeting in some abstract space, supermarket consumption is complex. Consumers engage with objects not
people, going from face-to-list to face-to-shelf (2007: 116), and whilst
they are aware of some merchants' tricks, such as how some products
(wine, beauty, pharmacy, clothing) are 'zoned' and laid out differently
to the standard use of aisles, they are unaware of others. Markets
operate through assemblages of humans, technology, institutions and
assemblages that comprise consumption. Here we see Cochoy developing the idea that humans are not the only actors with agency;
devices and technologies matter too. STS thinkers consider that
acknowledging the performativity of knowledge about markets and
the complex assemblages of market life matters to understanding the
processes through which value is qualified in markets (that is, how
prices are set, how products come to be seen as worth more than
those of their rivals and so on).

Assessing theories of markets

In this brief review, we have seen how different ethical judgements,
different methodologies and different understandings of what kinds of
things it matters to study, lead to writers producing different kinds of
accounts of markets and capitalism. We have seen how critical
responses, both to the effects of market action and to other writers'
perspectives, affect the arguments that scholars make. Whilst we may
disagree as to whether ethical or political views should influence scholarship, we are unlikely to disagree about the validity of critically engaging with other people's work as new ideas emerge from engaged
reflection on existing forms of knowledge. We saw how historical
analysis, paying close attention to the political, cultural and social
context of market activity, can provide important insights into contemporary life. We should note that the contemporary economic sociologists (NES and STS writers) tend not to engage in this kind of work,
but look more often to present-day markets. This reflects disciplinary
differences. NES scholars draw attention to the institutionalisation of
markets through embedding, only implicitly recognising that this
means embedding in a material world (Pinch and Swedberg, 2008).
STS scholars attend more directly to materiality, considering the
agency of things as fundamental to understanding how markets work.
Neither perspective assigns much significance to the lifeworld of the
consumers, to consumers' desires and subjectivities, to the mundane
and sensual encounters that consumers have with things. To understand this more thoroughly, we must turn to a different literature.

Conclusion

Capitalism is a mode of organising the production and exchange of goods and services. It varies between times and different places, is global in orientation and is affected by institutional governance mechanisms. In this book we foreground consumer capitalism: that part of global capitalism that produces and promotes goods, services and experiences for consumption by ordinary consumers looking to fill 'needs and desires', rather than the financial capitalism (capitalist accumulation through financial exchange rather than production) that is also so significant to contemporary life. We might want to be cautious about overstating 'global capitalism'. Presenting capitalism as an inevitable, inescapable primary force makes it hard to see those parts of social life that are outside of or resistant to capitalism (Gibson-Graham, 1996).

In discussing 'consumer capitalism', we should also recognise that more people are affected by their position in relation to global production than are active participants in branded consumerism. Nonetheless, consumer capitalism is global in three ways: because of the global links forged by commodity chains, because of the presence of a commercial culture of brands and marketing and because of the presence of sizeable numbers of consumers in many parts of the world, both 'developed' countries and those previously considered 'less developed' or 'peripheral' – including middle classes in Asia and South America. We have seen that theories of capitalism implicitly or explicitly incorporate moral claims. The idea that academic writing and theorising can reflect and develop a moral position about the world is important to remember in subsequent chapters, which discuss in more detail the rights and wrongs of work and consumption in global capitalism. To understand how capitalism operates, we need to understand its organisation, consumption practices and the work that produces this consumption. In the next chapter, we focus on consumers, consumer cultures, exploring the global dimensions of consumerism.

Research task

Investigate the supply chain of two products or services of your choice. Find out where the goods are designed and produced and consider what this tells you about 'global' capitalism. You might find it helpful to look at the producers' websites as a starting point. How would you explain similarities and differences between these products?

Discussion questions

1. This chapter has used history to understand contemporary global capitalism. What are the benefits of drawing on history for understanding contemporary capitalism? What are the limitations?

2. In what ways is capitalism 'global'? What is the significance of the local within the global? Fast food might be a good example to use when answering this question.

3. What are the implications of focusing debates and discussions of the gentle, destructive or feeble nature of markets and a capitalist system on studies of Western Europe and the US?

Chapter 3

Consumption

'Life is not complete without shopping', the former Prime Minister of Singapore, Goh Chok Tong, once said. This became the title of Chua Beng Huat's (2003) book on consumer culture in Singapore, in which he explored Singaporeans' apparent fascination with global brands and going shopping. This chapter tries to understand the sentiment behind Tong's statement by showing how consumer society emerged, and discussing the ways in which consumption seems to matter to individuals. This will provide insight into the power and importance of consumer capitalism. Consumerism, the ideology of consumption, is actively cultivated through commercial activities, through decisions made by states and through the actions of consumers and producers, and so we need a complex account of why (and for whom) life might not seem complete without consumption.

In 'What is consumer society?', we look at consumer capitalism. We consider the historical development of a 'consumer society' or 'consumer culture' in Western economies and its extension beyond these geographic and conceptual limits. Throughout this discussion, questions of the moral standing of consumption are explored. In the second section, we look at the extension of consumerism into a 'mass' market and explore sociological understandings of consumerism as part of modernity. These sections consider the kinds of production processes, institutional features and ordinary practices that comprise consumer capitalism, namely, the nature of 'mass' and differentiated consumption, self-service and the use of consumers as workers. In 'Explaining consumption', we look at the figure of the consumer, considering the uses of consumption, both as a dramatic signal of identity and in mundane practices of everyday life. In 'Production, consumption and promotion', we consider the interconnections of production and consumption and address the role of promotional activities like branding and marketing.

What is consumer society?

A consumer society is one where consumption has come to play a more significant role for individuals than that of production; that is to say that an individual's primary identification with the social world is as a consumer, not as a producer. A consumer society relies not just on these kinds of individualised meanings, but on mass production and consumption, material wealth, political and moral acceptance of, even support for, consumption, as well as legal and institutional frameworks that protect consumer rights or encourage the provision of goods and services as market commodities rather than homemade items or collective products (Lee, 2000). The US became a consumer society in the 20th century: 'consumption patterns, consumer consciousness, and the nature of daily life were significantly transformed, a transformation that corresponded to equally profound changes in production and distribution' (Strasser et al., 1998: 3). The term 'consumer culture' (Slater, 1997; Sassatelli, 2007) has different connotations. Whilst 'consumer society' is opposed to an imagined non-consumer (work) society, and so is a claim about the nature of the social world, 'consumer culture' refers to the means through which cultures are reproduced through markets, that is, how culture makes economy (Slater, 1997: 205). 'Culture' in this book is used as defined by Raymond Williams, as 'a whole way of life' (1958). Culture refers to how we live in communities, eat, arrange our living spaces, are educated and use consumer products. A consumer culture might exist where everyday life is inflected by market relations, where consumer products play a significant role in assigning meanings and where consumption is not a rare practice, nor restricted to the wealthy, but central to how individuals express their cultural identities. In this section, we will consider debates over the first emergence of consumer societies.

In Chapter 2, 'From global trade to global consumer capitalism', we referred to Braudel's historical studies that linked the economic to culture and the material. Historians inspired by Braudel's work have contributed a great deal to understanding the complexity of consumer capitalism, especially to unpacking the interconnections between production and consumption. A great deal of this discussion has been framed around two related questions: What is a consumer society? When did consumer society arrive in Europe? These are big and important questions in themselves, but may give the mistaken impression that consumer cultures only matter in the West, and that Americanisation is the key motif. This is not so. However, whilst many of the studies we discuss acknowledge that global trading patterns and exploitative colonial power were important to emergent consumer societies, these tend to imply that India and China, for example, mattered as producers of goods traded to the West, but not as importers and consumers. There is comparatively little research that looks at the emergence of consumerism beyond Europe and the US, and this does leave something of an empty space in our discussion. As we will see, writers like Chua (2003), O'Dougherty (2002) consider contemporary consumer cultures in Singapore and Brazil (respectively), and our focus will be less geographically narrow when we discuss contemporary consumption. But the particular trajectories of consumerism in these places are not well understood. As the historian Trentmann (2004, 2009) says, consumer culture has multiple histories and geographies and cannot be explained with reference to a definitive moment or event, such as the arrival of consumer society in the US and its subsequent mimicking elsewhere. And so, whilst in the discussion that follows I present a fairly standard story of the emergence of consumer culture in the specific case of Britain, with some comparisons to elsewhere in Europe and to the US in the 20th century, we should remember that this is a specific, local history that is not intended to imply that consumerism always emerges in the same way. We will begin by looking at 'supply-side', production-led explanations for the development of consumerism.

Production

In sociology, economics, geography and comparable disciplines, production processes are often privileged as the explanation for social and economic change. This implies that supply drives demand, and so that the explanation for a new 'consumer society' is that the factory system in 19th-century Europe, specifically Britain, generated 'surplus' products at ever cheaper prices that could be bought by the new class of wage labourers. New means of transporting goods between growing urban spaces were also a result of the apparent 'industrial revolution' and meant that retail infrastructure developed and consumption increased (Alexander, 1970). In this explanation, consumption is an outcome of production and technological change.

Many historians followed this kind of reasoning and positioned the coming of consumer society as an outcome of the industrial revolution (e.g. Fraser, 1981). They point to how fixed sites for shopping replaced hawkers, fairs and street markets (Alexander, 1970: 6–8), the growth in the size of shops and in the variety of stock and increasing numbers of multiple retailers (Fraser, 1981: 94), and how production and distribution were separated from the new shopping arenas. The simple story can be complicated in two important (and interconnected) ways. First, recalling the ideas about global trade discussed in Chapter 2 means we must pay a different kind of attention to what kinds of goods might be on offer, and how they might be brought to market. And second, that meaning, culture and identities were formed in relation to consumption. These complications mean that we need to unpick the historical story of the 19th-century 'revolution' to find a more complex, multilayered account of the intersection of production and consumption that might prove useful for exploring consumption in other times and places, as well as for understanding the moral and political consequences of consumer capitalism.

Culture: sales and desires

Sociologists like Sombart (see Chapter 2, 'From global trade to global consumer capitalism') who were writing in the early 20th century, like some contemporary historians of consumption, argue against the simple 'production-led' explanations for the coming of a consumer society. Neil McKendrick's thesis (1982) on the development of 18th-century consumer markets is perhaps the most important contemporary revision of the production-first argument. There was a 'consumer revolution in 18th century England' (McKendrick et al., 1982: 1). Only England had the right mix for a consumer society in the 18th century: a fluid social structure, rising wages, an emulative bourgeoisie, a culturally powerful capital city and intellectual environment. Intellectual changes included the spread of Adam Smith's arguments that economic growth could be furthered by expansion of production and consumption. McKendrick uses the example of the English potter, Josiah Wedgwood, to make his biggest claims about how consumption and production were interconnected. Wedgwood benefited from technological innovations in the production of china, and – a simple but very important development when you consider the fragile nature of the product – the new canals that enabled the china plates, bowls and vases to be transported smoothly from factory to markets. But he also was able to make his china fashionable amongst wealthy elites. He considered sales when he planned production and marketed his pottery to encourage fashions to change more rapidly. His sales rooms had tables set for dinner so potential customers could imagine using the items. McKendrick uses this example to show how emulation, and the rising importance of fashion, contributed to a consumer society. The McKendrick thesis is that consumer society developed through a congruence of production (new techniques), consumption (new markets amongst the growing upper middle classes) and distribution (new transportation and sales strategies).

Others suggest that McKendrick does not go far enough in moving away from productionist explanations. Colin Campbell, in *The Romantic Ethic and the Spirit of Modern Consumerism* (1987), draws on and critiques Weber's Protestant ethic to foreground culture, ideology and ethics, rather than production and sales. He argues that consumer culture did not arrive merely because of mass access to consumer goods, but because of changes to the judgements society makes about consumption. For Campbell, a consumer society relies on a revolution in production and consumption. Alongside a Protestant work ethic, there must be an ethic that legitimates consumption. He finds this ethic in phenomena which he suggests are often dismissed as trivial, such as fashion, romantic love, taste and fiction. Demand and desire generate a modern consumer culture through a new ethical and aesthetic attachment to novelty. The ethic of romanticism legitimated daydreaming, fantasy and self-indulgence, and was spread by one of the new commodities: novels. Daydreams involve looking forward in time from reality and create desires that – perhaps – consumer goods could fulfil. Actual consumption was not the key to pleasure; instead, private fantasies of what consumption might bring mattered:

> individuals do not so much seek satisfaction from products, as pleasure from the self-illusory experiences which they construct from their associated meanings. The essential activity of consumption is thus not the actual selection, purchase or use of products, but the imaginative pleasure-seeking to which the product image lends itself, 'real' consumption being largely a resultant of this 'mentalistic' hedonism. (Campbell, 1987: 89)

Consumer objects matter not for what they permit us to indicate to others, but for what intimate desires they speak to, for the excitement of a new experience. This argument foregrounds the sense of self of the consumer, that is, their subjectivity. However, in addition to imaginative desires, new opportunities to consume also matter.

Shopping

We can bring together the arguments about production and infrastructure, and about culture and fantasy by exploring the development of
consumption as an activity. Historical accounts of the development of
shops and shopping help us to see what a consumer society looks like.
A consumer society relies on access to a choice of goods and to shopping spaces. Designated shopping streets, covered shopping bazaars
and 'monster shops' offering fixed price sales are important to a new
consumer society, but the department stores, offering the 'world of
goods' under one roof, are the real symbols of a consumer revolution
(Leach, 1993). These developed from the mid-19th century in Europe
and the US and offered consumers the opportunity to browse. To us
this sounds quite ordinary, but browsing was not common prior to this.
Consumers learned how to engage in this new leisure activity and to
find pleasure in looking and imagining; a new kind of dream world,
suggests Wilson (2003). Instead of conversing with retailers, anonymous shoppers had more personal encounters with objects (Sassatelli,
2007: 27). The Bon Marché, founded in Paris in 1852, is seen as the
first department store (Miller, 1981), although similar developments
were occurring in the US:

> The department store alone did not lead to the appearance of a consumer
> society, but it did stand at the center of this phenomenon. As an economic
> mechanism it made that society possible, and as an institution with a large
> provincial trade it made the culture of consumption a national one. (Miller,
> 1981: 165)

The expansion of department stores mirrored the emergence of newly
wealthy middle-class households, who were the main clientele.

Divisions of gender and ethnicity are also visible in the 19th-century
department store. Department stores were places where 'respectable'
women could appear in public, drink tea together and purchase
necessities and frivolities from the 'world of goods' under one roof.
Middle-class women – the target audience of the new novels discussed by Campbell, and discursively constructed as virtuous (Davidoff, 1995) – were the new consumers, but their feminine weaknesses
caused anxieties. The lady shoplifter (Abelson, 1989), the shopgirl
who thinks too much of herself and the demanding 'tabbies' who ask
for service without being likely to buy anything (Rappaport, 2000)
were of concern at the time. These anxieties about the seductions of
consumption indicate that the cultural shift towards accepting consumption was not straightforward. Race was on view – and for

sale – in 19th-century Britain. The colonised countries of the Empire were represented by consumer goods, as in the case of the fashion for Indian cotton, and the patriotic consumer was urged to buy Empire goods (for example, during Empire Shopping Week in the 1920s and 1930s (Trentmann, 2007); in upstate New York at the same time, Americans used consumption to build national identity (Elvins, 2004). Colonial power was signalled 'back home' through the spectacular displays of 'exotic' objects like the Koh-i-Noor diamond on view in Harrods department store (Kinsey, 2009), as well as consumer goods for sale, and the new 'worldly' consumer looked differently at new objects brought from colonies (Mukerji, 1983). The consumer society did not just make consumers, but made for national and local belonging.

Culture, identity and subjectivity mattered in the new consumer settings, but these relied too on wholesaling and retail management and on new industries like advertising and management (de Grazia, 1998: 65). Economic shifts are always also shifts of culture, and the argument that the 19th- and early 20th-century department stores were emblematic of a new kind of consumerism is powerful. However, is it possible to speak of a consumer society if only middle-class households engage in this kind of hedonism?

The emergence of mass

We have seen so far that changes to the production of goods, to distribution, to the ideology and ethics of desire and consumption and to techniques of sales are entwined when understanding emergent consumerism. A consumer society, though, where identities are formed in relation to consumption, not work, implies that the pleasures and frustrations of consumerism are widely shared, not confined to the wealthy. Still with our focus on the West, in this section we see how a mass consumer society developed with mass production, mass consumption and rationalised distribution.

20th-century mass-consumer culture

The Fordist system involved mass consumption of mass-produced goods (Chapter 2, 'Post-Fordism'). It relied on greater political commitment to mass consumption, and this marked an important ideological shift (Ewen and Ewen, 1982). Understanding a mass market means asking questions about consumption as well as production. Why do consumers prefer to buy things than make them, or live without?

And how do producers learn about what consumers want? A mass consumer society is associated with marketing and advertising techniques, and with distribution and retailing that does not add excessively to the cost of the cheaply produced goods.

The development of chain stores in the early 20th century was an important contribution to the mass market, as grocery chain stores morphed into that most mundane and significant form of retail, the supermarket. Chain stores sold standardised goods in standardised outlets and used self-service. The significant developments in distribution and sales in the first half of the 20th century are summarised by Bowlby as the triumph of the 'silent salesman'. Shop windows, packaging, posters and other forms of advertising sold goods (Bowlby, 2000: 35) in new outlets: self-service chain stores and, increasingly, supermarkets. Supermarkets increased the amount of influence the retailer had over the goods and influenced the display of goods in store (both their packaging and their location in a store). Design came to matter in simple ways: self-service packaging had to be appealing and ensure that products could be seen without being damaged. It also mattered for how it generated and reflected cultural meanings, as when the streamlined 'jet age' designs of 1950s consumer products suited the engineering of those products and the spirit of the age (Votolato, 1998).

Supermarket baskets, and later trolleys, made it possible for the consumer to carry her selections to the till (and the gendered language is deliberate, as those who designed retail spaces imagined shoppers to be female (Humphrey, 1998)). Cochoy, an STS thinker (Chapter 2, 'Markets as moral projects') (2008, 2009) discusses the importance of 'market-things' in how consumer capitalism operates. Scholars often study consumer objects (branded goods, for example), but take for granted the devices that make shopping possible. Cochoy looks at the introduction of shopping trollies (carts) and asks what '[t]he grocer's property but also the customer's tool' (2008: 48–9) made possible. Customer behaviour is affected by trolleys, and by supermarkets' attempts to control the use of trolleys (for example, by adding coin-operated devices to prevent theft (Cochoy, 2009). Other devices like branded carrier bags are intended to travel further. The shopper does the work of carrying, packing and delivery, and in return, gets cheaper goods. Now the supermarket model is familiar to us, used for all kinds of goods in addition to food (for example, garden and DIY products, cosmetics and toiletries), and even small shops may follow the supermarket aisle layout. The flexible supply chains discussed in Chapter 2 are key to chain supermarkets, which rely on distribution networks that enable them to buy in bulk from suppliers, and hence negotiate discounts (Burke and Shackleton, 1996). Merchandising systems tend to dictate the flow of goods from suppliers to customers. Delivery schedules and EPOS (electronic point of sale) technologies facilitate production and stock control by enabling anticipated sales to be modelled. That this has been effective is shown by how concentration in the hands of big retailers has increased, particularly since the 1980s (Gardner and Sheppard, 1989: 162–3).

Once again, we have begun by focusing on the supply side. But productionist explanations of mass retail are not comprehensive. Consumer society relies on workers responding to rising wages by consuming more, not working less. Some of the reasons for the 'work-and-spend culture' (Cross, 1993: 5) can be explored by developing Campbell's idea of the 'romantic ethic'. New leisure activities of the 20th century, such as films, provide new sources for fantasy and different desires for consumer goods. Another reason may be that consumerism provides a source of belonging and is a cause and response to anxiety when geographical and class mobility changes communities: 'a Woolworth's culture guaranteed universal consumer participation while it confirmed a social hierarchy of consumption; it induced a seeming endless chase up the ladder of spending and working' (Cross, 1993: 176).

The necessary features of mass consumption emerged in the first half of the 20th century, but the phenomenon is most associated with the 1950s, when consumer goods like cars, televisions and refrigerators became common. This reflects a shift in cultural attitudes and practices of consumerism, and a restructuring of the economy to legitimate commercial leisure. May refers to 1950s consumer society as an 'American work-to-consume ethic' (1999 [1988]: 300), focused around a consumer-oriented suburban family life, where class divisions lessened, but gender divisions were reinforced. Political recognition that consumerism was a way of assimilating class and ethnic difference meant that mass access to consumer goods was supported as a means of ensuring social stability. Lee describes the 'mass availability of consumer goods' (Lee, 2000: ix) as *the* most significant transformation to ordinary lives in the 20th century. It brought whole new areas of social life under the sway of the market.

Critics of mass

In the 1950s, American economist J. K. Galbraith (1958) challenged the then typical rationale for mass production, that production was simply aimed at satisfying consumers' needs, instead suggesting that production created desires through advertising. He argued that, given its size and power and its technical apparatus, commerce cannot help but dominate over consumer power, with cycles of technical change and planned obsolescence (where a good is designed to have a limited lifespan) giving a rhythm to production and consumption. Vance Packard, an American journalist, developed a popular critique of the power of scientific marketing in *The Hidden Persuaders* (1957), and later Packard challenged the political and cultural obsession with economic growth despite the obsolescence and waste that came with it. However, a more powerful critique of commercial culture came from a group of German Marxist scholars, the Frankfurt School.

The Frankfurt School was a loose collective of German Marxist thinkers based initially at the University of Frankfurt in the 1920s and 1930s and who later migrated to the US because of Nazism. The Frankfurt School used a narrower definition of culture to the 'whole way of life' conceptualisation mentioned earlier, focusing on art, literature and music ('high' culture). They were critical of the effects of commodifying and commercialising culture, and were important to the development of 'critical theory'. Critical theory involves using conceptual tools (derived predominantly from Marx) to reveal inequalities, relations of domination and subordination and to advocate for changes to society. It is a value-laden theory which is explicitly aimed at improving social life.

Traditional Marxist theory suggested that the central antagonism of capitalist society was between those who owned the means of production and those who sold labour (the relations of production and the productive forces). Frankfurt School writers were concerned with questioning how the 'superstructures' of society and culture contributed to the exploitation of those who sold wage labour, as the extension of commodity culture affected home life and cultural consumption. Critical of Marxism's lack of attention to ideology and cultural practices, they argued that culture cannot reach its potential to be emancipatory when it is commercialised: 'The culture industry endlessly cheats its consumers of what it endlessly promises' (Horkheimer and Adorno, 2006: 53). Their argument (and fear) is that people are easily duped by commodities and promotional culture.

'Culture' becomes 'the cultural industry' when instrumental reasoning is applied to turn spaces of freedom and beauty into commodities. Art and music are glorious, but reproductions of prints and jazz records are not. Frankfurt School writers saw cultural commodities as agents of social control. They seem to promise relief from the burden of work, but instead reconstruct workers as consumers of commodities. The culture industry accrues value from culture, as though culture was a good like any other, amenable to streamlined production and the generation of exchange value. 'High' culture, synonymous with 'the arts', could be emancipatory as it was not in thrall to the standardised production methods of Hollywood or Tin Pan Alley. Popular culture was especially vulnerable to the accusation that it pandered to an already subjugated mass of the population. High culture reduces itself to low culture when it adapts to the market, when 'the listener is converted, along his line of least resistance, into the acquiescent purchaser' (Adorno, [1938] 1991: 32), as cultural commodities are then homogenous and predictable.

Consumption and modernity

We have looked so far at the history of consumer society. We have shown that historians have paid a lot of attention to its provenance and trajectory, and we have seen some of the anxieties that commercial cultures may entail. Sociologists who look at this historical story are tempted to make a different kind of claim to those above, to say not just that 'these are the important changes', but also that these changes reflect, and themselves generate, a different way of life. To put it differently, consumer society heralds a new modernity. In this section, we will discuss the ideas of those sociologists interested in explaining modernity, who suggest that consumption is key to the modern subject. As Don Slater says, 'consumer culture is a motif threaded through the texture of modernity, a motif that recapitulates the preoccupations and characteristic styles of thought of the modern west' (1997: 1). The precise nature of what the concept 'modernity' means needs careful attention. Modernity exists in opposition to the 'premodern', and in this definition tends to mean the era of industrial capitalism, Fordist and Taylorist production, social (class) stratification, and a political emphasis on rights, equality and some kinds of freedom. In addition, more contentiously and related to our earlier discussion of consumer society, modernity is an era where identity stems from consumption, not production. A 'modern self' is individualised for sociologists of modernity. Instead of seeing a self that is fixed and known from birth, they suggest that selfhood is an ongoing, reflexive project to which consumerism contributes in the absence of traditional markers of belonging such as class and family. Anonymous city living and secularisation also contribute to the growth of lifestyle and consumption as the means to self-realisation.

Georg Simmel (1858–1918), a German sociologist, explored the modern phenomena of city life by considering subjectivity and its relationship to the world of objects. His ideas are still important to how 'modernity' is thought about today. He reflects on the new spatial arrangements of modern life, the growth of cities and opportunities for shopping and other leisure pursuits that these provided. For Simmel (1903, [1997] 1904 [1957]), industrial capitalism increases the objectification and commodification of human life, and yet consumer goods are attractive for their novelty and for the sensual pleasures they provide. Consumption, fashion and city life are enduring sites of social and psychological struggle in the modern world. For example, Simmel says that fashion works through imitation (social conformity) and differentiation (individual distinction). Women (and again we see that consumption is gendered) are eager to adopt new fashions because they crave difference and individuality through consumption, being otherwise undistinguished. Wilson (2003), in a study of fashion, says Simmel shows us that modernity brings a more intense awareness of subjectivity. Fashion is part of how city life is mentally challenging. It offers an overload of stimulation to consumers that they balance by calculating, distancing and becoming blasé. Money makes it easier to be blasé, as it generates impersonality in economic relations. The features of modernity that Simmel emphasises are complicated and he shows us the ambivalences and complexities of modern life well. There is no simple claim that consumerism is bad in his work.

Contemporary writers have seen consumer culture as a defining feature of contemporary 'liquid' modernity, and are suspicious of it (Beck, 2000; Bauman, 2005; Ransome, 2005; Gabriel and Lang, 2006). Of these writings, those by Zygmunt Bauman are best known. Bauman uses the metaphor of a 'liquid' modernity to suggest that contemporary life is characterised by contingent, temporary and fluid attachments to the world around us, and to each other. Work is 'liquid', as people do not have jobs for life but move from job to job – perhaps even sector to sector – looking for something that fulfils who they are at that moment, and that provides them with the income they feel they need for their lifestyle. In 'a society of consumers' (Bauman, 1998: 2) identity is not derived from production, but from 'the aesthetic of consumption' (29). Consumption and lifestyle provide a means to create individual identity and social cohesion, but also cause division. The financially secure are seduced by consumption as individuals, and this shared security and seduction has the effect of creating them as a coherent group with similar interests. They encounter seemingly limitless consumption and are insatiable; 'Life is not complete without shopping' (Chua, 2003). They must be willing to be seduced and they must be offered new temptations. They have the freedom to consume, but it might seem like unfreedom; they have no choice but to consume. For the workless and the poor, being outside the charmed circle of consumers is a double burden. They may desire the fulfilment that consumption promises but are unable to get it. But also they are excluded and denigrated for their 'failure' to consume (Bauman, 1998).

Consumer goods themselves are volatile and temporary, and the satisfactions that quickly attained objects of desire provide wane equally quickly. The processes of consumerism are more stable: providers of goods and services work to seduce; economies are organised around desire, feelings and choice. The cultural processes that classify objects (as 'must-haves') are part of this modernity and are worked on by intermediary professions which encourage individualised expression in leisure time and self-fulfilment through work. Classifications also matter when consumer spaces are 'themed' (Gottdiener, 1997), when fashions are judged and when consumer experiences that are both aestheticised and standardised are offered. One marker of modernity, suggests George Ritzer (1998), is the rationalisation of leisure and pleasure characterised by the chain restaurant McDonald's.

Ritzer suggests that McDonaldisation is the dominant form of service production in contemporary societies, with rationality – efficiency, calculation, predictability and control (rather than quality) – governing production (Ritzer, 1998: 100–101). Customers know what to expect, workers know what they are expected to do, products are consistent. McDonald's uses production lines and the scientific management of workers and customers to produce and sell a limited range of products. Whilst there is some variation in products according to local cultural norms, the key principle is that the product is identifiable and similar. Such 'economies of replication' (du Gay, 1996: 102) generate predictable experiences for consumers and have extended beyond fast-food restaurants to other forms of consumption. Bryman marks a comparable process in his 'Disneyization' thesis (2004), showing how where cross-merchandising in themed leisure experiences is common (see Chapter 6, 'Emotion and capitalism'). Both writers tend towards overstatement, but point to the ongoing importance of standardisation in consumption.

Bauman's thesis tying consumerist individualisation to 'liquid modernity' (2000) is the kind of general narrative explanation of consumerism that Trentmann (2009) asks us to be cautious about. First, the 'modern' person of the early 20th century that Simmel discusses was also encouraged into self-expression through consumption, and Campbell (1987) suggests that there are antecedents to the contemporary reflexive self. So what is new in 'liquid modernity'? Second, Ritzer reminds us that a key means of 'self-expression' is rationalised, ritualised, formulaic consumption. This means that both 'mass' production and consumption persist in an era that others would call post-Fordist, and it means that consumerism is as predictable as it is seductive.

Modernity and consumerism beyond the West

The global workings of capitalism were obvious in our consideration of production in Chapter 2, but there is far less material available (in English) on Japan, China, India and other parts of Asia, and even less on other parts of the world where consumerism is increasingly significant. Europe and North America dominate. Does this matter? Trentmann (2009) says it does. Without this historical balance, the story of consumer culture appears clear, linear, coherent and universal: that a country will reach a stage of development that marks its transition to a consumer society, and that non-Western countries are simply later to develop. Further, the lack of research implies that Europe and the US are more interesting to study, and that other places matter for how they relate to the West – as providers of goods, or people, as the focus of colonial attention and as the 'rest' against which the 'West' can compare itself (Hall, 1992) – rather than in their own right.

If you are from China or have visited India or have friends from former communist countries in Eastern Europe, you will know that consumerism is not confined to the 'West', nor is it the same in all places that you know about. You might have witnessed the development of a new shopping mall or noticed a shampoo with its label written in several languages. These tiny examples might have increased in number during your lifetime, and indicate the global relevance of consumer culture, and the modernity that this reflects and produces. Sociologists might interpret qualitative changes in shopping and shampoo as reflecting a new modernity; economists interested in measuring development in 'emerging economies' use the pattern of consumption as an indicator of that development. Consumer culture has grown recently, especially in East Asia and in the emergent powerhouse BRIC countries. Table 3.1 indicates how the share of consumer expenditure is distributed between world regions. Europe and North America's share of global consumption decreased in the period 2009–2014, whilst that of other regions is increasing. It has risen most in the BRIC countries.

Table 3.1   Percentage of consumer expenditure, by region

	2009	2010	2011	2012	2013	2014
Asia Pacific	22.14	23.38	24.53	25.47	24.72	25.05
Australasia	1.80	2.07	2.22	2.30	2.19	2.10
Middle East & Africa	5.34	5.49	5.50	5.71	6.10	6.19
Eastern Europe	4.61	4.68	4.87	4.81	4.99	4.57
Western Europe	28.20	26.31	25.87	24.15	24.28	24.17
North America	30.00	29.21	27.95	28.41	28.54	28.80
Latin America	7.91	8.87	9.06	9.14	9.18	9.11
WORLD	100	100	100	100	100	100
BRIC countries	*12.15*	*13.58*	*14.87*	*15.42*	*16.13*	*16.54*

Source: Calculated from Consumer Expenditure: Euromonitor International – from national statistics/Eurostat/UN/OECD. Compares at current prices.

Qualitative evidence suggests that consumer identities are now more significant for middle-class Brazilians (O'Dougherty, 2002). The 'private paradise' of home ownership in residential areas of some Chinese cities shapes middle-class subjectivity as distinctive (Zhang, 2010). Comparable stories of the leisure and consumption practices that are associated with an emergent middle class can be seen in India (Fernandes, 2000; Brosius, 2010). In post-socialist Hungary, consumers look explicitly to Western Europe and the US for ideas about good forms of consumption (Fehérváry, 2002). These trends matter.

Established global corporations are targeting current and future sales efforts to elites and middle-income earners in emerging economies (London and Hart, 2004), and new kinds of global corporations are growing from within emerging economies (Guillén and García-Canal, 2009). Comparatively recent increases in levels of disposable income make new shopping complexes viable, generate new media industries (such as those making Chinese language material), and new markets for existing global chains (such as Subway and Starbucks) and for consumer products (such as imported bottled water) develop. So global consumer capitalism is more encompassing than is revealed by focusing on WESTERN countries, and is changing as disposable income, consumer subjectivity and consumption infrastructures increase. It's worth noting that those incorporated into global capitalism through being involved in the production of global goods are not always those who are consuming goods. Low wages and long hours for those making consumer goods do not always leave enough money for luxuries beyond subsistence (and actual pay packets may be lower than published wage rates (Chan and Siu, 2010)). This is a significant inequality. Worker rights campaigns and consumer activist groups like *War on Want*, *Labour Behind the Label* and the *Clean Clothes Campaign* work hard to demonstrate the way mass access to cheap consumer goods in comparatively wealthy countries is based on these goods remaining cheap. Employee wages are kept low to keep costs down, and even when manufacturers and consumer brands sign up to ethical codes, standards are not always maintained (Hale, 2000). We return to this problem in Chapter 8.

The accounts of consumer society we have discussed suggest that a visible consumer culture emerged in the 19th century and, that a mass consumer culture did not arrive until the mid-20th century, when cultural and economic changes extended consumerism beyond the wealthy classes. We have seen how changes overlap and co-create each other, and that patterns that seem from one angle to be new and dramatic have their precedents in the recent past. Contemporary consumption in the Western economies that we have focused on and in the more recently consumerist societies of wealthy Asia and South America can scarcely be described as Fordist mass consumption. How then, should we think about contemporary consumerism?

Explaining consumption

In this section, we look in more detail at what counts as 'consumption'. We define consumption and compare goods, services and experiences. We then look at key theories of consumption as developed by economists, sociologists of different kinds, cultural studies scholars and anthropologists. Then we consider how consumption is promoted by advertising, marketing and associated industries.

Commodities, goods, services and experiences

In its simplest definition, consumption is the use of scarce resources. Things are consumed as they are used up. As use implies waste, loss and destruction, this definition of consumption may contribute to the moral denigration that is attached to some forms of consumption. However, the term has other connotations. Consumption might mean household shopping, holidaying, making use of things, eating and drinking, interpreting cultural performances. It involves 'culture' and 'economy'; it is an inevitable part of living. Although 'intermediate' consumption, that is, consumption used for production, matters in global capitalism, as when tomatoes are consumed in the making of a jar of tomato sauce (Harvey et al. 2002) or computers are purchased in bulk for use in an office (Molotch, 2003: 131), our focus is on what consumers do. Consumption in contemporary society is largely conducted through market relations. Commodities are produced in order to be sold in the market and 'integral to our consumption is the act of choosing between a range of alternative commodities' (Slater, 1997: 25). Commodification is a marker of consumer society and many suggest that more and more of social life is marketed (Strasser, 2003), although as Williams and Windebank (2003) point out, consumption can move out of the sphere of the market as well as into it, that is, 'decommodification' may occur when market exchange is replaced by · another mode of exchange. Here, we focus on objects which encounter the market during their lifespan, that is, commodities.

I use the terms things, products and objects in this book somewhat interchangeably to refer to the goods, services and experiences bought and sold in consumer capitalism. Material things are at the heart of how we live as social beings. In the clothes we wear, the houses we live in and the food we eat, we engage with the social world, and with culture, through engaging with stuff. This means 'all objects are culturally meaningful and indeed that no objects can be simply functional' (Slater, 1997: 136). 'Things', 'objects' or 'products' may seem inappropriate terms when considering services and experiences, such as a haircut, a visit to the cinema or an open top bus tour of a city you're visiting, because these kinds of commodities have a different lifespan to a new pair of shoes or other good. But they are worth considering in the same terms because of how they are constituted within consumer capitalism as commodities. As with goods, the material and immaterial dimensions of services and experiences are important to understanding them as commodities.

In global capitalism, goods, services and experiences are consumed as commodities. We might choose between the array of 'FMCG' (fast-moving consumer goods) options in a supermarket, or between apparently clearly differentiated 'big ticket' items in a car showroom or furniture store. The moment at which a product goes from being generally available to anyone passing by with enough money to being the property of an individual is important. My table stopped being something you might consume from the moment I bought it. Ownership was transferred when I paid for it and, instead of having many potential users/consumers, it now has only a few, socially connected consumers (my family and friends). This is fairly reasonable of me. But what if I owned the street light outside my house and only turned it on when I needed to use it? This would not be reasonable, and public provision makes more sense in this case. What about my washing machine? In the UK it's normal to own one, but if you live in a flat in Scandinavia you might share one and have set times when you can use it. There are many possible relationships between ownership and use, and different ways of organising consumption. People may have strongly held beliefs about what consumption should be private and what should be provided by the state. As Gabriel and Lang say, 'In all of its meanings, consumerism is neither ethically nor politically neutral, and is therefore a terrain to be contested and argued over' (Gabriel and Lang, 2006: 9). When I have bought a table (or a coffee or a go on a rollercoaster) these have been private acts of consumption that rely on the infrastructures of production and consumption, and also on the meanings that exist in relation to these purchases. How can we understand these kinds of practices?

Rationality and consumption

In neoclassical economics (Chapter 2, 'Doux commerce'), consumers are conceptualised and modelled as sovereign. The choices they make are aggregated into 'demand' and their purchases drive the market. The simplest versions of economics do not question the meanings of consumer choices, which are deemed exogenous to their models, that is, determined by factors external to the model; preferences are seen as private. They assume that consumers are instrumental and maximise 'utility', the term economists use to refer to satisfaction. Consumption here seems just a question of 'decision making' between an array of choices; it's not a complex process. From this perspective, rational decision making by individuals leads to the efficient allocation of scarce resources. The traditional view of economists is that 'the individual consumer seeks to maximise utility at a moment in time, subject to an income constraint' (Roth, 1989: 37), with utility being provided from the goods consumed over time. A rational consumer knows which consumption 'bundles' he prefers (again, the gendered language is deliberate, as economists often assume the default actor is male), cannot have multiple preferences for the same bundles and is consistent in his preferences

(Roth, 1989: 37–8). Consumers who are 'savvy' in checking price comparison sites or consumer advice literature are engaging in this kind of rational consumption. Preferences are revealed through market decisions as to what people buy and how much they spend. The idea of the sovereign customer is important for how it gives rise to a politics of consumer power and consumer rights that is institutionalised in law.

Economics is always a more complex discipline than its critics suggest, and so this explanation is simplified. There are, of course, more sophisticated models used by economists that try to understand the derivation of tastes and preferences and how they change over time, and the constraints on rational decision making. Some economists try to model status effects, for example considering whether others' having something makes us more or less likely to want it ourselves (because goods are 'positional'). Nonetheless, it remains narrow in its understanding of consumers because of the assumptions of rationality and utility maximisation. We do calculate and make rational decisions about consumption – but only in some cases. Often we don't have time to calculate value, or we have to sideline our own preferences in favour of those of our family or we choose something for reasons that aren't about utility. One obvious critique of economics made by sociologists is that needs and desires are constructed not given, that they are historically and geographically changeable, and that a 'basic' need always takes a specific cultural form, expressing something beyond biology. For example, food is a basic need, but bread means something different to rice; beef would be acceptable to some, but inedible to others; some would want to choose branded goods. Culture and need are linked in all but the most extreme scenarios (Slater, 1997: 134–5). Indeed, 'necessity' needs to be reframed in contemporary consumer culture: shoes are a necessity, but they are not consumed as such (Schroeder, 2002: 7). Marketing scholars who work with 'consumer culture theory' (CCT) provide a critical assessment of how marketing goes wrong when it agrees with the economic construction of the rational actor. Holbrook and Hirschman (1982) argued for recognition of how hedonism, desire and the 'pleasure principle' drive consumers. Private experiences of consumption, and the sensory and emotional pleasures they contain, matter to understanding consumption. In the rest of this section, we consider how CCT and sociology have provided alternate ways of considering consumption, beginning with how social status generates 'needs' and preferences.

Consumption and social status

Sociologists think differently about the factors that economists treat as 'exogenous'. Social status is a commonly studied influence on consumption. In 1899, American economist and sociologist Thorstein Veblen (1857–1929) published *The Theory of the Leisure Class*. The 'leisure class' are those who do not do productive labour, who fill their days by engaging in conspicuous consumption. Conspicuous consumption involves extravagance and waste. The luxurious living of the leisure class creates 'status emulation' in those lower down the social scale, whose copying of new fashions creates a 'trickle down' effect. As lower status members of society adopt fashions, the leisure class searches for something new to differentiate themselves. (Wealthy) women, less likely to engage in productive labour, are the important conspicuous consumers, and Veblen finds their practices quite distasteful. Whilst Veblen's work has been criticised because 'trickle down' does not really explain changes to fashion and the 'leisure class' no longer exists, conspicuous consumption is a good example of how consumption can create differentiation and social cohesion. In recent times, for example, O'Dougherty (2002) describes middle-class Brazilians' desire for the 'car of the year' to indicate their status amongst friends, neighbours and colleagues and to show that they fit in.

A more sophisticated account of class, consumption and status than Veblen's is offered by French sociologist Pierre Bourdieu (1930–2002). *Distinction* (1984) provides a closely argued and detailed analysis and itemisation of the cultural habits and preferences in all class fractions of French society in the late 1960s, and has been very influential. It suggests that cultural knowledges and behaviours are class based, with different tastes reflecting and constituting the *habitus* of different groups of people. Habitus refers to the embodied properties of class and is the product of a slow and subtle socialisation process. For Bourdieu, class is expressed in the way a person thinks, speaks, walks, talks and acts and in the things they like. Those in different class fractions are likely to hold different levels of economic, social and cultural capital. 'Cultural capital' is particularly relevant to understanding the meaning of consumption. Tastes and preferences for some things over others indicate a person's social position. Thus tastes are socially determined; they are products of a habitus and a shared class understanding of what is desirable. For Bourdieu, class and social position are critical in influencing who wants to consume what. Consumption signals class, indeed it cannot help but define us to ourselves and to others; 'taste classifies, and it classifies the classifier' (Bourdieu, 1984: 6). Bourdieu suggests that cultural capital is used to maintain social privilege and exclude others by framing some sets of cultural knowledge as important and right. High-status class fractions arrange their homes differently, and engage in different leisure activities to lower classes.

Others share Bourdieu's observations that imitation and differentiation matter, as we saw with our earlier discussion of Simmel, that class matters, as Veblen suggested, and that consumption expresses and stabilises cultural categories (Douglas and Isherwood, 1996). Bourdieu offers two further insights. First, that consumption is a site of struggle and antagonism, as when 'symbolic violence' is enacted on those who engage in the wrong kind of consumption. Symbolic violence occurs when tastes are derided or others are excluded on the grounds of their tastes. Second, that the capacity of goods to differentiate is produced by some categories of workers: cultural intermediaries, discussed in Chapter 4.

Of course, social class is not the only marker of social status. Consumption may also mark differences of gender, age, race, sexuality and locale, and be used to include or exclude from social groups. Patterns and norms of consumption by some social groups may contribute to judgements made about them, as we saw in the discussion in 'Shopping' of how women were apparently vulnerable to the temptations of consumption. A comparable moral judgement is visible in accounts of consumption by minority ethnic groups, for over-consuming or for not consuming the right goods (see the discussion in Chin, 2001); others suggest that marketing strategies differ for non-white people (Molnár and Lamont, 2002). Cook (2004) points to how the values and meanings created by commercial cultures around childhood are also those through which childhood is culturally understood. For Cook, commodification isn't imposed on a pristine state of childhood, nor is it a process imposed on individualised children, but forms the basis for children's culture, as when the 'boundaries and exigencies of childhood have become market segments in and of children's culture – for example, in the particular styles and goods produced and consumed around the persona of "the toddler"' (Cook, 2004: 6, see also Kline, 1998). Childhood is thereby made in part through consumption, and social class can matter, as when Belgian parents in low-income families sacrifice their own consumption in favour of their children's desires (Kochuyt, 2004). However, the complex meanings offered by consumer goods may also be a source of self-identity, autonomy and power. Youth subcultures have used consumption to signal belonging, from the Vespa motorcycles ridden by UK 'mods' that separate them from others, to using white, not silver, eyeshadow to show to others in Shibuya district Tokyo that you are *Mamba* rather than *Celemba* (Kawamura, 2012: 54). These are examples from the discipline of cultural studies, which has long considered the consumer to create meanings in the world of goods.

Consumption and identity

In the 1980s, scholars in cultural studies, and those influenced by postmodern ideas (sometimes the same people) led a 'cultural turn'. The 'cultural turn' paid more attention to culture (and concomitantly less to economy and production). Postmodern writers like Lyotard (1984) and Baudrillard (1998) suggested that unifying and totalising 'grand narratives', such as the centrality of class in modernity, were invalid and untrustworthy. Instead, social life could only be thought of as fragmented, multiple and uncertain. Consumer cultures provide a source for fragmented and multiple identities: shop in the supermarket of possibilities for some inauthentic street style (Polhemus, 1994). For Fiske (1989), consumption may be transformative, as consumers adopt meanings that differ from those assigned by producers. From this position, consumption becomes a site of positive resistance to power structures (Willis, 1990). Those exploring defiant or playful approaches to consumption (de Certeau, 1984), who position culture as lived through daily life and who see something celebratory in the way consumption can generate identity, are countered by more negative accounts of postmodern consumer culture that deny the creative possibilities of consumption. In *The Consumer Society*, Baudrillard ([1970] 1998) describes the abundance of 'objects, services and material goods' as marking 'a fundamental mutation in the ecology of the human species' (25). Consumer culture is all-encompassing and transforms social life. Objects within consumer culture are comprised of signs that can be manipulated to generate meanings. Consumer goods, whether cars or fashion models' bodies, communicate meanings through 'sign value', a stage beyond use and exchange value (see Chapter 2, 'Destructive markets') that stresses symbolic meanings distinct from any reference to the real. Signs matter more than things and meanings consume themselves. The account of culture used by Baudrillard as he engages with Marxist and postmodern ideas is predominantly linguistic: communication and meaning exceed the material objects of consumption. Baudrillard brings 'culture' and 'economy' into a system that sees economic value as residing in the communicative ability of signs. Goods, services and experiences matter for the symbolic values that are attached, and so culture is a powerful source of identification. In CCT, these postmodern insights informed a shift away from the assumption that all that mattered for marketing was to know the consumer's mind, and towards attention to bodily experience (Joy and Venkatesh, 1994). Consumers were not passive, but active participants in making meaning, drawing on the sensory and aesthetic experiences of consumption and emotional responses (Addis and Holbrook, 2001). Lingerie, for example, is a hedonistic consumer good that contributes to women's self-actualisation and sensuality (Jantzen et al, 2012); 'retro' brands draw on the paradox of consumer nostalgia and the desire to benefit from innovation, and rely on consumer work to celebrate reinvigorating an old brand (Brown, 2001).

Consumption and relationships

However, as well as having symbolic values, the materiality of things matters – and is part of where symbolic values might come from. We want a coat that keeps us warm as well as makes us look nice. Daniel Miller, an anthropologist, suggests that the complex and different ways in which goods are brought to the market, and the many forms their consumption might take, make general theories of consumption difficult. Instead, it is important to study the specific contexts in which goods operate to stabilise culture and categories of meaning. In *A Theory of Shopping* (1998a), he explores the social and cultural functions of shopping as a form of consumption. By accompanying London families on their everyday trips to supermarkets, and asking them to discuss what and why they were buying, he is able to say something about how shopping constitutes a key element of family life. Most importantly, love is expressed through what is purchased ('treats' for children, a treat for oneself) and sometimes what isn't purchased. Meanings are shaped in particular local contexts through encounters with some kinds of goods. In work on consumption in Trinidad, Miller shows how consumers are not passive in the face of meanings targeted at them, in the case of a 'global' brand like Coca-Cola (1998b) or a global phenomenon like the internet (Miller and Slater, 2000). Their engagement in consumption forms and reforms possible identities, including what it is to 'be Trini'.

Anthropologists like Miller (see also Appadurai, 1986) think that materiality matters and is part of the rhetorical and social uses of goods. These uses change as flows of commodities bring new knowledge and new arenas for the construction of value and meaning. For example, a cookbook makes it possible to learn a new kind of cuisine from a different part of the world and contributes to demand for new food. Material-culture approaches help make sense of intimate settings where consumer goods appear. McCracken (2005) shows what happens to consumer goods when they are taken home, discussing how families create a sense of hominess by positioning objects, by preferring things that look old over things that are 'too modern', and by coordinating newly purchased goods with existing possessions, and so contribute to making family life through consumption.

A further strand in consumption studies that is explicitly critical of the consumption-as-identity position is the sociological literature on ordinary consumption (Gronow and Warde, 2001; Warde, 2005; Sassatelli, 2007). For these writers, consumer culture does not just refer to spectacular consumption, global brands and laminated customer service training sheets, but is mundane, routine, ritualised and requires attention to subtle practices. For example, going out to eat is a complex practice that requires manners, know how, knowledge of dishes and so on (Warde and Martens, 2000). More generally, this approach sees consumers as embodied subjects situated in time and space (Warde, 2005: 139; Sassatelli, 2007: 108), engaging in social action in ways that harness the emotional, corporeal, cognitive and discursive; compare this with the rational individual of economics. Consumer actions are shaped and mediated by the contexts in which consumption takes place, by material cultures and discourses about the consumer. For example, having an established habit may prevent consumers from being seduced by advertising. The practical, habitual and routine elements of consumption are powerful in influencing consumer behaviour. These writers use practice theory to show that the idea that consumption involves a conscious presentation of social status or reflexively acquired self-identity has some limits. A practice approach sees consumption as *'gratuitous and creative'* when people are consciously interpreting and recognising things they have bought, as well as a *'socially and culturally standardised activity'* (Sassatelli, 2007: 106, italics in origin).

Consumers, therefore, are complex creatures. At, at times victims to the lures of marketing, spending money they don't have on things they don't need (Schor, 1998), and at other times powerful, resistant and creative. And whilst consumers have agency through their choices and their routines, their actions are shaped by consumer capitalism. The next question we must consider is: How are these 'market segments' created and shaped? Meanings are not only assigned to objects by those who purchase them, but also by the agents of capitalism – marketers, branders, advertisers. How should we think about this?

Production, consumption and promotion

We have discussed production-led explanations for the development of consumer society, and considered also how consumer desires and identities have been formed in relation to the world of goods, services and experiences. In older literature, this is presented as reflecting a separation between 'economy' and 'culture', and yet, culture and economy are entangled in consumerism. Some of the seductive power of consumption seems to stem from the way it hides production, as when consumers can happily ignore the implications that cheap goods have for the wages of those who produce them, or when a marketing campaign subverts common strategies, say by using humour to promote products to people who don't think they are persuadable. The separation of production and consumption means that consumption can be transformed into something that enables self-expression and is comfortable and pleasurable (Leach, 1993: 148).

But there are many reasons for thinking that a clear distinction between production and consumption is unsustainable. First, the systems of provision that link the production and consumption of some commodities are distinct from those of others (Fine and Leopold, 1993). So food production/consumption and clothing production/consumption need different explanations, as the nature of the commodity affects production and consumption. Second, that production and consumption are linked by, and to, a range of other dimensions of the 'circuit of culture' (du Gay et al., 1997). A circuit of culture means that consumers and commodities reflect on and transform each other, through interconnections between production, consumption, representation, identity and regulation. Third, consumption is productive in many respects, including selfhood (Firat and Dholakia, 1998: 77). Strong accounts of how consumers engage in productive activity through consumption consider the 'co-creation' of value by consumers. Consumers' creative autonomy over the use of goods means they can actively engage in the social construction of value (Arvidsson, 2005: 241–2). Advertising, marketing and branding feed off consumers' immaterial labour. Immaterial labour (Lazzarato, 1996) refers to the practices that produce the immaterial content of commodities, including the social context of production itself. This is productive labour which creates and sustains the brand (249) by producing an 'ethical surplus' (Arvidsson, 2005: 251) in the domain of circulation. Marketing, obviously less critical of how consumers (or prosumers) are set to work like this, is keen to find ways to harness the value-creating potential of consumers, perhaps by setting them challenges to develop a new ad campaign. We will develop our discussion of this in Chapter 4, 'Beyond paid work'.

We make our decisions about what and how to consume in the context of markets, where sellers use all kinds of techniques to encourage us to buy, where those close to us might influence what we want, where our desires might have to be tamed because we do not have much money spare, and with reference to our principles about what counts as good consumption. A range of market and non-market influences matter. The later chapters of this book look at the way commercial work tries to influence our consumption practices (Chapters 4–7); here I just introduce and define the main kinds of promotional activities and their links to consumer capitalism, accounts that will become more complex as you read on and we explore the messy ways they mediate between production and consumption. How and indeed whether promotional culture works is an open question; when 'gut instinct' triumphs over market segment research to determine an advertising campaign (Davis, 2013: 2) and when consumers resist or dismiss campaigns designed for them, there can be no simple account of the power of promotion.

Promotional culture

The 'symbolic expertise' (du Gay, 1996: 100) of marketing, branding, advertising and design is essential to commerce and is part of what Andrew Wernick terms a promotional culture, where 'the boundary between sign and object is blurred' (Wernick, 1991: 184). Promotion lies at the intersection between the 'symbolic' and 'material' economies, bringing culture to the service of the market (Wernick, 1991: 186). Categories of promotion such as advertising, marketing and public relations are interconnected and interdependent. Whilst promotional culture has a long history (McFall, 2004), it is seen as more pervasive in contemporary society, affecting all kinds of commodities, goods and institutions (Davis, 2013). From discount coupons to self-branding, symbolic and financial values are created – and actively worked on – by advertisers and the like. 'Promotional culture' arguments position production and consumption as part of a general trend to collapse the social into economic activity. Promotional culture is related to design and the flow of fashion, and to the way commodities are produced as desirable goods, services and experiences. Meanings are made through promotion, but consumers are not passive recipients of these meanings; they are themselves part of how cultural-economic values are produced, used and reused in consumer capitalism.

The extension of branding ideas to nation states indicates how significant 'promotional culture' is to our daily lives beyond the directly commercial. Nation branding is directed towards a long-term alteration in internal and external understandings of what a 'nation' is about (Aronczyk, 2008), relevant both to political practices and to commercial tourism. If complex geopolitical historical entities are eligible to be branded using techniques honed on bottled water and electronic products, then promotional culture is powerful! Contemporary life in advanced and developing societies is marked by a consumer culture and a consumerist attitude to aspects of life often assumed to lie outside the realm of the market and to things that ethically we may prefer not to see corrupted by market life. Comaroff and Comaroff are amongst those who describe this extension of market life as part of neoliberal culture that 're-visions persons not as producers from a particular community, but as consumers in a planetary marketplace: persons as ensembles of identity that owe less to history or society than to organically conceived human qualities' (2001: 13). And yet, as when Italian migrants to Canada buy expensive Italian furniture in order to have something of 'home', consumption can be about belonging (Joy et al., 1995).

Promotional activities

Advertising   Advertising involves the explicit production of apparent differences between products in order to make them appealing. Traditional strategies include billboard posters, magazine pages, 30 seconds of television time – 'interrupt and repeat' advertising (McStay, 2010). Adverts are familiar elements of the spectacle of consumption, providing us with ideas about what we might and might not buy. Advertising draws on and re-forms the culture around it; Schroeder (2002) describes this as ideological: advertising disguises existing inequalities. Sponsorship (say of sport teams) and product placement are advertising activities that point to the blurred line between advertising and marketing. This has a long history, as hinted at in 'Shopping'. Early department store advertising was bold and spectacular. The British store *Selfridges* used window displays, adverts, in-store demonstrations of technological products and stunts (Rappaport, 2000: 154–70). Later uses of 'scientific' marketing, with close links to psychology, developed in particular in the 1950s and aimed to tap into the 'mind of the buyer' directly, without the need for a salesman (Bowlby, 2000: 57). Recent trends in advertising aim to capitalise on the communicative possibilities of the internet, offering seamless advertising mingled with other 'content', and attend to producing experience AS WELL AS providing information.

Marketing   Moor (2007: 2) suggests that scholars have paid too much attention to advertising and not enough to marketing, branding and other forms of promotion. Marketing involves observing and understanding (and sometimes creating) social differences, and segmenting the population in order to target those with disposable income, in order to reduce competitive uncertainty (Corley, 1987: 66). Marketing's key tool is market segmentation, where different methods of communicating an atmosphere or lifestyle and an image of a product are seen as appealing to different social groups. Social class, geo-demographics (where residential neighbourhoods are classified), and psychographics (using personal values and opinions) are common approaches for classifying (segmenting) consumer types, each of whom must be seduced using different strategies (Fischer and Bristor, 1994). More recently, mining purchase data, customer relationship management, sentiment analysis and social media promotion have been used, enabled by web 2.0 (Knox et al., 2010) as part of 'rethinking marketing' (Rust et al., 2010). For Schroeder (2002) and other CCT writers, marketing provides myths for consumers to make sense of consumer objects and everyday life, to imbue objects with aura and meaning, to create relationships rather than merely to facilitate transactions.

Branding   Branded goods developed from the 19th century. Logos and trademarks were used on packaging to indicate a standardised product of knowable quality; branding was thus used to generate trust. Brands are intended to attract and attach loyal consumers who will identify with, buy and promote branded products. Branded retail, leisure, tourist and service spaces are designed to contribute to the experiences of consumers. In the 1980s, the culture of branding changed radically, and it is now common to see corporations, employees, charities, nations and even individuals described as brands. New ways of accounting for brand value in company balance sheets, stock market trading, mergers and acquisitions and other financial activities were developed, including strategies for measuring the value of a brand to consumers. This is a part of the ideology of neoliberal market capitalism and structures global market activity (Askegaard, 2006). As part of this refined brand culture, the values, emotions and aesthetics of a brand are objects of scrutiny and concern: brand messages and brand narratives are controlled to create attachments.

Moor sees branding as a meeting point between design, marketing and advertising, with branding as part of an increased aestheticisation of production (2007: 9). Design refers to the form and aesthetics of products and the selling environments, both online and on the high street (Molotch, 2003). It steers consumers to particular kinds of understandings of what a product can do, and to the connotations it has. Product placement in media channels, infotainment shows and 'brand ambassadors' are examples of how branding makes media consumption a part of promotional culture. But branding's significance is its potential for bridging production and consumption – not only the messages transmitted by brand managers, but the consumer's labour in creating shared brand meanings (Banet-Weiser, 2012). 'Real', authentic life and commodified culture are interconnected through brandscapes; brand meanings are mediated and often ambiguous.

Service   Service here refers to customer services of many kinds, from managing the transaction to advising on purchases to providing assistance, and to personal services that are bought in commercial spaces. Shop assistants, website designers, waiters and bar staff contribute to the sale, marking the meeting point between buyer and seller, acting as the seller's representative and present at the ultimate point of commodification: where money is exchanged at a given price. Their work is not only to manage the transfer of ownership, but to contribute to how consumers adopt the good, including by producing spectacles of consumption. Customer service therefore contributes to consumer capitalism, as it presents products as desirable and makes exchange possible. Service is part of branded environments and is used commonly as a basis for promoting the comparable virtues of a good or service, and to producing a spectacle of consumption.

Conclusion

In this chapter, we have considered consumption, consumerism and consumer society as elements of 'consumer capitalism'. Consumer capitalism is historically and geographically varied, and the impetus to consume is produced through a complex set of practices and inter-actions within global capitalism that draw in work, consumption, social difference, technology and many other elements of the world. Slater's words summarise why it is worth thinking about this:

> The specific arrangements arrived at, the way in which relations of production and relations of consumption mediate each other, place consumption at the heart of questions about what kind of society we are: how is access to objects of consumption regulated: what is the logic that determines the nature of the goods provided to the everyday world; how are our notions of needs, identity, ways of life defined or identified or mediated? (Slater, 1997: 4)

The consumer, in consumer culture, is part of a mediated world, con-tributing to and being formed by the consumer experiences that sur-round them. The exchanges, interconnections and mediations between the work of production and the work of consumption are at the heart of consumer culture. Too much emphasis on consumption, however, means that the work that makes consumption possible is neglected. In the next chapter, we consider what kinds of work produce con-sumer capitalism. Given the complexity of consumer society as we have discussed it here, we explore the many and different forms of work which produces the experience of consuming: that which makes shops attractive spaces, generates desire for goods and makes exchange possible.

Research task

Interview someone aged 50 or older about their experiences of shopping and consumption, for around 20 minutes. How has con-sumption changed in their lifetime? What do they think about those changes? Did they notice the rise of brand culture, and if so what do they think about that? How do they compare themselves to younger generations?

OR

Investigate the history of retail in your local area. Which are the oldest forms of retail that still persist? What can you tell from old buildings about how shopping used to happen? When did super-markets first arrive in your area, and what effect did they have?

Discussion questions

1. Do you think contemporary consumption is 'mass' consumption? In what ways is it mass? And in what ways is it differentiated? What markers of difference are most significant?

2. Consider your last purchase (no matter whether it was of a bottle of water, a night in a casino, a haircut or something very different). Which of the ways of 'explaining consumption' help you to understand this purchase?

3. Consider a recent 'place branding' campaign (look online for examples). What does this tell you about what branding can and cannot achieve?

Chapter 4

Work

The goods, services and experiences of consumer capitalism are produced by different kinds of workers. This chapter explores the forms of work that are most directly involved in the production of consumption. It looks at the ways in which this commercial work has been studied and explores some of the interrelationships between different commercially oriented occupations. In Table 1.1, I provided a list of occupations that contribute to work in global consumer capitalism, derived from reading research from a range of disciplines. I called these occupations 'commercial work'. These are jobs that in some way contribute to the consumption practices that were discussed in Chapter 3. Expanding consumer markets in pursuit of profit is fundamental to global capitalism, as discussed in Chapter 2, and workers in these commercial occupations play important (and different) roles in making this happen. This chapter considers ways of theorising commercial work, exploring the similarities and differences between commercial work occupations.

The key questions of 'Services in global consumer capitalism' are: what is 'service' and how useful is it to understanding commercial work? This section explores theories from economics and business studies, including the traditional 'tripartite' division of the economy into primary, secondary and tertiary sectors, and considers the role of the tertiary 'service' sector in a post-Fordist era. In '"Culture" and work', we discuss theories that start from a focus on culture rather than economy and explore the work of consumer capitalism as being about the production of culture. We consider how commercial work is

74

distinctive because of how it works on and with culture, and discuss the implications of this for understanding culture and capitalism. In 'Conditions of work', we explore what work is like in global capitalism, looking particularly at conditions of work and how commercial workers are encouraged to be flexible. Finally, in 'Beyond paid work', we consider consumption a form of work.

Services in global consumer capitalism

Many claims have been made as to the apparently increasing dominance of services as a significant part of the shift to a post-industrial economy (e.g. V. Fuchs, 1968; Bell, 1973). Arguments about services come from economists, geographers, business studies scholars and sociologists. Scholars have argued about what terminology to use to describe an economy dominated by services: post-industrial (V. Fuchs, 1968; Bell, 1973), post-Fordist (see Chapter 2, 'Production and consumption'), 'informational capitalism' (C. Fuchs, 2010, 2013), a knowledge economy (Herzenberg et al., 1998; Benner, 2002), an experience economy (Pine and Gilmore, 1999), a new economy (Leadbeater, 1999) and more! Each of these terms draws our attention to different dimensions of a similar observation of the world: that developed economies do not make as much 'stuff' as they once did, and have moved from being economies dominated by manufacturing to economies dominated by services. This is a well-established argument, although consumer historians, such as Barnett (1998), writing about London in the late 18th century, suggest that services have a long history of making consumption possible. We will focus on exploring the particular nature of 21st-century economic life. A post-industrial economy is one dominated by services, not manufacturing, where most people are employed in services and where more GDP is generated by services. Services may be culturally as well as economically dominant (Mort, 1989).

The defining features of 'services' are, firstly, that they are not extraction or manufacturing (that is, services are a 'residual' category), and secondly, that services are, to a great (if variable) extent, intangible and ephemeral or 'weightless', to use the term advocated by business guru Charles Leadbeater (1999). Service is what we get in a restaurant when we order a meal or from our bank when we use them to pay a bill; it is an act that needs to be produced at the time of its consumption. We begin this section by discussing official measures of services and then discuss criticism of these measures, to see how the 'weightless' immateriality of services is complicated by a number of factors. We then consider the idea of a 'service economy'.

Official measures

You may have already come across the idea that there are three main sectors to an economy: primary (extraction and agriculture), secondary (manufacturing) and tertiary (services) (Jansson, 2006: 7). This typology is taught in secondary school geography classes and originated in the 18th century (Illeris, 2007). It is sometimes called 'stage theory' for the implication that economies develop from primary to secondary to tertiary (Brenner, 1977). Such a label makes the value judgement that countries with a higher proportion of tertiary (service) activities are more developed. Decreases in manufacturing employment are said to be associated with occupational 'upgrading' (higher-skilled professional jobs) for some, but also a higher proportion of low-skilled, low-status jobs for others (Moynagh and Worsley, 2005). This varies between countries, and men and women experience this change differently (Webb, 2009). The International Standard Industrial Classification of All Economic Activities (ISIC), developed by the United Nations, marks out services as: trade; repair of household goods; hotels and restaurants; transport and communications; financial activities; real estate, leasing and business services; public administration; education; health and social services; community activities (such as waste treatment, membership associations, recreative, cultural and sport activities); domestic services; diplomacy and international organisations (Illeris, 2007: 29). That's quite a list. There is a comparable International Standard Classification of Occupations (ISCO), which includes the following workers: professional, technical and related; administrative and managerial; clerical and related; sales; service (Illeris, 2007: 31). These official measures are important, but as many writers acknowledge, creating typologies of service industries and occupations is hard to do well, given the great complexity and diversity of this economic activity (Bryson et al., 2004; Jansson, 2006). How useful are these measurement exercises?

Complicating 'services'

Several writers find the official measures limiting and provide alternatives. Sayer and Walker (1992) suggest that, for example, retailing is as much as an extension of the manufacturing and production process as a service industry, commenting that '…circulatory activities… cannot be sundered from the industrial base by relabeling them either service outputs or service labor' (Sayer and Walker, 1992: 58). Jansson (2006) suggests measuring household (final) consumption of goods and services and paying attention to the flow of goods and services between 'primary', 'secondary' and 'tertiary' sectors across networks and chains of supply. Daniels and Bryson (2002) note that manufacturing does not take place in a vacuum away from services. Take car production and sales. This incorporates business-to-business services that sell parts, marketing services that assess and create demand for vehicles, such as the marketing and branding discussions that preceded the decisions to re-make 1960s small cars like the Mini or the Fiat 500 (see Simms and Trott, 2006, on the Mini and Ciravegna, 2011, on the Fiat), and so on. The division between the physical process of manufacture and the knowledge-based part of production is blurred and it's impossible to tell when the manufacturing process ended and services began (Daniels and Bryson, 2002: 983).

Allen and du Gay (1994) developed a related set of arguments from a different starting point. They were concerned to think about the separation of 'culture' and 'economy' (developing new economic sociology discussions in Chapter 2) and used this concern to argue that services have a distinctive, hybrid identity where 'the boundaries between the economic and cultural are blurred' (1994: 266). Economic value and cultural meanings are entwined (du Gay and Pryke, 2002: 1). For example, retail services are characterised by the mobilisation of workers' 'capacities and dispositions aimed at winning over the hearts and minds of customers … in order to produce certain meanings for customers and thus a sale' (2002: 3). We'll develop this idea in Chapters 6 and 7. These are part of a broader 'contingent assemblage of practices' (2002: 3) that engender economic action through and with culture. That is, services are tightly bound into production because they are means through which 'culture' is captured in the production of consumer capitalism. We'll discuss this argument further when we look at how goods and services are made desirable through 'culture work'.

These discussions suggest that a more complex set of categories that distinguish between the different consumers of services and different modes of consumption might be a helpful way to think through services. Bryson and Daniels (2007: 4) provide a typology that delineates the different kinds of services and distinguishes between the effects that each kind of service has:

1. Consumer services (final end users)
2. Producer and business services (providing inputs for other organisations)

3. Public services (provided by the state or by private or not-for-profit organisations)
4. Services provided by not-for-profit organisations that go beyond national boundaries
5. Informal and unpaid everyday services.

Societies differ as to what kinds of service fit in which category. For example, care work may be in categories 1, 3 or 5 (Lyon, 2010). For the most part, the services that are directed at producing consumption fit in categories 1 and 2. Services often provided by the state to end users (such as healthcare and education) are excluded from our consideration of consumer capitalism, even though in many places there is a market for health and education and you might have the experience of being relabelled 'customer' when you thought of yourself as a patient, and you might be studying at a university that has spent a lot of money marketing the quality of its education to you. These examples should remind us that typologies and sharp distinctions should always be treated with caution, as tools to think with, rather than as fixed and true. Accounting, auditing and financial services are not the focus of this book as they are business-to-business services that do not imagine an end consumer. However, advertising, marketing, design and communication services that create markets, understand final consumers and contribute to making goods and services desirable are of great interest. They are producer services that add symbolic value to goods and services. Let's consider now what 'service' work might look like.

Questioning service work

Services are scarcely ever immaterial, relying on all kinds of infrastructures for their production. Infrastructures, such as ICT that provides the tools to reintegrate services that are produced separately to other parts of a production process, are central to the service economy, even though they may seem to be 'black boxed' (Latour, 1994) and hidden from many accounts of service. Recall the discussion of ANT in Chapter 2, 'Markets as moral projects', where we argued that material objects were agents in economic life. Service processes rely on these non-human agents, enmeshed in networks; economic processes do not work through abstraction alone, nor through human agency alone (Warf, 2007). Further, as we saw in Chapter 3, 'Consumption and relationships'), sharp distinctions between 'symbols' and 'materials' are not viable, as materials carry meaning. So remember this well: just because we are talking about a 'service economy', we're not suggesting that materials don't matter. Goods, services and experiences all involve engagement in the material world: in how services are designed and produced, and in the materiality of the bodies of the workers.

One of the most important dimensions of the materiality of services is how they are produced by highly 'material' human bodies. Services demand people-based skills, both in the sense that skills and competencies are embodied in the workers (and so substituting one worker for another changes the nature of the service) and because service work tends to have some kind of contact with clients or customers. Often this means interaction with customers, but it can also involve being asked to absorb the preferences and mindset of some abstract group of customers in order to think about how to sell to them. The social characteristics of the individual worker matter in service economies: gender, age, ethnicity, class, sexuality, (dis)ability matter. 'Personality', 'attitude' and other forms of self-presentation are very important to working in a service economy, which was described by C. Wright Mills (1956: 183) as a 'personality market' (see also Cremin, 2011; Nickson et al., 2012), as we'll discuss in Chapters 6 and 7. Working bodies come to have multiple meanings and are part of the flow of global capital. Client-based service work, such as that provided by brand agencies, demands attention to workers' own bodies (Chan, 2000) and to personal relations between workers (Bloomfield and Best, 1992) and with clients (see Edwards, 2011, for a discussion of PR clients). Let's now consider what a society dominated by the provision of services looks like, and how a 'service economy' can be produced. How might we think about the interconnections between this work and other activities, including the production of the goods and services that are for sale in a 'service economy'?

Service economies in global capitalism

Economies are linked by flows of people, services, goods, knowledge and so on; the commodity chains discussed in Chapter 2, 'Production and consumption', are also chains of services. Where production is 'vertically disintegrated', as post-Fordist theorists would say, different dimensions of production are separated and may be produced in dispersed locations. For example, high-skill services may be located in global cities like Toyko, London or New York, with 'back-office' services such as software support in areas where wages and other costs are lower. The global sourcing of services is an important feature of capitalism, and reflects some of the 'contradictory, contingent and contested' (Warf, 2007: 383) processes that form global capitalism, both supply chains and the 'cultural circuit' (Thrift, 2005) of capitalism.

Emerging economies often aspire to develop a service sector of some kind, often a high-tech, knowledge economy. In the 'capitalist archipelago' (Arrighi, 1996: 13) of Asia-Pacific, service industry policies have been linked to policies that support the cultural industries, knowledge economies and higher education (HE) and are intended to make it possible for that country to compete to provide global services. Seoul, for example, has both high-skill and routine IT service work (Park and Choi, 2005). Morshidi (2000) discusses the Malaysian government's desire to generate 'world city' status for Kuala Lumpur (KL) (see also Felker and Jomo, 2013). Producer services are seen as key to being able to compete in a global economy, and so there have been marketing campaigns to make KL look attractive to investors, support for export-oriented local service providers and new infrastructures (most dramatically, the Petronas Twin Towers, which you might recognise from films). Many other countries responded to the desire to develop a service economy by deregulating, for example, removing regulations to limit overseas ownership of firms, to encourage foreign direct investment (FDI), as this seemed like a way to compete in a neoliberal, global economy.

KL is one of Asia-Pacific's 'hub' cities, along with Hong Kong, Seoul, Melbourne and Singapore (Hutton, 2007). These cities are often multicultural, and are regionally and globally important, measured by indicators like an increased share of global air passenger numbers (Shin and Timberlake, 2000), as well as by the development of the full range of service activities: personal assistants, bars and restaurants, global retail brands for the well-paid workers to spend their spare cash and so on. The relationship to manufacturing, the kinds of services that are present, and the kinds of global relationships that different places have, all matter to how we might understand an economy that is shifting towards services. India, for example, is a favoured destination for corporations whose customers speak English and who want to outsource call-centre services. India's former status as a colony of Britain means many citizens have English language skills (although they may still be expected to take 'mother tongue' accent reduction courses – see Mirchandani, 2012), but earn lower wages.

In Chapter 2, 'Production and consumption', we also described the coming of post-industrial and post-Fordist production in Western countries that had undergone a comparatively slow industrialisation process since the 19th century. The post-industrial economy dominated by services appeared to Western-oriented commentators (used to seeing manufacturing production as the source of value) to be novel. In the Asia-Pacific states discussed above, in 'transitional economies' (moving from communism to capitalism) and in other places where new middle-class consumers have emerged, a different kind of explanation is needed. Stare (2007) suggests that post-communist states, accustomed to focusing on producing goods, did not initially consider the contribution of services to other forms of production and to economic development. Over time, demand for producer services increased, specifically in marketing, advertising and PR, as a result of increased competition within transitional economies. In Bulgaria, modern advertising emerged after 1963, reflecting the socialist state's partial acceptance of the demand for consumer goods and their recognition that advertising was a useful promotional tool to support the state (Ibroscheva, 2013). Lin (2005) and Hutton (2007) argue that a time-compressed version of the Western model of Fordism to post-Fordism does not make sense to explain the growth of services in Asia-Pacific. Rather, services and manufacturing grew together and are co-dependent. In Guangzhou, services developed in response to state policies, making Guangzhou 'a distinct globalizing city-region that blends the legacy of a socialist Third World city with the new forces of marketization and globalization' (Lin, 2005: 296). These research findings should force us to rethink established theories about the stages of development into developed post-industrial economies. We need to think about different relationships between state and industry, the role of big cities, the importance of intra-regional exchange to see how services matter.

Whilst services are important to understanding global consumer capitalism, and their growth is significant to economic development, 'service' has its limitations as an explanation for understanding the production of consumption. It does not provide a sufficiently fine-grained framing to enable drawing out differences and similarities between different forms of service or the relationship between good and service. Using 'service' means it is quite easy to miss the complexity of the different occupations that directly produce consumption: we can identify both retail and personal service industries and occupations in the official typologies, but spotting marketing and promotion is much harder. To identify and critically assess the characteristics of this kind of work requires different kinds of theoretical tools, ones designed for a sharper focus on the kinds of occupations that produce consumption.

'Culture' and work

In the previous section, we explored how the work directed at producing consumption can be framed if we categorise activities using the tools of economic geographers and similar researchers. The idea of different kinds of services was helpful in thinking this through, and enabled us to see different industries and different forms of work. But this way of thinking does not recognise that consumer goods, services and experiences have a cultural content that affects how work is done. In this section, we turn to ideas generated by scholars working from a starting point that positions 'culture', especially 'commercial culture', as central to global capitalism. We look at how two, interrelated, ideas offer some insight into the nature of 'producer' services aimed at end consumers: culture/creative work and cultural intermediary work. We then consider consumer services and sales work.

Culture industries and culture work

If we are to understand consumption, then we must pay attention to the production of commodified goods, services and experiences. We saw in Chapter 3, 'Critics of mass', that the Frankfurt School criticised the culture industry – commercialised, mass culture – for offering false promises and banal blandishments. Whilst the focus of the Frankfurt School was on the products themselves, researchers inspired by these ideas later came to investigate how culture industry products are made by cultural workers. How are the creative and risk-taking capacities of culture workers (Garnham, 1990) used to meet consumers' desires for new pleasures?

What is included in the definition of culture industries varies between writers. For example, the collection edited by A. Beck (2003) includes TV and film production, the music industry, radio and 'performance' in general; the culture industry comprises media and immaterial products. McRobbie (1998) and Skov (2002) consider fashion design to be part of the cultural industries. Stranger (2011) considers surfing subcultures to be a cultural industry made up of surfing tourism, media, surfing schools, professional surfing, clothing and fashion accessories, and surfing kit. Advertising and marketing of surfing lifestyles produce the cultural form of surfing. More formally, Miege (1987) suggests there are three distinct ways in which value is manifested by cultural products: physical products with cultural value (books, for example, but perhaps also clothing); broadcasting and other media products (funded by advertising); and public performances funded by ticket purchase. The materiality or tangibility of the product and the mode of economic exchange mark out the different parts of the culture industry. Using 'culture industries' to understand the production of consumption means exploring what might comprise the economic and cultural value of goods, services and experiences.

Hesmondhalgh suggests that cultural industries are marked by three features. First, the cultural industries make and circulate texts (2007: 3–4). Hesmondhalgh uses 'text' as a synonym for 'product' and asks us to think of films and songs as texts, as well as written texts such as newspapers and magazines. Text here is a term for the 'works' that are made in the culture industries, what might often be called 'content' in the occupational settings we are interested in. In later work (Hesmondhalgh and Baker, 2010), 'texts' are more tightly defined as invoking symbols, so that 'in the general social division of labour, workers in the cultural industries are involved in the creation and dissemination of very particular kinds of productions, ones that are mainly symbolic, aesthetic, expressive and/or informational' (Hesmondhalgh and Baker, 2010: 60). Second, the production of these texts involves creative acts to produce symbolic products (Hesmondhalgh, 2007: 4–6) that carry rich meanings. Third, texts influence people's sense of who they are, their identity, their relationships with others and therefore contribute to economic, social and cultural change (2007: 6–8). Hesmondhalgh goes on to list the 'core' cultural industries as broadcasting, film, internet content, music, publishing, digital games, advertising and marketing (2007: 12–13), although design also fits the definition and is considered in this book. Note here that advertising and marketing produce symbolic texts that refer to other kinds of consumer goods. In the language of service economy researchers, these are producer services doing work directed at final consumers.

Hesmondhalgh and Baker's (2010) exploration of 'good' and 'bad' work in the cultural industries shows that it is important to pay attention to the specificities of particular kinds of labour when understanding the experience of work. In particular, workers in the cultural industries differ from other knowledge workers (defined in Chapter 5) because the key feature of their work is the production of symbols. Their careful empirical study of media work – specifically television, music recording and magazine publishing – considers the organisational and occupational divisions within each sector that mean that not all workers engage with culture and creativity in comparable ways, and there are hierarchies within industries often based around how closely cultural workers engage with the 'creative' production of

symbols. The story so far suggests that culture work in culture industries is distinguished for its symbolic content. What, though, of how
culture workers operate?

Creative work

Many researchers consider that creativity is a key feature of culture
work, and 'creative work' is sometimes used interchangeably with
'culture work', with 'creative industries' treated as a synonym for cultural industries (for a critical discussion of the reduction of 'culture'
to 'creativity', see Garnham, 2005). Creativity is often associated with
the production of culture, as when artists and composers are creative.
'Creativity', in many languages, is a term that carries a heavy moral
load; most of us think of being creative as a good thing, and so it
becomes something to aspire to. Being described as 'creative' and a
'creative worker' is therefore positive, particularly when many other
forms of work are known to be apparently uncreative, being routinised, repetitive, tightly managed and controlled (although routines and
repetition are important to creative workers, for example when a new
design emerges from drawing and redrawing). We can start to see that
there is a politics to creativity. Managers are urged to be 'creative', with
creativity linked to innovation and hence economic growth, and this
gives rise to a different kind of organisational culture (Ross, 2004).
Here we see that creativity is not the property of the lone artist, but
is contextual and negotiated, and relies on social relations, networks
and technologies for its particular manifestations.

The politics of creativity has been associated with the politics of the
industrial structure in a very explicit way by many nation states, who
are keen to tap the possible benefits to economic life of doing creative
work (see Ross, 2009, on China). Recall how the post-industrial society
was one dominated not by manufacture but by services, and by post-
Fordist production in which product differentiation was key. So forms
of work that produce symbolic values come to matter in a post-
industrial society to create differentiated consumer products. Policy
makers answering the question 'What would make a good post-industrial economy, if skilled manufacturing has been replaced by technology or moved overseas?' looked to creative services.

An influential argument was made in evangelical terms by Richard
Florida, whose 2002 book *The Rise of the Creative Class* appeared to
many policy makers to solve the problems that resulted from de- or
post-industrialisation. Florida's idea is that creative quarters within
cities could regenerate poverty-stricken areas, as new workers with

expertise in the production of symbolic values would move there, attracted by cheap rents. Internet start-ups, small-scale clothing and homeware design companies, artists and musicians would congregate in cultural quarters of cities, joined perhaps by small companies working in more established industries like media production, and by independent retailers serving complicated coffee products. Creative 'clusters' are located near universities in regenerating areas. Evans (2009: 1007) lists 'spaces of invention' in Poblenou (Barcelona @22), Fashion City and World Jewellery Centre (Milan), Orestad (Copen-hagen), Digital Corridors (Malaysia), Digital Media City (Seoul) and campus-based science/R&D and creative precincts in Brisbane (QUT, South Bank), Berlin (Adlershof), Helsinki (Arabianranta) and Toronto (MaRS).

In some places, local and national policies supported the develop-ment of an explicit, top-down cultural-economic policy framed as developing 'creativity' (Peck, 2005; Kong and O'Connor, 2009). The 'Cool Britannia' movement in the UK (1997 onwards) emblematises this move, and state policy supported a shift to creative work. Com-parable policies can be seen in the rest of Europe, in Australia and Canada, in South Korea and, more recently, in the emergent econo-mies like Taiwan and Malaysia, developed by governments of quite different political viewpoints to those of the neoliberal 'New Labour' party of 1990s Britain. In Singapore, for example, Western ideas of individualised creativity have been reworked as 'managed' or 'bounded' creativity, reflecting the pull of the strong state towards maintaining conformism whilst increasing the numbers of Singapor-eans in the creative industry occupations (Green, 2001). Yue (2006) sees this shift as being about promoting 'Asian values' through the new Singaporean creative industries. 'Creative work' is thus closely tied to specific political projects, far more so than 'culture work'.

'Creative work' and 'creative labour' are common terms to refer to the kinds of occupations that produce consumption. The term is prob-lematic, however, in the extent to which it defines and promotes 'creativity' as the main attribute of this kind of commercially oriented work. Creative acts – as a marketer melds old ideas in an original way to develop a new branding strategy, or as a graphic designer refines the colour palette associated with a brand or product (Moor, 2008) – are applied in relation to the broader social, cultural and symbolic values. 'Creative' acts rely on understandings of markets, so that the people working on the branding strategy acquire knowledge of their competitors, what the 'market segment' is like and so on (Moor, 2008). The graphic designer knows how similar books are sold and might want to differentiate her product a little, but not so radically that potential consumers won't pick up the deliberate clues. Knowledge matters and relationships matter.

'Culture' and 'economy' revisited

The concepts of culture and creative work help us to understand how consumption is produced, especially when 'culture' is seen as embedded in economy, and cultural products are understood as commodities. The idea that culture work generates new commercial activity in a straightforward way is complicated by the convergence of different kinds of cultural products, and by the overlaps between cultural production and promotion. As researchers have paid more attention to the materiality of symbolic goods, and as the nature of cultural consumption has changed with new ICTs, stronger arguments for the impossibility of separating 'culture' from commerce have been made. Lash and Lury (2007) characterise the 'global culture industry' as being marked by a radical shift of culture into economy which means that 'culture' is not only symbolic and representational, but culture must be thought of through things, and things through culture: 'Cultural objects are everywhere; as information, as communications, as branded products, as financial services, as media products, as transport and leisure services, cultural entities are no longer the exception: they are the rule' (Lash and Lury, 2007: 4). Brands are constituted through things and as things, and are the key markers of the global economy. Cultural commodities too have become more thing-like: real, material, embedded in everyday economic activity. That is, material commodities and services come with atmospheres, symbols, images, icons and auras. There are many examples, like that of the Japanese brand 'Hello Kitty', where all kinds of interlinked products – some faked – draw on and reproduce the symbolic value of the cute cat. Hello Kitty is a TV show and a series of things, and market value lies in its 'kawaii' (Japanese for cuteness) (Yano, 2009). A distinct moment for 'culture' is hard to identify.

The cultural forms that are made by marketing, advertising and other 'promotional industries' are instrumental (in being intended to sell products), and other cultural producers may consider their creative outputs to be distinct from market pressures. Slater (2011) suggests that the promotional work of marketers looks different to cultural work only if we accept culture as something separate (or in principle, separable) from formal rationality, or material motives and constraints, that is, from the economic sphere. Cultural production for the cultural industries occurs in relation to other modes and forms of production, mediation and consumption, and such work is incorporated into consumer culture. For example, media work overlaps with the promotional activities of commerce. In an account of fashion design in New Zealand, Molloy and Larner suggest that 'the boundary between culture making, cultural mediation and cultural consumption is increasingly blurred' (2010: 362), and occurs throughout the commodity chain. So 'culture work' is not only done when producing cultural products, but also when mediating markets.

However, when extending concepts developed to explore a specific kind of work to apply to other kinds of work, we should also think what we lose by collapsing those differences. For example, organisational and occupational specificities make promotional activities a different kind of work to media work; advertising creatives work on several projects at once, and require different knowledges and skills to music producers. The next section moves away from the concept of culture work to consider framing advertising, marketing, branding and other promotional work as cultural intermediation.

Cultural intermediaries

The idea of 'cultural intermediaries' derives from Pierre Bourdieu, whose work on the impact of class and taste on consumption was discussed in Chapter 3, 'Consumption and social status'. Bourdieu carried out correspondence analysis, a quantitative technique designed to explore associations between categorical variables on survey data that asked about cultural tastes and preferences, to divide French society into 'class fractions': small groupings within the commonly used categories of 'working class' and 'middle class'. Cultural intermediaries belong to a class called the 'new petite bourgeoisie', workers who engage in representation and in producing cultural and symbolic goods. They are taste-makers and interpreters, and serve the function of transmitting 'cultural capital' (embodied, inherited and institutional knowledge and resources), even as they lack 'economic capital' (income and wealth). Other 'cultural intermediary' occupations in this original formulation are activists, musicians, television and newspaper producers, journalists, critics and teachers (Bourdieu, 1984: 351, 359). Cultural intermediaries, suggests Bourdieu, often produce 'middlebrow' cultural products for mass media: 'a whole series of genres halfway between legitimate culture and mass production' (1984: 325–6). For Bourdieu, cultural intermediaries are thereby different to cultural producers working in 'legitimate' cultural forms (art, classical music and the like). Bourdieu's categorisations are particular to the time and place of his study: France in the late 1960s. For Bourdieu, fashion designers tend to have low educational capital but privileged upbringings that provide them with the cultural capital to be an arbiter of taste. In contrast, in London (McRobbie, 1998) and Hong Kong (Skov, 2002), fashion designers are educated to degree level and are not from class-privileged backgrounds. For Nixon and du Gay, 'practitioners in design, packaging, sales promotion, PR, marketing and advertising' (2002: 496) also make (and manipulate) 'middle-brow' culture, and hence are considered as cultural intermediaries.

The 'cultural intermediaries' concept has been discussed and developed by many researchers interested in understanding how music producers (Negus, 2002), advertising executives (McFall, 2002; Nixon, 2003), magazine editors (Crewe, 2003), graphic designers (Soar, 2002); branders (Moor, 2008) fashion designers (McRobbie, 1998; Skov, 2002; Larner and Molloy, 2009; Molloy and Larner, 2010), fashion buyers (Entwistle, 2006, 2009) and others operate. The concept is sometimes seen as too fuzzy and broad, and researchers suggest that it's important to consider what differentiates different occupations that count as 'cultural intermediation' (du Gay and Nixon, 2002). One thing you may note about this list of research subjects is just how important these occupations are to making consumption happen. These are workers who decide what is appealing and what may be worth buying. The symbols they produce are attached to, associated with or encapsulated by, consumer goods, services and experiences. Cultural intermediaries mediate the categories of culture within commercial contexts. Cultural intermediation is thereby a more specific category than 'culture work', and works well as a way of thinking about commercial culture.

Bourdieu's definition associates cultural intermediation with a class position, but 'intermediary' refers not just to an 'in-between' class status, but also to being in-between production and consumption, interpreting ideas, trends, symbols and artefacts. Keith Negus describes cultural intermediaries as workers who are 'continually engaged in forming a point of connection or articulation between production and consumption' (2002: 503–4). That is, the content of the work matters more than the class position, although cultural intermediaries may share some social characteristics and are willing to blur the distinctions 'between personal taste and professional judgment (or leisure and work)' (2002: 504). Horne, discussing cultural intermediaries in the context of sport, says their tastes, values, lifestyle and identities have tremendous influence on 'the production of contemporary consumer culture as a way of life' (2006: 120). Crewe (2003) goes further and says editors of men's magazines lived the lifestyle discussed on the pages of their publication. The idea here is that personal tastes and consumption practices are brought into the workplace.

A more subtle account of the idea of cultural intermediaries operating in some sweet spot between production and consumption comes from Anne Cronin's work on advertising. For Cronin (2004a, 2004b), cultural intermediary work involves mediating within multiple 'regimes' of practices and discourses around what will sell and how to sell it, but within contexts that are not fully controllable, as when intermediaries misunderstand differences between cultures, or when consumers assign different meanings to goods. Advertising executives, for Cronin, are less powerful and more reactive than the hype suggests, and struggle to achieve their aims of mediating to create sales. Similarly, Moor (2012) and Skov (2002) both use design to discuss cultural intermediary work, and show the complexity of this mediation. In Moor's reading, branders design the symbols and artefacts of a product or organisation, and so the aesthetics of the brand are fundamental to the consumption of that brand. Brands are not designed before or after the products they are attached to, but alongside: they mediate the cultures of production as well as consumption. Skov's work provides a complimentary insight into where symbolic values are produced. Fashion designers are marginal to the organisational structures of Hong Kong design companies. They work with little interference as long as their designs are marketable and not too expensive to produce. Designers in Hong Kong, suggests Skov, understand that design work is not about free-floating creativity, but about making sales. Whilst they may think of themselves as able to see the whole picture, rather than being obsessed by the bottom line like the 'pig headed businessmen' (Skov, 2002: 563), they recognise that their work is commercial as well as creative. Rather than producing culture by extending their own preferences into their work, cultural intermediaries are aware of the commercial settings of their work. They do work that is 'shaped by their aesthetic senses, industrial codes of regulation and experiences in familiarity and difference within a specific local context of cultural production' (Kobayashi, 2011: 729).

Extending the concept

We've seen already that cultural intermediaries are considered by Bourdieu to belong to a class fraction. By thinking differently about the class and status associations of cultural intermediary work, some researchers have suggested that quite unexpected occupations can be understood using the cultural intermediary lens. Wright (2005), Pettinger (2004), Gregson et al. (2003), Smith Maguire (2008) and Sherman (2010) have all used the concept to explore workers in occupations that do not require much training or educational capital, and that are low paid and low status. Booksellers, sales assistants, retro retailers, personal trainers and personal shoppers are thought of as mediating consumption. For example, the personal shoppers studied by Sherman had few relevant qualifications and incomes way below those of their clients, but imposed their sense of good taste when purchasing presents on behalf of their clients or selecting furnishings.

David Wright (2005), who interviewed booksellers, indicates the 'cultural capital' of this kind of intermediary work:

> Being a well-read person was considered to be an important aspect of the workers' role which had greater resonance than the simple (or apparently simple) technical appreciation of numbers of books in stock, or dealing with customers ... Interviewees saw themselves as expert consumers, able to communicate their expertise to grateful customers, or to demonstrate their expertise to customers who shared their orientations to objects informed by similar levels of cultural and symbolic capital. A genuine appreciation of books, as opposed to one informed by commercial imperatives, was considered crucial. (Wright, 2005: 115)

Gregson et al. (2003) show that specific knowledges and tastes also matter in retro retailing (we discuss knowledge further in Chapter 5). Retro retailers count as cultural intermediaries because they understand their market. Pettinger (2004) suggests that even low-status retail workers in chain stores mediate consumption insofar as they are employed to represent the brands of their employing organisations. They thereby contribute to the production of symbolic meanings in commercial contexts. Like the personal trainers studied by Smith Maguire (2008), they are exemplary consumers and skilled body workers. The cases described here problematise the celebratory constructions of the cultural intermediary workers as active agents in consumer capitalism, by drawing out a more complex dynamic between production and consumption. Can all jobs involved in the production of consumption be described as cultural intermediation? Only if care is paid to understanding the position of such workers in relation to other producers, consumers and dimensions of the commodity chain. It is important to specify similarities and differences within cultural intermediary categories to avoid making them too diverse (Moor, 2008).

The researchers who have developed the 'cultural intermediary' concept have looked at consumer-facing occupations. So we can say straightforwardly that cultural intermediaries generate consumer culture through their interventions in consumer markets, although they do different things depending on their occupation, the projects they work on and the organisation that employs or manages them. They have in common an orientation to taste making: as musicians, sommeliers and graphic designers, they shape symbols and ideas. As disc jockeys, ad executives, journalists, critics and bookstore workers, they manage relationships between the producers of cultural forms and consumers. Extending the concept of cultural intermediation to comparatively routine and low-skilled work brings us to thinking more carefully about the way customer-facing services, as well as producer services, contribute to the production of consumption. The next section considers sales and service workers.

Sales and service work

Many kinds of workers are implicated in the production of consumer culture, particularly as 'culture' and symbolic production extend into so many parts of economic life. Consumer-facing service workers are sometimes referred to as 'frontline' workers, and are significant to the workings of consumer capitalism. They provide commercialised services, manage transactions for consumer goods and generate leisure and tourism experiences. In the 'culture' stories discussed so far in this section, we did not pay much attention to what happens once symbols have left the design studio or briefing room and are materialised in commercial spaces. How is promotional activity carried out in front of customers? How are routine transactions managed and what are the implications of a brand strategy that goes all the way down to the point of exchange? A key argument in this book is that understanding consumer culture means looking not only at high-status culture workers and intermediaries, but also at low-paid service workers, sales and marketing strategists and face-to-face salesmen (gendered language deliberate!). The body of the tourism rep enacts the 'Club Med' or 'Club 18–30' brand as much as the carefully designed brochure or website does, and perhaps more tangibly to the holidaymakers (Guerrier and Adib, 2000); a kitchen salesman has brochures and guidelines but needs to be able to persuade potential customers (Bone, 2006).

What does sales and service work entail? In 'Services in global consumer capitalism', we drew a distinction between personal and customer services and business services. Now these need retheorising. Two common framings are 'customer service' and 'interactive service work'. Both carry the connotation that the service matters most, over and above the provision of goods. Service here is, as Bell says, 'a game between persons' and contrasts to industrial society, characterised as 'a game against fabricated nature...centred on the relationship between man and machine' (1999 [1973]: 17). Customer service is the term commonly used within organisations. Customer service may refer to workers who answer the telephone in a call centre to assist with personal banking, to the clerk who provides tickets and directions in a leisure centre, to the smiling assistant who packs shopping and takes money, to a waiter or hairdresser and so on. The relationship between customer and worker is privileged as the key feature of work, and the worker is framed as focused on supporting the customer to meet their desires. This term is often to be found in management advice literature, which focuses on 'meeting' and 'exceeding' customer expectations.

Researchers interested in these kinds of occupations tend to use the term interactive service work (ISW). Here, rather than the customer demanding and the worker providing, we have the recognition that many services are provided via 'social interactions in spaces where the service provider and service purchaser are *co-present*' (McDowell, 2009: 8, italics in original), as hairdressers cut clients' hair, care workers clean patients' bodies and call centre workers respond to customers' complaints. ISW may be highly routinised, as in the case of fast food, where service worker follow scripts and customers have been well trained to understand how to order, how to pay and how to eat (Leidner, 1993). Alternatively, it may be highly personalised, intimate and unpredictable. In the case of many personal services, such as care work or hairdressing, the demands for intimacy may conflict with the imperative of the market transaction: speed and care do not necessarily make comfortable bedfellows.

'Culture', and how it is manifested in personal interactions, is deemed the central characteristic of ISW. Everyday culture, as a 'whole way of life' embedded in economic relations, in gender, age and ethnic difference, is drawn on and made in this kind of work, so that cultural understandings of what service should include, and how strangers can talk to each other, matter. 'Interactive' is often taken to mean that talk matters most, and sometimes that is the case (as in the example of call centre work). But symbols also matter (as in the culture work discussed above), and these symbols may be bound up with the worker's own body. Consider the smile that we often expect from service workers. The aesthetics of the smile and the social messages it contains (of welcome, of hierarchy and subservience) are incorporated into the service experience. ISW is therefore related to commodified services.

As Wolkowitz (2006) and McDowell (2009) say, a great deal of the 'interaction' is between bodies. The hairdresser, for example, may chat as she cuts, but is paid to change our appearance. Co-presence (in time if not space) means that interactive service workers need to be available when customers demand them, so that call centre workers stay up all night.

Whilst some forms of service work incorporate sales (as when service workers are expected to do 'upselling' by persuading customers to purchase bigger versions, extra features or extra products), sales work is worth thinking through in its own terms. Sales shares features of both cultural intermediation and customer service. Studying sales indicates some of the interesting similarities and differences between the kinds of selling that happen through general promotional activities and transactions that rely on interactive encounters. Face-to-face sales work, whether of the kind done to sell 'big ticket' items like houses, cars or kitchen showrooms, or to sell small and everyday household goods, relies on interpersonal relationships between seller and buyers. For example, Strickland et al. (2013) studied winegrowers who sell in part 'at the cellar door', that is, on the site where the wine is produced. Here, there is less need to pressure and persuade customers to buy: tastings, the aesthetics and marketing of the vineyard as a happy family-run organisation do the work of selling. Sales, especially direct sales outside of fixed retail spaces, may be a one-off transaction, as in the case of kitchen sales studied by Bone, in which case a 'casual and routine approach to deception' (Bone, 2006: 19) may be present. Alternatively, they may be longer, relationship-based encounters, as in the case of cosmetics sales. Selling techniques that increase the 'cost' to customers of not buying by making them feel guilty or worried that they are missing out, or that add to the pleasure of the purchase, may be attempted. For the American encyclopaedia sellers studied by Schweingruber (2006; Schweingruber and Berns, 2003), getting sales meant working hard at having a 'PMA' (positive mental attitude) and young sellers actively consumed motivational material to help them find and keep this emotional state even when they went for long periods earning nothing.

Direct sales organisations that rely on door-to-door solicitation, product parties and catalogues, or on referrals and appointments, tend to operationalise sales worker's personal characteristics (as friendly or persuasive). Sales workers tend to rely partly or wholly on commission from sales, and this means that they, more than the organisations whose products they sell, face risks. In the case of cosmetics, women in Ecuador (Casanova, 2011), Brazil (Abílio, 2012) and Thailand

(Wilson, 1998) all mobilise friends, family and work colleagues in informal consumption. Notably, although the women work informally and for commission, the companies whose products they sell are large, formal organisations. *Avon* has operated for over 100 years and recruits Thai women (and some men) with the promise of income and by offering entry to a professionalised, entrepreneurial, clever and independent global identity (Wilson, 1998). In contrast, *Yanbal*, a company that distributes mostly in South America, uses a familial analogy to refer to relationships between consultants (mothers and daughters), reflecting the clear feminisation of this work (Casanova, 2011). Abílio (2012) describes how the demarcation between sales work and consumption is not clear cut for women selling *Natura* products in Brazil: selling gives them a chance to consume products comparatively cheaply. She suggests that the women face a double exploitation: they carry the risks of the work by having to pay up front, and they do unremunerated work to promote the brand in their social circles. In the case of sales work, then, social relations are collapsed into market relations and consumption and production are not separated. Instability, precarity, the demands of performances are presented in these cases, and workers may compensate by supporting each other, for example, by exchanging ritualised compliments and admiration to compensate for some of the negative aspects (Biggart, 1989), or exchanging banter and macho bravado about their own and others' performance (Bone, 2006). In these cases, we can see how culture, in the form of the symbolic meanings of material goods and personal interactions, contributes to how goods and services are bought and sold. Having differentiated between commercial work occupations, let's now consider how work is organised.

Conditions of work

Scholars interested in the nature and experience of work have long argued that work is difficult, demeaning, alienating and damaging. As we saw in Chapter 2, 'Destructive markets', Marxist thinkers suggest that the experience of selling labour in exchange for a wage involves a loss of autonomy, as workers become under the control of managers (representing employers, the owners of the means of production), and involves the exploitation of workers' efforts. Buying and selling labour power in exchange for a wage is not value free, nor are capital and labour equal parties to this exchange. Many scholars writing about the experience of work take such ideas as their starting point, especially those associated with 'labour process theory' (LPT). Others focus on understanding the implications for work of neoliberal capitalism. We consider this in the second part of this section when we discuss flexibility.

Work and the labour process

At the heart of making sense of the wage relationship is understanding that labour power is bought and sold. Labour process theory was developed to provide helpful insights into the unequal relationship between buyers and sellers of labour, and draws attention to three interconnected dimensions of the organisation of work: the act of working (and the employment contracts that govern that), the thing that is worked on (with goods or services that have both use value and exchange value in Marxist terms), and the technology used to make that thing. These elements are interconnected. Whilst a craftsman must understand the different activities needed to produce a finished item, industrial capitalism 'dismembers' (Braverman, 1974: 54) the worker by permitting him (and we would now also say 'her') only to contribute to one part of production. He becomes a detail worker and is paid less, as less skill is demanded of him: 'every step in the labor process is divorced, so far as possible, from special knowledge and training and reduced to simple labor' (Braverman, 1974: 57). Deskilling through this enhanced division of labour reduces wages, and is made possible through technological innovation. Much of the service provision in mass consumer services (such as fast-food restaurants, call centres and supermarkets) is routinised, and this affects the kind of skills, work processes and conditions of employment for workers (Jordan, 2011). Technologies – tills that prompt workers to say set phrases to customers, or computers that guide workers through a preset workflow – affect work. Such routinisation may be described as deskilled, as formerly skilled work becomes less skilled. It may also be considered degraded, that is, the work is less pleasant to do because workers have lost autonomy and because they see only a small part of the overall production process. For Smith and McKinlay (2009), culture work is usefully thought of in these terms, but this mode of rationalised organisation and routinised work is more commonly applied to sales and services workers.

Management, hiding its antagonism towards workers by calling its practices 'scientific', extends employers' capacity to control workers by dictating how work is done. This is noticeable in the computer-led workflows of call centre workers, for example. More generally, work is controlled because conception is separated from execution: those who decide how work is to be done are not those who carry it out. We see this in service work in the form of customer service training guidelines, design briefs sent out to retail stores to govern how items are displayed, portion size regulations in chain restaurants and so on. This presumes that the work is ripe to be deskilled, as the worker possesses no tacit knowledge, no understanding that cannot be captured by the consultant or predicted by such regulations. Culture work is based on tacit knowledge, as we will discuss in Chapter 5, and so appears to be different. In LPT, management and control of workers is at the heart of antagonistic relationships between capital and labour and can engender conflict and resistance.

Other scholars look at workers' sense of who they are, their subjectivity, and how it can be captured and worked on by management to encourage them to choose to do things to benefit their employers without direct control. Work groups can come together to work out a collective way of getting through work (Burawoy, 1979) and workers might go through extensive (re)training programmes to become the right sort of people (Sturdy and Fineman, 2001; Sosteric, 1996). Working subjectivity may also explicitly refer to and draw on subjectivities formed in relation to consumer culture (du Gay, 1996), so that workers understand how to provide service because they are also reminded by managers that they too are consumers. In the case of creative industry work and cultural intermediation, many scholars show how workers come to operate in conditions that look far from ideal: accepting short-term contracts, celebrating long working hours and instability (reviewed by Gill and Pratt, 2008). Managerial functions are internalised for workers who feel like work never stops.

How is work organised?

Recall the idea of flexible specialisation (Chapter 2, 'Post-Fordism'), with production changing to meet consumer demands; both production and consumption are flexible, and this means that work too must be flexible (Harvey, 1990). Labour is urged to be flexible in three ways: flexibility of activity, number and time. Workers may be moved between tasks; more or fewer of them may be employed to deal with changes in demand; and their contracted hours may vary according to complex shift patterns. 'Non-standard' employment contracts, including part-time and zero-hours contracts, outsourcing, temporary project-based contracts and so on, may be used. Other features of flexible work include personalised pay structures, jobs that are not tightly demarcated and on-the-job training.

There has been some dispute as to how common the changes associated with post-Fordism are and how widespread flexible work is. In the 1980s, when the discourse of the flexible firm (Atkinson, 1984; Atkinson and Meager, 1986) was heard for the first time, researchers found little evidence of its importance (Pollert, 1988; Bradley et al., 2000), and some are still convinced that claims are overstated (Doogan, 2009). Others suggest that there has been a clear substantive shift in conditions of employment (Gallie et al., 1998; Marchington et al., 2005; Gallie, 2007), whereby both labour market flexibility and flexible organisations have changed the nature of work. The flexible organisation of work and production includes lean production, where organisations focus on their core products and rely on networks with other firms to do other things. This alters the external boundaries of the firm (Marchington et al., 2005). Culture workers are particularly likely to operate via networks, connections and short-term contracts with each other. Networks make for different kinds of employment relationships: suppliers and distributors, designers and marketers may be outside of the core firm, or moved back in-house if the outsourcing or network relationship does not seem to work.

The discourses and practices of contemporary global capitalism have changed the nature and experience of contemporary work. The 'Anglo–Saxon' model of neoliberalism (Harvey, 2005: 88) is often referred to as the explanation for the push towards flexibility changes, although such ideas have purchase beyond the US and UK. For example, neoliberal ideas are present in the EU's pillars of economic growth and in the European employment strategy which, until 2003, referred to employability, adaptability, entrepreneurship and equal opportunities. The success of multiple versions of neoliberal economic practices means that capital has tamed labour by making it vulnerable. Labour market reforms introduced by governments influenced by neoliberal understandings of the benefits of the free movement of capital, and the inefficiencies that result from controlling capital, shifted the nature of the relationship between capital and labour in favour of the former. Legislation to change the nature of employment contracts, reduce the rights of labour to organise and bargain collectively and to reduce the support of the welfare state, including sickness pay and protection from dismissal, are all part of neoliberal destabilisation of labour (Kalleberg, 2012; see Molé (2012) for a discussion of the Italian case and Lefresne (2012) on young French workers). This research counters the idea that enforced flexibility does not damage, but benefits, workers. Researchers studying the impact of flexibilisation have found it to have negative implications for people's sense of security, belonging and happiness (Sennett, 1998). A flexible worker must learn not only to cope with, but to celebrate, this flexibility. He makes himself employable; she rushes into work to do some extra hours; both are concerned to stay flexible in order to get and keep work. Without a stable and certain employment contract with the income this guarantees, the flexible worker leads an uncertain life.

Culture work is seen by some to be in the vanguard of the shift to organising work in this manner (Ross, 2001), although other service work has long used temporal flexibility. Ross describes the ideal 'knowledge worker' as:

> comfortable in an ever-changing environment that demands creative shifts
> in communication with different kinds of clients and partners; attitudinally
> geared towards production that requires long, and often unsocial hours; and
> accustomed, in the sundry exercise of their mental labour, to a contingent
> rather than a fixed routine of self-application (Ross, 2001: 81).

Culture work is often project-based with workers employed on temporary contracts (Christopherson, 2008), perhaps for a few hours (as the models who attend promotional events) or for as long as it takes for the project to be completed (as a film's art director) or for a few months (as an intern in magazine publishing). This way of organising work generates insecurity and is described as 'flexploitation' even when it is normalised (Morgan et al., 2013). Culture workers are not alone in working on temporary contracts, although there is more research done into the instability they face than that of workers in other sectors. Even culture workers in economies where labour conditions are generally better (such as the Nordic countries) work in increasingly precarious environments (Vinodrai, 2013). Being part of a network is increasingly important to workers' chance of accessing decent work – and is hence a source of discrimination based on race and gender (Christopherson, 2008).

The 'flexible' labour market may also be referred to as a 'precarious' one. These two terms mean something similar, but have different political and moral connotations. Whilst describing employment as flexible makes it sound positive, precarity indicates more clearly that uncertainty has a cost. Precariousness or precarity are increasingly used to capture the way in which job security is compromised and workers have less protection in neoliberal global capitalism, and are defined literally by Ross (2009: 6) as begging or praying for work. Precarious work is common in an era when the social value of full employment is challenged. Although public discourses encourage workers to celebrate their own flexibility and their status as free agents, Ross's research finds such workers to be and to feel vulnerable. Creative workers are in the 'vanguard' of the precariat, most willing to celebrate their own precarity. However, service workers also confront the 'brave new world of work' (U. Beck, 2000) as not set up in their interests, facing zero-hours contracts, split shifts and unsocial working hours when they can even find paid work.

Beyond paid work

The discussion so far has assumed that it is paid work that counts. But if we take a step back and ask what work is, then we draw attention to another important dimension of the production of consumption: that unpaid work, including that done by consumers, matters.

What is work?

The answer to the question 'What is work?' may feel obvious: work is what we do to make a living; it is manipulating materials to produce goods or provide services. We can make a joke, as does Donkin (2001: 4), that many people's definition of work is 'something I would rather not be doing', although this means we cannot understand the idea that work can give pleasure. More seriously, Lars Svendsen discusses how hard it is to avoid circular definitions of work, as we have a commonsense understanding that only some kinds of effort should be labelled work and tend to 'intuitively grasp what constitutes work and what does not' (2008: 7). However, working out how to mark the boundaries (or fuzzy areas) that might demarcate between work and non-work involves considering some political questions, as definitions are never neutral statements of fact. It's worth doing this to understand that 'work' is a complex concept that encompasses multiple dimensions and is not the same in all times and places.

Most people would think that 'work' means paid work. Workers are paid 'at work' for doing a set of tasks, usually determined by someone else and agreed to in a contract. For the period of work, this contract determines what you do. That is, you sell your labour power in return for pay. You may get a weekly wage for the hours you work, or a monthly salary for use of your skills and capabilities. At the end of the day (or night), you stop and are no longer at work. In the simplest way of thinking about this, there is a strict demarcation between work time and non-work time (leisure time, sleep time, family time).

Colin Williams complains that '[c]asting one's eyes along the book-shelves of our academic libraries in search of information on the economy, it is as though there is only one form of work that is now of any importance, namely commodified work' (Williams, 2005: 25, see also Pettinger et al., 2006). When labour market statistics are gathered, paid work is the work that is counted. But not all work is paid work. As we will see in later chapters, many of the kinds of work that produce consumption depend on the non-work activities that such workers do – including their own consumption – and that consumers too do 'work'. In the 1970s, feminist thinkers questioned the status of domestic labour and asked whether housework was work. The articles in Malos (1980), for example, draw attention to the ways in which the nominally 'private' sphere of the home was connected to the public sphere of work, as when cooking, cleaning and care within the home 'reproduced' the wage labourer for <u>his</u> public role. For some, work within the home was not seen as a system of exploitation based around capitalism, but as a system of exploitation based on patriarchy, with men 'appropriating' the labour of women. For others, then and now (Fortunati, 2007; Weeks, 2011), invisible domestic labour was fundamental to the workings of capitalism. In addition to domestic labour, other kinds of work exist outside of paid employment, including voluntary work, informal work, consumer work and internships (see Taylor, 2004; Williams, 2005). These forms of work contribute to global consumer capitalism in important ways, as do the 'play' activities of commercial workers that contribute to their abilities to create commercial cultures, as in the case of the cultural intermediaries discussed in 'Cultural intermediaries'. In the section that follows, we will focus on consumption as work.

Consumption work

Consumption work is central to how consumer capitalism operates. Prior to purchase, consumers 'work' to make consumption happen. We saw in Chapter 3 how the development of self-service transformed consumption. Consumers loaded and unloaded their shopping trolleys, and now they may also operate self-service checkouts. Customers doing this are 'quasi-employees' (Koeber, 2011: 4). Internet retail is an obvious recent example of consumption work. Internet users spend time booking tickets for trains or concerts, updating software that enables them to download songs and films, and so on. This work keeps our lives going. The work that consumers do after purchase has been framed by Glucksmann (2013; Wheeler and

Glucksmann, 2013) as part of the process of production. Glucksmann draws on Karl Polanyi's ideas (Chapter 2) about the interconnected-ness of economic processes (the 'instituted economic process') and argues that consumers are implicated in economic processes when they complete production at home (for example, by building flat-pack furniture or cooking partly prepared food). Consumer work is distinct from paid work in the public sphere, although it is an essential part of the process through which goods, services and experiences are made consumable.

The kind of consumption work we do varies over time and between places. Goods accessed through formal markets in one place, or at one time, may be accessed through informal markets elsewhere. For example, you probably have a mobile phone that belongs to you, having chosen a model of phone and a payment tariff. In Botswana, however, owning a mobile phone would give you a chance to set up a small business renting out your phone to paying customers (Sechele, 2011). Limited access to landlines in Botswana and the expense of a mobile make this a potentially profitable enterprise. In large cities in Korea, Taiwan and elsewhere, eating out is normal and kitchens may be very small to save space. Many people living in Taiwan prefer not to drink tap water and buy water in bottles or from water stations that look like petrol stations (Harvey, 2012). Cultural norms, com-modity forms and infrastructures combine to affect the kind of work consumers do, and we might learn from paid work about new ways of consuming: for example, using computers at work preceded and encouraged home computing (Firat and Dholakia, 1998: 54). There may be a division of labour in consumption work. For example, whilst building flat-pack furniture may be gendered as men's work, food consumption work is often done by women for their families, and has a different meaning when done by paid domestic servants (Devasahayam, 2005).

These examples of consumption work are mundane and reflect the forms of 'ordinary consumption' discussed in Chapter 3. They are sociologically interesting because they are instances of the small and ongoing changes to everyday life that emerge through consumer activity in global capitalism. The patterns of production and con-sumption we are accustomed to are not universal nor going to endure. The examples are also reminders of how many acts of consumption occur outside of the seemingly dominant industrialised consumption of the supermarket, shopping mall, branded leisure complex and the like. All kinds of informal economic activity persist in consumer capitalism.

Consumer work and value

In addition to asking about the location of work, we can also explore how the work that consumers do may contribute to the production of value in consumer capitalism. Status brands may explicitly try to appeal to (potential) employees as well as customers, and see customers as the best employees. Yeran Kim (2013), discussing the current fashion for South Korean cultural products in Asia, describes how fans of Korean popular culture from Taiwan and other countries in East Asia come to Korea to study or work and gain cultural capital. They may end up employed in Korean media organisations, but are more likely to get involved in independent media, often as translators. This involves workers in 'pragmatic precarity', suggests Kim, whereby the only way to work is to accept precarious work. For Kim, as for Hye Kyung Lee (2012), creative consumers are important to the operation of the cultural industries. The manga 'scanlators' (scanning + translation) studied by Lee are new kinds of intermediaries, using different distribution channels to mainstream manga publishing. As consumers, they do translation, editing and dissemination of products, contributing to the spread of manga whilst also substituting for paid workers.

Koeber (2011: 4) refers to consumers as 'quasi marketers' when they wear branded goods, but 'co-creation' and 'prosumer' are more common and powerful terms. Co-creation is currently popular with marketers and other commercial workers and refers to how branded corporations try to access and mobilise the knowledge work and lifestyles of consumers to create value for their own products. Rather than 'taming' customers, co-creation suggests that marketing should follow customers and encourage them to promote companies themselves (see Prahalad and Ramaswamy (2004) to hear more about how marketers speak about co-creation). The prosumer exists between production and consumption, a consumer who is put to work by the brand or corporation, participating through consumption work or on social media platforms (Beer and Burrows, 2007; Ritzer and Jurgenson, 2010). Brands present on social media sites such as Facebook or Twitter and encourage co-creation by asking customers to 'like' the brand page or 'retweet' to get a chance to win a product. By doing this, brands access customers' existing social media networks. Offline variants of co-creation are also common, for example in immersive consumer-as-producer experiences, such as 'Build-A-Bear' shops where children select a 'basic' model bear and then customise it (see Zwick et al., 2008 for a critical discussion of this and other dimensions of co-creation), or the 'American Girl' shops where shoppers can take their doll to the hairdressers or to watch a film (Moore, 2007). Consumers engage not just in the production of symbolic brand values (through, say, making a brand seem cool to their peers), but in the individualised production of goods, services and experiences per se. And as workers, our nominally non-work time can be co-opted into our work, when we shop to buy the stuff we need to be a good worker (Pettinger, 2008), or when we work for a company that explicitly demands our lifestyles be used to help it build distinction (Land and Taylor, 2010). A clothing company where workers are encouraged to use their leisure time to go surfing, or do other sport, and so produce stories that can appear on the company website is one where the boundaries between public and private, and between production and consumption, are no longer visible.

Conclusion

Commercial work is a significant part of a service economy, and includes business and personal service occupations. However, the work that produces consumption requires attention to the cultural context of consumption. A wide range of workers make goods, services and experiences desirable, valuable and saleable, many of whom are involved in the production of commercialised cultural forms or in explicitly 'mediating' between production and consumption (we have seen many ways in which it doesn't make sense to think of production and consumption as separable domains, but as constantly interwoven). These workers are often employed on flexible contracts and many have normalised this. It is important to make visible the service workers who have the power to influence transactions and experiences and thereby to contribute to symbolic values alongside other kinds of commercially oriented 'culture work'. If you have ever walked out of a retail space without buying something because of poor service, you will have a sense of this. Interactive service occupations that mediate consumption and that make consumer markets operate are part of the process of making consumer markets and contribute to the enchantment of the customer. In comparison with other forms of commercial work, they are low-paid, flexibilised and (often) feminised forms of work. The work that consumers do to make possible their own consumption of goods, services and experiences is also important, when consumers produce the objects they consume and produce value through co-creation.

In later chapters, we'll look at the details of how this work is carried out and how it seeks to affect the emotional and aesthetic dynamics of consumer cultures. In the next chapter, we will consider what attributes and abilities commercial workers need in order to do the work that produces consumption.

Research task

Look up official statistics to work out the percentage of employees who work in commercial work occupations. Official statistics are produced by government agencies and are usually published on the internet. Which occupations are easy to locate? Which can't you find, and why not?

OR

Take the end credits of a film and investigate the different occupations listed. Which of the categorisations discussed in this chapter could you use to characterise these different occupations?

Discussion questions

1. What do you understand by 'creativity'? Is advertising a form of creativity? Does the label 'creative work' help to understand advertising work?
2. Consider the discussion of cultural intermediaries in 'Cultural intermediaries' and 'Extending the concept'. Do you think the concept 'cultural intermediary' is useful to understanding retail service work?
3. What forms of 'consumption work' have you done recently? What 'values' have you produced? Consider your use of branded products, your consumption of services and experiences and your social media practices.

Chapter 5

Doing Work

Work, Consumption and Capitalism takes the view that we get worthwhile insights from considering the ways in which consumer capitalism is actively produced by many kinds of work. In this chapter, we examine key concepts that help us to see how the work that produces consumption is done, that is, how working bodies operate. What kinds of skills do commercial workers have? Indeed, is 'skill' a helpful concept for making sense of what work in consumer culture is like? Some have characterised contemporary capitalism as a 'knowledge economy': are the interrelated concepts of 'knowledge work' and 'knowledge economy' insightful for understanding how consumer markets are created and enacted? Would understanding this work as a form of craft provide a nuanced understanding of some of the dimensions of commercial work, such as sensing what will appeal to a target market or designing a brand strategy? We consider 'doing work' by discussing how working bodies contribute to generating sales, whether by creating desire through advertising, by designing the selling space, by working on goods to make them saleable, or by managing the exchange of goods and services. An important argument in this book is that working bodies are also consuming bodies. This dual engagement with production and consumption influences the sorts of bodily competencies which are possessed by workers in consumer capitalism.

In common with the rest of the chapters in this book, this chapter starts by looking at a key philosophical concept. In this case, we consider how to conceptualise 'the body'. We will look at how active, living, breathing biological bodies needs to be put at the heart of thinking about bodies in work, and consider how technology changes and enables work. The discussion of bodies sets the scene for a detailed exploration of three concepts that are commonly used to understand work. 'Skill' considers how skills can be understood as the attributes and resources of individual economic actors, and addresses how skills are socially constructed knowledge and craft. 'Knowledge' explores 'knowledge' and 'knowledge work' as significant in the discourses of work in contemporary capitalism, and asks what a focus on knowledge can help us understand about how consumer capitalism operates. 'Craft' foregrounds working bodies by looking at craft, and considers whether this concept can contribute to an understanding of the complex activities of commercial workers.

Bodies

The key concept of this chapter is 'the body'. It would be hard to think about doing work if we did not understand how bodies work and how work affects bodies. Philosophers have provided some useful tools for helping us to think about what a body is and how it operates in social spaces. In this section, we'll look at ideas about the body and at ways of thinking about working bodies and their relationship with technology.

Theorising bodies

Descartes' famous phrase 'I think, therefore I am' (*Cogito ergo sum*) summarises an idea central to much Western philosophy: mind–body dualism, that is, a hierarchical split between mind and body. The philosophy of mind–body dualism can be seen in understandings of work that distinguish between manual and non-manual ('mental') labour (Sohn-Rethel, 1977). As mind and rationality are linked and are the source of a thinking self, those forms of work which involve thought ('non-manual labour') acquire higher status. In contrast, the apparent lack of thought needed for 'manual' jobs assigns them low status. Such jobs are also often tightly controlled or managed, to remove the need for independent thought by the worker. Trying to assign occupations to the category 'manual' or 'non-manual' reveals these categorisations as unsustainable: design work, for example, requires an embodied competency (such as an ability to draw) that is inseparable from the creative capacity of the designer to think of new ideas; apparently routine work like serving in a restaurant also relies on thinking bodies that can prioritise customer demands and manoeuvre around the kitchen and dining area without incident. We need to conceptualise the relationship between mind and body as altogether more complex (whilst acknowledging the legacy of this mind–body hierarchy in many of the categories and ideas we work with).

An alternative philosophic heritage derived from phenomenology provides a different way of theorising bodies, suggesting that we know and understand the world through our bodily engagement in it, so that conscious awareness of our body in the world gives us a sense of who we are (Diprose and Reynolds, 2008). Some writers suggest that we are aware of our biological, fleshy body only when it is forced to our attention (Leder, 1990), perhaps when we try to change it, as when we learn a new skill (Lande, 2007). Slavishak (2010), for example, says that workers come to be aware of how their bodies are controlled by production techniques when they experience and discuss the pains and demands of work. So how can we think about bodies in a way that gives weight to biology and culture, to blood and feeling? Frank's definition is pretty comprehensive; a body is a 'fleshy, verdant, carnal, sensate, engaged organism that is composed of bones, blood, organs and fluids, as well as status, hopes, fears and anxieties' (1997: 27). Bodies are inseparably biological and social, inseparably thinking, feeling, moving and acting things. For Turner (2008: 245), the experience of embodiment is comprised of three dimensions. First, there is 'having' a body; a body is a thing, it is seen and perhaps judged by others, not least for its gendered, 'raced', classed and aged appearance, and it needs feeding and caring for. Second, there is 'being' a body, where the body is a project we might work on, perhaps to reflect a changing sense of who we are. Third, there is 'doing' a body, where our body is produced through time. These three dimensions help to understand different dimensions of work. The idea of 'having' a body makes us notice that overwork might damage bodies. The body as a project is evident in cases like the fashion models studied by Mears (2011), where bodies are worked on to suit the demands of clients (see Chapter 7). The idea of 'doing' helps us to recognise that bodies change over time in order to do work and because of the work they do – including how they acquire new skills, knowledges and craft ability, as we'll consider in the sections to come.

Bodies and work

Although there is extensive scholarship on the topic of the body, only a few of those who study work have brought the body to the forefront of analysis. Morgan et al. (2005) draw a distinction between embodied and disembodied work. Work can be more or less embodied according to how much awareness of the body of self and other is needed (2005: 5). They suggest that care work is 'more embodied' than advertising work, because the body of the worker encounters and works on the body of the care recipient in the case of the former. The latter, in contrast, is disembodied, and 'disembodied pleasures may involve the opportunity to daydream, or to think creatively' (2005: 7). Given the critique of mind–body dualism, however, we might want to be cautious about the idea of the more and less embodied worker, and the implicit *dematerialisation* of the body that is entailed by that idea. Remember what Turner (2008) said: having, being and doing are *all* part of embodiment. Rather than investigate the 'degree' of embodiment of a form of work, it is more interesting to ask how the body is transformed through work and how it makes work happen.

All work is 'body work' in a general sense, relying on the engagement of a thinking, acting, moving being with a set of tools and technologies to produce something, whether an object or an interaction. Work needs a capable body. Wolkowitz (2006) is an exception to the common neglect of the body when thinking about work. She developed the concept 'body work' to refer to the work human beings do on their own and other's bodies (2006: 174), as a specific dimension to the way bodies are regulated by work. Gimlin (2007) suggests that there are four different types of body work: the work performed on the worker's own body (discussed explicitly in Chapter 7); paid labour on the bodies of others (by health care workers and the like, developed by Twigg et al., 2011); the management of embodied emotional experience and display (discussed explicitly in Chapter 6); and the production or modification of bodies through work. I suggest that it is worth considering two specific dimensions to this latter category: what embodied capabilities are needed for different occupations? And how is an ability to do work acquired? We will answer these questions by exploring three important conceptualisations of how working bodies produce consumer capitalism: skill, knowledge and craft. An important dimension of the skill, knowledge and craft of commercial work is its understanding of, and location within, consumer capitalism: body work, therefore, is in part also consumption work.

Bodies, work and technology

Before we look at doing commercial work, we should note how technology affects how work is organised and experienced. New technologies change what work is done, and by whom, for example, by substituting bodies with machines. This substitution often involves deskilling. One instance of deskilling in commercial work is the shift from personal services to self-service to the use of technological devices. Grocers who previously weighed out the food that customers wanted were superseded by factories that pre-packed that same food and enabled the customer to pick it off the shelves themselves and put it in that fundamental technology at the supermarket, the shopping trolley (Bowlby, 2000). Internet retailing is a further step in the shift from personal service, combining consumer work with a complex backstage production of consumption that uses ICT to manage the distribution infrastructure. Note how there's no simple substitution of worker by machine; the production process is transformed and different kinds of workers are needed, including software engineers and low-skilled product pickers. Some forms of interactive service work can be, and have been, substituted with technology and consumer work (self-service checkouts, for example), or do not require co-presence in space as well as time (hence the use of overseas call centres). Technological substitution is never complete, and many of these kinds of occupations demand a full, embodied encounter between worker and customer.

Technologies also mediate how established activities are done. For example, the development of new software packages changes how culture workers do 'creative' work, as Manovich (2011) shows when he looks at Photoshop. Customer loyalty programmes, customer-relationship software, computer-aided design and so on may generate a shift in the kind of knowledge a cultural intermediary can have, or what a creative worker can or should do. As consumers leave trails of information behind them (for example, by promoting brands on social media or using loyalty cards), data mining to understand and influence consumer practices emerges as a new kind of work, requiring new skills. Technologies make possible the creation of different kinds of knowledge. Well-established technologies like EPOS that are central to post-Fordist flexible production make it possible to know and respond to consumer tastes. Newer innovations like computer bot brokering further change the experience of work and consumption. Product brokering is used by companies (like Amazon) to make recommendations to customers based on their purchase history; merchant brokering enables customers to compare prices (Brown and Duguid, 2000: 42–4). In both cases, technology provides new information, and knowledge about, and produced by, consumers in the course of their consumption is a significant source of value. Technological change means that knowledge moves between different agents, including from commercial workers to technology itself. This means that skill needs change and new kinds of objects are encountered by craft workers. Doing work, therefore, is contingent on how work is organised.

Skill

Skill is an important concept for thinking about work, and one that is commonly used outside of academia. We need to explore the different ways it is used to see what it offers us for understanding the production of consumption. In this section, we will explore the derivation and use of the concept. Being skilled and having an economy made up of skilled workers sounds like an unquestionably good thing. It seems that a politician could not go wrong by calling for 'upskilling' (a workforce gaining more advanced skills), as skill seems likely to produce economic growth. Certainly, without labour competent in doing and making, production is impossible and so skill, the embodied capacity to perform tasks, is central to economic activity. How, though, can we say whether one job requires more or less skill than another? To what extent is 'skill' a clear and useful concept for understanding commercial work? To answer these questions we will consider what counts as a skill, what kinds of skills are scarce, how policymakers think about skill, and how this relates to intimate experiences of participating in the labour market.

What counts as skill?

Lists of what counts as a skill might be familiar to you; look at some of your university documentation to see statements about the kinds of skills your degree promises you. Lists of desirable skills are used to argue for a shift in training provision to meet economic development goals. For example, if policymakers decide that more people with the skill of 'computer literacy' are needed, then training can be introduced. Lists of skills enable readily understandable arguments to be made about shortages and desirable skills. Skill lists also recognise the relationship between the skills possessed by individual workers (or potential workers) and local, national and supranational economic development. However, such lists can soon become outdated, and do not reflect how 'skill' is historically and geographically contingent.

Itemising skills does not offer much scope for understanding how skill is used within specific work contexts. Indeed, it is hard to imagine the very abstract 'skills' in NGO documentation or employers' reports unless you think also about the contexts in which such skills take place. 'Computer literacy', for example, means something very different when thinking about how a retail worker comes to understand EPOS technology compared to how a brand designer learns how to use photo-editing software. And the difference is not merely one of complexity of a specific skill; the context of the work matters too. There are few occupations or activities that require just one skill; most rely on a range of skills, and it is often the combination of skilled activities that makes a job count as high- or low-skilled. So it is important to consider the context and interconnections in order to judge whether (or more importantly, how) something is skilled. Further, advocates of 'transferable skills' often neglect how many skills are specific to a context.

A more complex theory about skill is desirable. Green (2011) argues that 'skill is a personal quality' and has three features:

i. **P**roductive: using skill is productive of value.
ii. **E**xpandable: skills are enhanced by training and development.
iii. **S**ocial: skills are socially determined. (Green, 2011: 5)

Green suggests that economists, especially human capital theorists, have a tendency to stress only the 'productive', while sociologists are very good at understanding the 'social'. Both, along with psychologists who also study skill, agree that skill can be enhanced, although they would explain this differently. This 'PES' (Productive, Expandable and Social) understanding is a good way to think through different dimensions of skill, and we will consider each feature in turn.

Productive skills and human capital theory

Human capital theory (HCT) sets out to explain why individuals acquire skills and why they acquire some sets of skills and not others. The economist Gary Becker, a key figure in the field, described the development of human capital as: 'activities that influence future real income through the imbedding of resources in people. This is called investing in human capital' (Becker, 1962: 9; Becker, 1964). Human capital is a form of investment in production, where the individual is the unit of production. HCT presumes rational action by those involved in the labour market. People have the incentive to invest in human capital, measured as educational qualifications or years of schooling, because it will mean they can get a better job, defined as a better-paid job. Education and training raise productivity and productive workers may expect – if not get – higher wages. Individuals who invest in human capital make use of state institutions such as schools and universities to garner generic human capital. Human capital is also something that firms invest in, on the presumption that well-trained workers will be more productive. The general presumption is that firms will be willing to train workers in 'firm specific' human capital, but have no reason to train workers in generic or transferable human capital that they can use in other employment. Transferable human capital makes it too easy for that worker to leave the firm before the company has recouped its training costs. Some economists suggest that there is a further kind of capital, 'semi-specific' human capital, which might be relevant to an occupation (retail) or sector (interactive service work) (Neal, 1995, 1999), and this is a helpful refinement.

HCT prioritises upgrading the technological capability of individuals and therefore economies. It rests on a mechanistic view of the person in the production process. Individuals are not thought of as having complex lives; their motivations are simple: to make more money. Societies, too, and labour markets, are not seen as very complex, but presumed to have a simple desire to maximise productivity, with workers facing few structural barriers to benefiting from the skills they have. The reality is more complex: skilled workers cannot necessarily circulate between jobs; their competencies may not be easily transmitted to new workers; and firms sometimes make deliberate decisions to sideline workers with high levels of human capital because they're expensive! The use of unpaid interns in branding agencies to develop new ideas is a contemporary example of how expertise may be sidelined in favour of cheap workers without experience but with the uncredentialised benefits of youth, energy and enthusiasm (Daniel and Daniel, 2013; Siebert and Wilson, 2013).

As industries grow and decline, and as jobs move between places, workers with skills that were once in demand will find getting decent work harder. The skills of a miner are not much use if the mine has closed and the big local employer is now a call centre that expects 'communication', 'problem-solving' and 'teamwork' skills. Other labour market factors matter too, as when job design mediates the demand for certain kinds of skill rather than others: the Russell Sage Foundation studies of low-wage work (e.g. Gautié and Schmitt, 2010) found that little formal training was offered in many retail, hotel and catering or call centre jobs, as these had been made as routinised as possible. The discourse of skill individualises responsibility for getting decent work and tends not to pay attention to embedded structural inequalities. For example, 'vocational training' in skills specific to an occupation is only a solution for unemployment if there are relevant jobs available for the newly trained worker. This means that workers, training providers and firms need to share an understanding about what skills are needed, and what the timeframe is to acquire them.

As well as the troubling assumptions of the rational worker and the rational firm, there is an array of research to show that HCT does not explain individual and firm behaviour well enough. Not only do higher wages not always result from higher educational levels, but mechanisms to ensure that the supply of skilled labour matches employer demand are flawed. Brown (2001) suggests that HCT focuses on individual 'employability', at the expense of a more complex account of skill formation that recognises that particular skills are interdependent and embedded in structures such as training institutions and firms; how skills are acquired, evolve and are measured as skills is quite complex. Nonetheless, HCT is popular amongst policymakers, not least because it enables a focus on the production of value (Green, 2011).

Expandable skills: education and training

The second feature of Green's concept of skill is acquisition. Education and training are the most common routes to acquiring skills, and educational policy is often directed at ensuring that the level and content of educational provision is suitable for the current or projected demands of the labour market. Vast agencies ('Cedefop', Australia's 'Industry Skills Council', Singapore's 'SkillsConnect' and so on) are devoted to assessing vocational and educational training (VET) and to planning in order to ensure that demand and supply are not mismatched. Keep and Mayhew (2010) are critical of how skill comes to be monitored by state institutions, suggesting that by being too narrowly vocational, 'skills policies' reflect a limited understanding of what might comprise an educated workforce.

The state, via its provision or monitoring of training instructions, plays an important role in the production of skilled workers. Nation states vary as to how training is managed. What sorts of apprenticeships are available in firms and how are these managed? Is on-the-job training credentialised (and hence transferable)? What is the school system expected to do to make workers 'job-ready'? The formal vocational training institutions in the Netherlands and Germany make for a quite different system to that in the UK, or US. Germany, a coordinated market economy in the 'varieties of capitalism' language (Hall and Soskice, 2001), with its long-established apprenticeship-based vocational training system, treats skill acquisition as collective. Companies have incentives to train and workers to acquire specific skills. In liberal market economies like the UK and US, the responsibility is on the individual to participate in 'lifelong learning' to keep their skills current, and – economic theory tells us – firms do not have incentives to provide intense training in generic skills in a flexible labour market where workers might leave. The flexibility that dominates in liberal economies fosters general skills, transferable between industries, for example through high rates of university education rather than vocational training (Culpepper and Thelen, 2008: 24, cited in Mayer and Solga, 2008). Sector specialisation and levels of development also influence the proportion of firms investing in on-the-job training. Rates are higher in northern Europe than in Southern Europe. Northern European apprenticeship systems locate training in the firm. In southern Europe, school-based training mean employers fill in training gaps (Elias and Davies, 2004).

However, country-level comparisons are flawed, say Brockmann et al. (2009), because 'skill' and other key terms are understood differently by different languages. Further, general comments about economy don't help with sector-specific work, such as culture work or cultural intermediation. Accounts that compare skill 'regimes' between countries make it possible to compare 'manufacturing' and 'service' sectors but are limited by how they treat the actual work being done (and the skill involved) as measurable and abstracted from the occupational and organisational context; we cannot gain much insight into the particularities of commercial work from this macro-analysis. What happens to our understanding of skill when we pay attention to context?

Skill is social

The third dimension of Green's typology of skill involves considering the social construction of skill. Feminist work and activism aimed at identifying the skilled components of women's work and hence claiming fairer remuneration, demonstrates why it is important to consider the way in which skill is socially determined. This work challenged taken-for-granted assumptions about what counts as skilled work (e.g. Cockburn, 1983) and sought to unpick the relationship between a skilled person, a skilled job and the social construction of the idea of skill. For example, it questioned essentialist understandings of the capacity to care, that is, suggested that care is not something that women do naturally but is a skill that is slowly learned over a long period of socialisation into gender roles. We will discuss this further in Chapter 6 when we consider women's apparently natural ability to manage emotion. In-depth ethnographic work has been used to work out how specific tasks might be judged skilled or unskilled. As ethnographers who research work have to learn the tasks themselves, they can end up counting quite a lot of occupations as skilled! For Payne (2009) this is troubling, as it overextends the meaning of skill, even as far as including workers' knowing how to comply with management demands as a skill. Nonetheless, unpacking skills that are tacit, uncodified and embodied is an important process. This 'social constructionist' critique of skill as geographically and historically contingent is one of the important contributions made by sociologists to understandings of skill. It hints at how we might want to think about skill as a complex concept.

Consider the following activities that are part of the paid work that produces consumption: folding jeans for a display; preparing a cocktail; choosing the colour of a brand logo. Which are 'skilled?' What dimensions of skill are involved? The first, folding jeans, sounds unskilled, although there might be an argument that in the context of branded stores which demand that their jeans are all folded just the same, this is a task that needs training and dexterity (would you be good at it? I know I am not (Pettinger, 2006)). Similarly, preparing a cocktail is easy to make sense of: you could learn the recipe and get it fixed into your mind, and you might even acquire some of the commitment and flash that some bartenders display (Ocejo, 2012). The work involves learning and skill, but many of us could work out how to do this fairly quickly, so it seems the skill level is low – until you started developing your own recipes, and so your bodily ability to understand flavour and create new tastes would come into play. However, even in the case of just making the cocktail, the 'articulation work' (Strauss, 1985) done by individuals and work groups to ensure that these activities fit alongside all the other tasks to be done is in itself a skill, albeit one that is not captured in formal credentials (but is perhaps reflected in job adverts that demand 'experience' for jobs that are apparently low-skilled). 'Articulation work' reminds us that work is dynamic, not itemisable; it is situational and processual, not fixed; it is done by groups, not individuals. Competence is not merely the property of individuals but collective and situational (Boreham, 2004). Skills, be they the management of feeling or technological competency or the ability to address a complex problem brought by a customer, are not enacted by bounded individuals. Instead, they are operationalised in specific workplace environments, where they may have been acquired and developed. Situated workplace learning produces workers with tacit and uncodified skills (Lave and Wenger, 1990), and this is important to being able to do specific work tasks in the set environment. New recruits learn to fold jeans the 'right' way:, a tiny skill, but one that is part of more complex workplace processes and practices. This is by way of saying that restrictive understandings of skill do not provide in-depth understanding of doing work.

Choosing a colour needs a different kind of discussion. On the one hand it seems quite easy: just think about what you like the look of most. But there's a whole sub-industry devoted to thinking about the relationship between colours, fashion, affect and market success ('colour marketing manager' and 'colour consultant' are real job titles); those involved might argue strongly that having the right colour to signify particular brand values is very important. For example, given longstanding associations between greyness and dullness, there might be skill in knowing what shades of grey could be rehabilitated to show a serious – but still interesting – business. So choosing a colour that will appeal to customers might count as skill for those in design and marketing, and comes with a kind of science behind it (see Kauppinen-Räisänen and Luomala, 2010 for a study of colour marketing). This type of skill is technical in some respects and also aesthetic and creative, capabilities which tend not to be extensively considered in discussions of skill. Skill, knowledge and feeling in the body are entwined in doing this work.

However, of the 'social' dimensions of skill, it is the soft skills of working with people – clients, customers and colleagues – that require particular attention. The next question about skill that we face is what to do about understanding skilled and unskilled tasks within the context of occupations. How can sets of skills be aggregated into judgements about 'high-' or 'low'-skilled occupations, and how can these be aggregated to judge the point at which an economy becomes 'high-skilled'?

'Soft skills' and interactive skills

So-called 'soft skills' are prized in consumer capitalism. In contrast to the 'hard skills' of technical competency, soft skills are more nebulous (and naturalised). They are the qualities of being a certain kind of person, able to communicate clearly, having personal attributes like 'adaptability, motivation, cooperativeness' (Thompson and Smith, 2009: 16). These might be nicely described as 'interactive skills'. In advertising, soft skills are itemised as critical thinking, persuasion, interpersonal communication and presentation by Windels et al.

(2013). Soft skills may be harder to train people for, and are not as easily measured or readily credentialised as technological competences, physical abilities or cognitive capacities. We might come to question whether 'skill' is the right term at all for these personality attributes, which we may, as customers or as colleagues, notice by their absence rather than by their presence. Soft skills are used, for example, to manage customers by managing the personality of the worker. Traditionally feminised, soft skills are often unacknowledged and devalued by being naturalised as something that women can readily do.

In Chapter 4, we saw that employers wanted a flexible workforce. Flexibility, enthusiasm, creativity, passion and suchlike sometimes appear in lists of desirable attributes for potential employees. To some extent these are not skills at all, but indicate something about a worker, such as their willingness to respond to the demands of their employers, to not cause upset, to be willing to work hard. It is not the capacity to do specific tasks that is exchanged in the labour market, but the act of being (and becoming) a particular person (Adkins and Lury, 1999). These are examples of how modern work 'governs the soul' (Miller and Rose, 1990), requires commitment to 'enterprise' (du Gay, 1996) and demands self-exploitation (Gill, 2007; McRobbie, 2002; Perrons, 2003; Reidl et al., 2006; Tennant, 2012; Ursell, 2000).

Now, it may be the case that you would want to argue that neither the soft skills needed to work 'well' in consumer capitalism, nor the personality traits demanded by a flexible and individualised way of organising work are enough to make a job count as 'skilled'. In the case of culture work and cultural intermediary work (defined in Chapter 4), technical skills, creative capabilities and interpersonal skills may combine. Such workers are often considered to be high-status workers and are well recompensed for their work (even as they face poor working conditions). It is harder to make a case that sales and service work can be thought of as skilled, and indeed much of the work done by those in such occupations is routine, low-paid and low-status. The case for skilled status rests partly on the articulation work needed, and partly on the soft skills needed to manage interactions with customers. This is not to say that such work is not skilled at all, as we have seen that it is easy to naturalise attributes as 'unskilled' when they need training and practice, but it means that it's worth being cautious about making such claims, for example, by recognising that different dimensions of an occupation can require different levels of skill.

Recognising 'soft skills' suggests that workers' sense of themselves and their bodily capabilities are changed as they develop and use new skills: in Turner's phrasing, that 'doing' with a body (for example, acquiring skills) affects having and being embodied. This may demand an understanding of 'skill' that does not view skill as an attribute that is separate from, and then added to, a person. It is easy to see that we are deeply socialised into the 'soft skills' that are part of our bodily encounter with the world and of our understanding of how to get and keep work, and that these affect our experience and knowledge of the world. It is also the case that technological skills might usefully be thought of not as capabilities added on, but as transformative – the act of 'doing' with a body, say, acquiring a skill, re-forms what it is to have a body. 'Skill' is a concept that tends to individualise and codify a worker's capability to do a specific task, and such an atomising idea does not get at the complex constitution of work in consumer capitalism. Understanding that commercial work involves the skilled co-option of specific knowledges may provide a more grounded account, and we now turn to discussing this.

Knowledge

Knowledge is a key component of a capacity to do work. In this section, we will assess understandings of how different kinds of workers possess, use and produce knowledge about consumer markets as part of their work. Can 'knowledge work' help us understand work in consumer capitalism? In order to answer this question, we must first think about the context within which knowledge work happens, that is, we must consider the 'knowledge economy'.

A knowledge economy?

Information society thinkers such as Castells (1996, 1997, 1998) and Lyotard (1979), despite their different philosophical groundings, suggest that contemporary society is characterised by flows of information. Networks of people and technologies make information (often in the form of data) readily transferable. In an information society, knowledge is the principal force of production and, for Castells, it is a component of comparative advantage. A knowledge economy comprises: one, a trade in knowledge products, such as knowledge about consumers derived from loyalty card sales data or internet browsing patterns, or even knowledge about knowledge – such as management or marketing advice texts; two, capital markets that make investment in or acquisition of knowledge firms possible;

three, a labour market in knowledge workers (Harvey and McMeekin, 2007). Information society relies on knowledge workers to circulate knowledge, using technological infrastructures to enable information exchange. Knowledge work is thought of as highly skilled, produced through the 'knowledge factories' of education, especially higher education. The advanced services that Chapter 4 described as business-to-business services are components of a knowledge economy.

Various definitions of knowledge work and knowledge economy are used, differing as to how much attention they pay to highly educated workers and to information and communication technologies. Some definitions may include the manufacture of knowledge-capturing machines, while others stress the service work that makes possible the flow of information through ICT (which might include routine knowledge-processing jobs). CRM systems, or feedback software, are knowledge-based ICT systems that produce consumer capitalism. A 'knowledge economy' may also refer to knowledge-intensive service industries – this is a useful definition for this book, as it incorporates the producer services that make consumer markets work (as well as financial services, education, health and so on). Despite these different stresses, Casey suggests that techno-scientific knowledge, specifically instrumental economic reasoning, is dominant in knowledge economy discourses (2012: 15–16). Consumers come to be knowable and manageable, not least because their consumption practices are trackable.

Developing a knowledge economy is seen as a desirable way to generate economic development by global organisations such as the OECD and UN, and by regional governance institutions such as the EU or the Asia Development Bank. Whilst Fordism demanded comparatively low-skilled workers to carry out routine work, post-Fordist flexible specialisation contributes to increased demand for newly 'upgraded' skilled workers. Walby describes the apparent benefit of a knowledge-based economy as providing 'higher skilled jobs with greater autonomy, flatter hierarchies, flexible schedules and improved quality of working life' (Walby, 2007: 4). Work that is demanding, that enables the worker to make their own decisions without being tightly managed by layers of senior managers, and that is flexible in time and space sounds like desirable work (although knowledge economy ICTs may also create poor-quality jobs, as in the case of call centres (Mirchandani, 2012)). Whilst the different 'varieties of capitalism' influence how the policies are enacted and what kinds of development are possible (Walby, 2007), nation states and para-state institutions have adopted similar policies designed to encourage the development of knowledge work, in particular, to increase the supply of high-skilled workers. The massive expansion of higher education is the most visible of these policies in the EU, OECD and UN (Casey, 2012: 17). Casey suggests that this reflects how the knowledge imperative is connected to dominant neoliberal economic policies and discourses of the 'new economy' (2012: 32). For example, *Europe 2020* (Barroso, 2010) endorses the pursuit of competitive knowledge and innovation and the expansion of education in the same breath as it encourages the liberalisation of labour markets, and the Asia Development Bank promotes knowledge as 'essential to closing the productivity gap' (Jagannathan and Geronimo, 2013: 3. Education is reconfigured as important insofar as it produces a skilled workforce and hence contributes to economic growth; it is not seen as beneficial for its own sake (Casey, 2012: 2).

Achieving a high-skilled-knowledge economy means eliminating low-skilled jobs, perhaps by outsourcing them overseas. Those displaced are expected to gain new skills. However, knowledge work is not uniformly highly skilled, and knowledge work that involves information transfer may involve less status than information production. Carla Freeman's (2000) research into women working in travel-industry information processing in the Caribbean reveals the complex effects of engaging in even routine knowledge work. Her 'pink collar' interview respondents felt that they benefited from their new knowledge of, and proximity to, global travel, as well as from the comparatively high wages that made them powerful consumers, even as they were also frustrated by routine work and strict management. Both better and worse working and living conditions are possible in the shift to knowledge work. There remains in the most developed economies a large range of low-, and mid-level skilled work, much of which is necessary to support the high-skilled, flexible knowledge workers (Perrons, 2003) too busy to clean their own houses or buy their own birthday presents (Sherman, 2010). Low-level service work produces the infrastructures for the knowledge-rich economy.

Moulier Boutang (2010, 2012) provides insight into questions of the status and desirability of a knowledge economy, although he prefers the term 'cognitive capitalism' to 'knowledge economy: 'in cognitive capitalism the value of knowledge depends on an ability to *selectively use* information' (2010: 322). Further, selective use of information challenges the idea that production and consumption are distinct, separate spheres. In cognitive capitalism, there are multiple devices, spaces and opportunities where information about consumption is reinserted into production. We saw JIT production that responds to purchases described as one of the features of post-Fordism. Prosumers, discussed in Chapter 4, 'Consumer work and value', are another, reflecting how marketing harnesses public opinion and attention, for example, through creating 'water cooler' advertising moments (that is, content that people will talk about with their work colleagues). The collective production of information, feelings and buzz is central to economic exchange, as in cognitive capitalism, innovation and knowledge are continually produced and appropriated. Whilst the costs of knowledge and innovation tend to be borne by individuals, communities, households and states, the benefits (the positive externalities) are co-opted by neoliberal economic orders.

Considering a specific commodity is a useful way of seeing how consumer capitalism relies on knowledge work and knowledge networks. Knowledge shapes the journey of commodities to the point of consumption. In the case of cut flowers, Hughes argues that 'knowledge plays a vital part in reshaping the morphology of a commodity network' (2000: 179), that is, the commodity chain and the form the final consumer products take are affected by the competing and complimentary knowledges held by workers and embedded in processes that make up the chain. What kinds of knowledge mediate between production and consumption? Production for the European and North American cut flowers market often occurs in developing countries where multinational corporations and development agencies circle round each other. Hughes' (2000) research shows that buyers from multinationals reject products if they do not conform to the retailer's specification, as determined by market research into customers. However, it would be wrong to imagine a simple linear model of knowledge flowing from customers to retailer to flower grower. Customer knowledge and demand is influenced by the kinds of products they have seen and so flower designers may be consulted to understand and anticipate new trends and fashions, that is, to imagine and influence customers' future desires. Growers need to know what future demand might look like, as cut flowers are not amenable to JIT production! Hughes concludes that the circulation of commodities is only possible because of a knowledge-intensive production network. Horticulture and technological knowledge, including genetic knowledge of flowers, and knowledge of the cultural meanings of markets and gift giving are both significant, and these multiple circulating forms of knowledge are used by retailers to strengthen their own position (Hughes, 2000: 184–5). Knowledge work is embedded in knowledge processes which may be termed part of a knowledge economy, information society or cognitive capitalism. In the next section, we will explore the features of knowledge and ask: what is knowledge work in consumer capitalism?

Knowledge work

The widest definition of knowledge work refers to those who handle and distribute information (McKercher and Mosco, 2008). Alvesson provides a more precise account: 'the use of judgement backed up to a high degree by theoretical, intellectual knowledge' (2004: 1), although he notes that this may be too narrow, given that what counts as knowledge is ambiguous and contested. Knowledge work may draw on intellectual, communicative and symbolic skills, and knowledge workers tend to have autonomy over some parts of the content of their work – if not over labour contracts and conditions of work. Under this categorisation, advertising would count as a form of professional service work in a knowledge-intensive sector (Alvesson, 2004: 18). Nonetheless, neither 'knowledge work' nor 'knowledge-intensive firm' are precise categories (Alvesson, 2004: 26–7), the 'knowledge economy' even less so. One of the weaknesses of the 'knowledge work' concept is how it collapses important differences in its overgeneralised categorisations: '[i]t makes little sense to generalize about work conditions across a classification that is plausibly shared by high-salaried research scientists and data-entry workers' (Ross, 2003: 34). The knowledge work that specifically contributes to global consumption includes: knowledge about consumers, knowledge about kinds of consumption and knowledge of clients. Knowledge-intensive service work is a category that encapsulates many forms of the work that produces consumer capitalism, including design, retail management, professions and creative industries, whilst also including some that do not directly contribute (financial services) and excluding some that do (interactive service work). In this section, we will look at how knowledge work is organised, and how it influences the flows of commodities in global capitalism.

Knowledge work, like other kinds of work in 21st-century capitalism, is characterised as flexible. Some commentators argue that workers benefit from this flexibility and from the new kinds of careers that are possible in a knowledge economy (Castells, 1996; Quinn, 1992). In Chapter 4, we saw how temporally and spatially flexible work was a common feature of 21st-century work. Knowledge work is an exemplary case of this, not least because of how some forms of knowledge work involve project and piece work (Ross, 2009). Even where knowledge workers are employed on permanent contracts, how their knowledge and knowledge work maps onto organisational and institutional infrastructures affects what they do at work, and their experience of work. Knowledge work may involve being 'always on', ready to take advantage of a new contact or new idea, and many workers in knowledge-intensive jobs spend time pitching for, or bidding for, future work, or maintaining the social networks that make them likely to get such work (Blair et al., 2001; Gill and Pratt, 2008). In addition to this individual flexibility, and given that labour is less mobile than capital, capital can discourage states from instituting laws that protect labour by threatening to leave (Martin and Schumann, 1997). An economy dominated by knowledge work can become a low-wage, low-skill economy with little protection for workers, as work can be moved between geographical locations. The extent to which nonstandard work is used in the knowledge sectors is variable between occupations, countries, the dominant class, gender and ethnicity of workers.

Work across geographical borders is a common feature of knowledge work, facilitated by ICT and other technologies. Muller's (2005) insights into the success of the Bangkok advertising industry tell us something of the global exchange of knowledge work. Advertising is a complex product that relies on understanding local cultures, and promotional strategies must be adapted to local contexts. In Thailand, global advertising agencies make up 75% of spending on advertisements, and these adverts are produced in Bangkok by Thai workers employed by the global agencies. Muller suggests that the standard interpretation – that these are peripheral workers being told how to do the work by their American bosses – is wrong. Rather, decision making is decentralised and intelligence is distributed; Thai creatives make the (sometimes award-winning) adverts autonomously. However, many have worked overseas and been trained in the US or UK, and the transnational advertising agencies use this kind of mobility to create shared standards. So knowledge of both global and local advertising styles informs this knowledge work. The Thai adverts, 'characterized by strong visuals, minimal copy and a quirky sense of humour' (Muller, 2005: 133), are then produced with the aid of local producer services (such as market research or print, web and TV ad production). Ad agencies are thus embedded in the economy of Bangkok, are connected to global networks of 'creative' work and generate adverts that work in the local context. Similarly, UK-based advertising agencies create adverts for the Nigerian press (Alozie, 2009).

Whilst knowledge is embodied in individuals, organisations matter. A key characteristic of knowledge work is that it tends to require cooperation, communication and community, rather than control and hierarchy; flat hierarchies and networks are seen as desirable, and workers are configured as 'human resources', considered as useful for what they offer global corporations (Walby, 2007: 17). The organisational infrastructure influences how knowledge work is done, as Chiat/Day advertising agency found when it tried hot-desking (where employees do not have an assigned work desk but must find somewhere suitable each day). The experiment did not last long, not only because people feel comfortable sitting somewhere familiar, but because of the kinds of incidental learning that happen when workers sit next to a colleague (Brown and Duguid, 2000: 72).

Knowledge workers are, on the one hand, powerful because they embody specialised knowledge, skills and capabilities, but on the other, must prove and re-prove the worth of their knowledge. Relationships with clients are important to understanding this insecurity. Workers must invest time in relationships with clients, and are vulnerable when clients are struggling or when they must depend on a small group of clients and cannot build extensive but time-consuming networks (Gottschall and Kroos, 2007: 177). The advertising workers interviewed by Nixon (2003) worried about reputation and status in the workplace, measured according to their recent successes, reflecting how discourses about good workers in this kind of field stress individualism and meritocracy. In a study of new media workers, Gill (2002) identifies the problems for workers expected to be entrepreneurial: portfolio working offers limited security and protections, and workers must invest a great deal of time in finding new work and in upgrading skills. Women suffered more than men from the way work was organised, working on fewer, less lucrative jobs and being more likely to have to move into other occupations. For Andrew Ross, work never ends: 'Modern knowledge workers no longer know when they are on or off the job, and their ideas – the stock-in-trade of their industrial livelihoods – come to them at any waking moment of their day, often in their most free moments' (Ross, 2009: 204).

Embodied knowledge

Whilst information may be a disembodied process, translatable into software code and bytes of data and transferrable through ICT, knowledge is not easy to separate from the knower. Knowledge needs to have been 'digested' (Brown and Duguid, 2000: 199) by an embodied knower. Collins (2010) and Nonaka and Takeuchi (1995) draw a distinction between explicit knowledges and tacit knowledges. The former can be easily communicated to others, for example, through training programmes, but explicit knowledges do not always make much sense without tacit knowledge. For example, when assessing the (likely) effectiveness of a marketing campaign, promotional workers draw on the explicit knowledge of what customer research has told them and what the client expects, but also on tacit knowledge about what works in this context. A few years ago, HSBC's advertising campaign ('the world's local bank') tried to create distinction by pointing out that it understood (made explicit) the tacit cultural knowledge required to do business in a range of different cultures (Koller, 2007). In doing so, it reduced complex, tacit cultural knowledges to simple slogans and hence pointed out the difficulties of translating culture.

Within work environments, shared knowledges might exist that are neither tacit nor explicit but specific to that 'community of practice', in Lave and Wenger's (1990) term. Working in such an environment means understanding the norms and habits of that community of practice, for example, understanding what kind of aesthetics a client prefers. As Catherine Casey has argued, the key problem with knowledge is that it is sticky and hard to diffuse. The 'extraction, codification and transmission of tacit knowledge into knowledge products that may be exchanged' (Casey, 2012: 54) may be a key aim of management seeking to reduce dependency on specific knowledge workers, but tacit knowledges are not readily amenable to extraction; as Michael Polanyi (1967: 4) says, we know more than we can tell. Tacit knowledges are deeply embodied. The desire to audit and codify tacit and practical knowledges stems from the repositioning of knowledge as a tradable asset, as a contributor to economic development. Whilst practical and tacit knowledge cannot always be easily decoded and commodified, it may be valued through labour markets, with workers using past success and reputation to claim their worth. Indeed the tacit and embodied nature of knowledge may be a source of privilege and occupational closure – and so the question of whether someone is skilled, knowledgeable or creative (or none of those things) is political. Marketing advice literature is an example of making codified knowledge and experience exchangeable, as when Tréguer (2002) explains how to sell to older people or Gesterland and Seyk (2002) advise on selling 'across cultures'. Similarly, an improved version of a product codifies a designer's expertise in solving a problem.

What kind of knowledges are relevant in the context of consumer markets? Appadurai (1986) writes about the 'social life of the commodity' as involving three kinds of knowledge: knowledge that goes into production, knowledge required to consume and the knowledge which feeds commodity circulation and exchange. Each of these knowledges may be technical, social and aesthetic. Technical knowledge may refer to the production of goods and service, but may also be important to understanding the circulation and consumption of goods, as when a consumer explicitly looks for a fridge-freezer that defrosts automatically (the consumer has technical knowledge about what a freezer can do, and finds out if a specific freezer has this attribute; a salesperson may also be expected to know this). Aesthetic knowledge, which we'll discuss in Chapter 7, is not only important at the moment of consumption but throughout the process of production (as in the case of cut flowers, where the aesthetics of individual flowers plus an understanding of how they might be combined in bouquets matter to understanding what is grown). Social knowledge, which might include how different kinds of people might use a good or service, informs each part of the flow of commodities. Moor (2008) suggests that designers consume as they imagine target customers do as an exercise to think through customers' lives and hence understand how customers might use products or respond to branding. Such attempts to uncover customers' feelings might mean that some kinds of customers are excluded; they are unimaginable and so their needs and preferences are untranslatable. For example, older customers' needs and preferences may be neglected; the 'Good Grips' range of kitchen utensils now popular with older people who have lost strength was designed by a young man whose wife struggled with other equipment (Postrel, 2004: 43). The diverse forms of knowledge that are relevant through the lifespan of a good, service or experience may be held (differently) by several key parties, including 'knowledge workers' in business services, sales and service workers, and consumers. Appadurai's ideas about the complex knowledge involved in commodities is important for understanding the production of consumption, as it makes clear that the act of exchanging knowledge is only one part of how consumption is produced. As Hesmondhalgh and Baker put it, focusing on the exchange of 'knowledge' ignores 'the specific importance of *culture*, of *mediated communication*, and of the *content* of communication products' (2010: 58, italics in original). What is communicated, and how it might mediate understanding and experience, matters.

And what of the low-skilled knowledge work? 'Many of the new jobs that have appeared in the highly competitive, information and knowledge-intensive economy and deregulated labour markets are found in an expanded lower-skilled, poorly paid and poorly protected service sector,' says Casey (2012: 117). 'Knowledge work', partly because of its discursive claims to being good work, and partly because it privileges one part of the process of doing work, cannot provide an adequate account of the work that produces consumption as it downplays significant dimensions of work. These include understandings of the way work is connected to other areas of social life, how working bodies are produced in relation to work and to consumption, and the complex relationship between things, people and bodily capability to act. We have seen that knowledge work is inseparable from the body of the knowledge worker. In the next section, we consider a theory that foregrounds the body more explicitly: craft.

Craft

In the course of the 19th century, industrial production became the dominant way of organising manufacturing. New occupations developed and old ones changed or declined. Commentators at the time were saddened and angered by the loss of craft occupations. Thorstein Veblen referred to craft as the *Instinct of Workmanship* (Veblen, 1914). These writers were observing the movement of production from craft and guild workspaces, organised around long apprenticeships, to factories. Whilst a craft worker needed to understand how to make something from start to finish, industrial workers needed only to master a small element of the whole process. Recent writers have looked to craft to provide a source of meaning and identity in a world where many workers are alienated, frustrated and isolated. In *The Corrosion of Character* (1998), Richard Sennett sets the scene: the flexibility demanded of modern workers actively damages their potential to live a good and happy life. His later book *The Craftsman* (Sennett, 2008) looks for a form of work that could be more fulfilling. Sennett, discussing a range of occupations, from musician to baker to architect, each of which requires hand, eye and brain to come together if something good is to be made, defines craft as 'skill, commitment and judgement' (2008: 68), where the quality of the results of work is not predetermined, as it would be by a finely calibrated machine, but dependent on the worker. Other definitions of craft invoke judgement, with Pye adding dexterity and care (1968: 12–13), and Campbell adding skill, knowledge and passion (2005: 23). The idea that judgement is a central part of craft is important for recognising the contingency of work. Craft is body work that involves skill and knowledge.

Extending the idea of 'craft'

Is craft a useful concept for thinking about the work that produces consumption? There are three possible reasons to be cautious about this. First, the moral overtone of craft work as good work (rather than degraded industrial production) and the hierarchy of what counts as craft may limit the extent to which we can imagine the concept as useful in different contexts. Second, as with skill, only some kinds of workers get to be counted as craft workers: Cobble's (1991) account of American waitresses trying to get craft status in angry negotiation with male-dominated culinary unions is illuminating. The waitresses ended up drawing a distinction between themselves and low-status female-dominated occupations like cleaning. Sennett excuses the gendered assumptions in the title of *The Craftsman,* saying that the alternatives are clumsy; I'm not so convinced. Third, craft focuses attention on the material objects that are the end product of craft work, rather than the human relationships that surround material objects, and this goes against dominant understandings of this kind of work that stress knowledge, creativity, culture and interaction. These caveats aside, what use can 'craft' be for understanding work?

'Craft' has positive connotations and taps into the contingent elements of work. This means that it has been used by researchers considering work that is not obviously about the production of material objects, despite the heritage of the concept, including the work of judges (Kritzer, 2007) and DIY car mechanics (Dant, 2010). For our interest in producing consumption, we can look to work on performers (Godlovitch, 1998), advertising executives (Morais, 2007), journalists (Deuze, 2005) and call centre operators (Whalen et al, 2002), amongst others.

Kritzer (2007) offers five dimensions to craft work. Three are external to the craftsperson: the production of something that has utility; its identification as valuable by a customer or clientele; and the production of a consistent product. These dimensions are worth noting for how they position craft work within an economic and social context. Internal to the craftsperson are aesthetic standards and identifiable skills and techniques. If we reconsider our discussion in 'Skill is social' about cocktails and choosing colours for a brand, then Kritzer's version of craft can help: utility and value refer to a drinkable cocktail that can be sold for a profit or a saleable product that the client likes and that future customers will demand. The cocktail must be produced consistently; the redesign may well be notable for being innovative but it must still be rolled out consistently across different parts of the business. Aesthetics and skills are needed to create these products and, crucially, the products may vary according to which craftsperson made them and so the embodied capability of the craft worker is a part of the finished product.

Craft makes it easy to understand the tacit abilities, knowledges and capacities needed to do work that are not readily definable and credentialisable as skill. The judgement needed to work out the best way of doing something must be learned. Craft workers are able to make adjustments without really thinking through what they're doing: the craft becomes held within the body. The idea of craft makes it easy for us to see that skills in work are often multi-layered, complex, hard to verbalise and interwoven with other capabilities. Craft gives us a sense of the contingency of doing good work and how work is caught up in working bodies. Craft is not readily replaceable by machine work, as it relies on the worker's sensory engagement with the thing being worked on: a 'complex repertoire of gestures, a variable and responsive emotional tone, and a developed capacity for gathering knowledge of particular objects through all the senses' (Dant, 2010: 2.6). The teleservicing work studied by Whalen et al. also implies the importance of sensory and emotional engagement with what is worked on, in this case the customer's needs:

> If we define 'craftsmanship' as work where the quality of the result is not predetermined, but depends on the judgement, dexterity and care which the worker exercises as she/he works, and further, that the quality of the result is continually at risk during the process (Whalen et al., 2002: 256).

Here, commercial workers are expected to use judgement and employ 'soft skills' to generate particular outcomes; objects and working bodies are entwined. The symbolic and cultural dimensions of commercial culture have a material dimension that can be crafted.

Morais refers to some elements of advertising work as craft: clients craft briefs, the agency crafts copy and negotiations between agency and client are a craft (2007: 155). In these uses of craft, both interactions and products are crafted, and rely on judgements and skills that are themselves produced through commercial workers' engagement and investment in consumer capitalism: having a consuming body matters. The way marketers 'craft' words and stories to match brand narratives and create 'brand myths' (Kniazeva and Belk, 2007) is part of how marketing makes markets. Knowledge of target markets is gathered from market research, but is also embodied by advertising workers themselves. For example, explicit knowledge about why people buy a particular brand is acquired through market research and this feeds into the sales strategy for that brand, influencing the promotion work, the sales environment, the likelihood of other consumers buying it and so on; however, skill, judgement and care are needed to translate such codified knowledge into a brand strategy or marketing campaign. Nixon (2003) discusses this in terms of the cultural capital possessed by workers, which involves a capacity to reflect either on their own desires and preferences or on those of people they know, and hence craft campaigns in relation to these. Kuipers (2012), looking at transnational buyers of television programmes, suggests that whilst cosmopolitan cultural capital is key to their understanding, these intermediaries maintain different degrees of aesthetic and professional distance from the TV products they sell. The craft of TV buying means understanding what audiences might like whilst not being persuaded yourself. Overall, craft incorporates a working body with skills, capacities, tacit and explicit knowledges that work to produce consumer capitalism. It involves knowing consumer products, and responding to customer and client demands within the constraints imposed by organisational controls.

Conclusion

Each of the three concepts discussed in this chapter provides some insights into doing work, and the way that doing work relies on having a certain body, and on being embodied (Turner, 2008). The concept of skill allows us to distinguish between more and less skilled activities, occupations and economies, and to make comparisons between nations, regions and occupations. However, we must be careful about how measures of skill are identified and applied because judgements about what count as skills are not neutral. We saw that the operation of consumer capitalism relies on knowledge work within an economy of knowledge about consumers and showed that knowledge workers create, gather, hold, use and transmit knowledge about consumers and consumer products. This concept situates commercial work within a broader economy of knowledge, which is helpful, but it offers comparatively little insight into understanding what working bodies do. In contrast, craft work focuses attention on the specific enactment and capabilities of working bodies in relation to other objects and people. Craft work is therefore useful to us in looking at what work is like, but not in locating commercial work within its setting. Overall, these three concepts illustrate different dimensions of doing commercial work and mean that we can understand something of what commercial workers do when they produce consumption. In the next chapter, we look specifically at a key feature of consumer capitalism, the harnessing of emotion, and consider how consumer capitalism relies on emotions being produced and managed.

Research task

Investigate a marketing campaign that has caught your eye. Consider the work that has gone into it. Who produced it? What knowledges did they need? What skills were involved in its production? What research is it based on? What can you find out about its production from the marketing agency?

OR

There are many national and supranational skills councils (for example, Cedefop): organisations seeking to understand skill needs. Investigate how one of these considers the skill needs for a 'high-skill' 'service economy'. How do they understand the 'knowledge economy'?

Discussion questions

1. Choose two different commercial work occupations. What kinds of skills are involved in each occupation? Include soft skills and tacit skills in your consideration.
2. Critically assess the idea that the main attribute commercial workers must have is knowledge of, and an ability to understand, consumers.
3. What is gained by thinking about commercial work as craft work? What are the limits to this idea?

Chapter 6

Emotion

Emotion is fundamental to social life and to consumer capitalism. We may often assume that our emotions are individual, internal, natural and inevitable. We also often assume that emotions exist in opposition to reason. But to understand the importance of emotion to social and market life, we must interrogate these assumptions. We must ask: what is the relationship between emotion, mind and body? Are emotions universally felt? Can emotional states be shared? Most importantly for the purpose of this book, we must ask: how are the emotions we feel affected by our social practices and positions, including commercial activities? We look at how markets are formed through emotion and affect, exploring how advertisers actively work to generate emotional states in customers, how customers feel and perform emotions in their consumer activities, and at the emotions at play when customers and workers meet in selling spaces. We consider that whilst commercial workers might try to generate emotions, emotions are slippery and easily exceed attempts to control and constrain them.

In 'Understanding emotion', we look at ways of conceptualising emotion, exploring its relation to reason and rationality, and look at how different intellectual disciplines address emotion and affect. In 'Emotion and capitalism', we consider exploring how emotion is central to both the experiences of spectacular consumption and to ordinary consumer practices. 'Work and emotion' discusses the idea of emotional labour, particularly in relation to interactions between workers and consumers. Finally, 'Culture work, emotion and affect' looks at emotion in higher-status commercial work occupations. The discussion will show that emotions are not trivial, uncontrollable and primitive urges that must be amended into rational responses, but are important ways of knowing and living in the world. They are simultaneously part of our very intimate experiences of living and they have an enormous affect on how we are brought into social worlds.

Understanding emotion

For much of the history of Western thought, individual emotions have been considered to be the wayward cousins of reason and rationality, requiring curbing and restraint and careful management if they are not to overwhelm social order. Becker, for example, discusses how understandings of modernity rely on a series of 'dualisms', including the mind–body dualism (Chapter 5, 'Bodies'), as well as oppositions between nature and culture, and subjective feelings and objective reason (2009: 201–2). 'Modern' society is marked as distinct from other, uncivilised places, and from traditional societies. Reason – the action of a rational, individual mind – is superior to the uncontrollable, natural body:

> Because the emotions are viewed as embodied sensations, they are considered to be the antithesis of reason and rationality. From this perspective, the emotions are impediments to proper considered judgment and intellectual activity. (Lupton, 1998: 3)

That is to say that the dualism of reason–emotion may map onto those of culture–nature, mind–body and male–female in an insidious way that marks those without social and political power as troublesome.

Becker argues that this dualism of reason and emotion is central to how modern society has defined itself and so emotion is readily seen as incompatible with modernity. He argues that this simplistic characterisation denies the observable importance of emotion to modern society, as when wonder and passion are part of the 'rational' work of scientists (Barbalet, 2009: 42–4). Further, some argue that reason and emotion are both part of cognitive processes. They are a way of knowing the world. Philosopher Martha Nussbaum says that emotions are judgements, 'suffused with intelligence and discernment' (Nussbaum, 2001: 1). Emotion can be a way of knowing and involves reasoned judgements about others, and so emotional states have a public resonance beyond their significance for an individual.

Gender, reason *and emotion*

This cultural and rhetorical separation between reason and emotion has been discussed by feminist writers interested in developing an account of women's lower status in society. The association of women with nature, emotion and bodies has a long history in Western thinking, stemming from Christianity and from Enlightenment science and philosophy (Jordanova, 1991). It reflects a complex interplay between gendered social relations, science's understanding of sexed bodies and the differences between women and men (such as the 19th-century belief that disorders of the womb made women hysterical), the commonplace truth that women give birth and how philosophers envisioned the differences between the sexes. The association of men and masculinity with rationality (as in the belief of some 19th-century scholars that only men should be educated) and of the feminine with emotion influences the longstanding denigration of women. This matters to making sense of work in consumer culture – including why women are more numerous in interactive service work and men in knowledge work.

As we saw when considering the comparatively developed consumerism in Western Europe in the 19th century (in Chapter 3, 'Shopping'), gender, emotion and consumerism are entwined. The new department stores offered a place for women to be visible and yet safe in public, but they also generated controversy. Given women's childish emotionality, the bright lights and the worlds of goods were considered too seductive. A woman who spent too much on fripperies was seen as engaging in wasteful consumption and might damage the status of her hard-working husband; a woman without money (or perhaps with money, but out of control) may be seduced into shoplifting by the beautiful displays of luxury goods (Rappaport, 2000; Reekie, 1993). The inverse of these gendered assumptions, that men are 'less' emotional, or have less facility with emotion, is also restrictive.

Knowing emotion

Philosophers, psychologists and sociologists have different takes on emotion (see Goldie, 2010; Lewis et al., 2010; Wetherell, 2012), and vary in their engagement with biologists' accounts of emotion. Cognitive accounts of emotion stress that emotions are more than unspecific feelings, and suggest that each individual infers emotions from feelings. Cognitive understandings of emotion are important to biological scientists of different kinds, and to psychologists, not least because seeing emotions as cognitive makes them amenable to measurement. Neuroscience, for example, explores how feelings travel through neural pathways and so shape how we live in the world (Damasio, 2006). Neuroscience provides clear insights into biology and brain activity, but tends to operate with quite restrictive and limited ideas about culture. For example, neuroscientists often distinguish between emotions they deem to be 'basic', universally shared emotions and those they consider to be culturally specific.

Psychologists also tend to conceptualise emotion as natural (not social) with a common biological inheritance. They also accept the idea that emotions have to be thought in order to be felt (they are cognitive) (Clore, 1994, cited in Barbalet, 2009: 51). Conceptualising emotion like this means that feelings are readily amenable to scientific study. Marketing and other business sciences are interested in the results of this sort of research, and have used it to try to understand the science of selling and the science of buying. For example, Paco Underhill in *Why We Buy: The Science of Shopping* reports on the anxiety older customers in a supermarket seemed to experience when trying to get to the painkillers when they were located next to the drinks 'cooler' where teenagers would congregate. The older customers bought more painkillers when they didn't have to pass the teenagers (2000: 28–9). Anxiety is the emotion that makes sense of the behaviour to Underhill; the cognitive understanding of emotion means it is knowable by ourselves and by others. Another implication of the cognitive understanding of emotion is that emotions are states that can be redefined and regulated through will and work (Becker, 2009: 217). Acting rationally in contemporary society doesn't mean acting unemotionally. It means acting with careful use of emotions to achieve an end. It involves monitoring your own emotion.

Beyond cognitive emotions

So far, we have understood emotions as appearing in response to something or someone: an object, a situation, an experience or perhaps a memory. Psychoanalysts add another layer of complexity to this understanding of emotion by considering the unconscious, that part of each individual that is intrinsic to them and yet operates outside the conscious 'ego' or 'I'. Impulses, fantasies and wishes come to us and we are not sure why. This implies that there are feeling states that influence who we are now, and how we behave, but which we cannot access. We repress painful experiences so these are detached from emotion, but they may manifest themselves in other ways. The 'enigmatic messages' (Frosh, 2011: 32) of early childhood socialisation are very important to understanding where our sense of self comes from and is a possible source of some of these unknowable and unpredictable feelings.

In both cognitive and psychoanalytic accounts, emotions are held by individuals in response to the situations they are in or have faced previously. Sociological accounts of emotion locate individual feeling states within the social context, noting how the pursuit or avoidance of some feelings drives our daily lives, and how what counts as emotion is conditioned by our social and cultural milieu. Sociologists influenced by symbolic interactionism, a set of ideas that explore the social and individual meaning that interactions with people and things may have, discuss how we seek to avoid shame and embarrassment as part of our presentation of self (Goffman, 1990). Thomas Scheff develops Goffman's ideas to argue that pride (which we seek) and shame (which we try to avoid) are the emotions most significant in producing social bonds. We feel these without knowing or naming them, even using other words to refer to them. Feelings of shame are shared and exchanged between individuals, but are also an 'inner contagion' (1990: 76), as when the memory of feeling ashamed goes round and round in our thoughts (as in the case of the young girl who wore the wrong kind of clothes, discussed by Nenga (2003) (Chapter 1, 'Fordism')). Emotion, in this way of thinking, is not purely an individual experience. Consider how manners, and the emotions attached to manners, change over time and between places. Whilst European understandings of 'good manners' are now freer than they were in the 19th century, internalised self-control has increased in order to avoid the shame of being seen as behaving badly (Wouters, 2007). To put it another way, emotions are generated not merely in the bodies of individuals, but through our engagement with wider social and cultural norms and practices, and so consumer capitalism permits and encourages some emotions and not others.

Research into emotions in non-Western contexts challenges the certainties that emotions are universal and natural, amenable to scientific scrutiny and in opposition to reason. Anthropologists such as Abu-Lughod and Lutz (1990) reveal that the emotions common in developed Western countries are not visible in comparable ways elsewhere. The French philosopher Vinciane Despret takes these kinds of findings to argue that '[w]e fabricate our emotions so that they will produce us' (Despret, 2004 [1999]: 20). She means partly that our version of scientific knowledge gives us an understanding we live up to, and partly that emotions are not mere reactions to events, but moods we cultivate ourselves (individually and socially). Emotion is not merely a response to attempts by others to generate a reaction, but something we want to feel, and that we feel here and now in a particular form that may not be matched elsewhere. Despret's ideas give us a complex account of emotions in consumer capitalism; a child's response of wonder to visiting a Disney theme park is in part a reaction to the attempts by the Disney corporation to produce wonder, in part about how the child has learned that delight and wonder are the right reactions to big treats, and in part about how wonder is a pleasant individual and communal feeling state.

Feelings that matter

As if the story was not already complicated enough, it's worth making a couple of observations about what kinds of feelings matter and where feelings come from. It is striking how few emotions have been explicitly named in our discussions so far: shame, pride and wonder are named. But many of the other emotions you might feel in the course of a day are not on the radar, not even love or anger. Instead, 'emotion' is named as a generic category. Lazarus and Lazarus (1994) say that emotions can be nasty (anger, envy, jealousy), existential (anxiety, shame), empathetic (gratitude, compassion, those aroused by aesthetic experiences), and refer to conditions of life that are unfavourable (sadness, relief, hope, depression) or favourable (happiness, love, pride). Further, banal 'ugly feelings' such as animatedness, irritation, paranoia and disgust (Ngai, 2005) or the sombre or light-hearted moods we might feel in response to our environments are also worth thinking about. The boredom, amusement, compassion and camaraderie that might be part of working in consumer capitalism reflect a further dimension to the idea of 'emotion'. So whilst in this chapter we might often speak of emotion in the generic sense, we should remember that emotions are specific.

We must also think about the kinds of encounters in the world that generate emotions. Nussbaum's ideas about emotion, cognition and judgement as important to moral reasoning stress how emotions relate to people. Emotion also has a relationship to material things and to actions. Specific artefacts conjure up emotions of different kinds, and the instrumental uses of these artefacts, along with their symbolic and aesthetic resonances, affect both our expectations of a thing and our response to it; if we expect a gadget to enable us to do something, then we may be irritated when it fails, or feel stupid that we can't get it to work (Fuller and Goffey, 2012). Emotional attention and commitment are needed when repairing broken cars (Dant, 2010). The manipulation, control and mastery of the craft of this kind of work (discussed in Chapter 5, 'Extending the idea of "craft"') relies on, and generates, an emotional tone. Dant does not discuss the irritation that arises when things go wrong, but we may well empathise with that feeling! Emotions are physiological and sensational, yet also social and cultural. They are cognitive, yet have unconscious aspects. They are influenced by experiences and guide future experiences, providing motivation and behavioural norms. They are felt as uncontrollable, and yet are managed and manipulated. I am now going to add another layer of complexity to the discussion, by considering affect.

Affect

Affect is a term used to discuss mood and atmosphere, and the kinds of feelings that are not easy to name. Whilst writers interested in affect use many different definitions, affect is commonly distinguished from emotion by its focus on bodily sensation and feeling, and by an interest in flows, potentials and uncertainties. Understanding affect means moving on from considering the relationship between emotion and reason, and between mind and body. Affect is seen as a complex physiological state produced when bodies encounter the world. It is the colour we experience the world as having, it is mood and atmosphere: 'a world experienced without any affect would be a pallid, meaningless world. We would know *that* things happened, but we could not care whether they did or not' (Tomkins, 1995: 88). For the psychologist Silvan Tomkins, and those influenced by him (Sedgewick and Frank, 1995), affect is a physiological response which may or may not translate into emotion. Affects vary in their intensity and their duration, and paying attention to affect means considering fleeting moments.

Wetherell, rather critical of the more nebulous and abstract conceptualisations of affect, considers affect theory to be useful to understand how 'affective practice mobilises, recruits and stabilises brain/body states' (2012: 159), that is, to make sense of how we are grounded in feeling, how feelings help us understand meanings and our bodily encounters with the world. Studying affects involves seeing how biological bodies engage in meaning making. The concept of affect suggests that individual bodies do not have fixed and demarcated boundaries that mark a distinction between self and other. Instead, bodies are connected. They move dynamically in relation to each other and to other objects, and they may be affected by momentary encounters with strangers and strange places in the public world (Stewart, 2007). Our attempts to make sense of what's happening to us and what feelings we have now may help us make sense of other events at other times. There is a dynamic social interplay between the person and the world and so it is not easy to predict what an affect might do to the person feeling it.

In the course of the day, you may experience many affects which do not always fully register with you, and other affects might be the source of stories about the emotions you are conscious of (Clough et al., 2007: 2), as when you tell your friend a story about walking into a room and sensing an atmosphere (say, of tension). Other affects might feel like emotion, verbalisable as well as felt in the body: perhaps if you dropped your bag on the floor and everything spilled out and you felt a blush spread over your face, a corporeal state which you know to describe as embarrassment (as for the interviewee in Nippert-Eng, 2010: 119–20). Affects are thereby influenced by all kinds of phenomena in the world, including consumer culture and the work that makes it possible. The market system encompasses feeling; feelings are made, bought and sold. In this book, emotion tends to refer to the *cognitive* manifestations of feeling, whilst recognising that cognition sits alongside bodily feeling. Affect tends to refer to bodily sensations of being in the world which are not directly conscious.

Following this discussion of emotion and affect, let us now consider how such concepts can help us understand consumerism.

Emotion and capitalism

Contemporary marketers say that brands and branded goods are designed to generate emotion, especially emotional attachment. For example, 'creating emotional brand attachment is a key branding issue in today's marketing world' (Malär et al., 2011: 35). A recent fashion in marketing, 'lovemarks', explicitly draws on the emotional association of brands, as this extract claims:

> Lovemarks are the future beyond brands. They deliver beyond your expectations of great performance. Lovemarks reach your heart as well as your mind, creating an intimate, emotional connection that you just can't live without. Ever. (http://www.lovemarks.com, accessed 13.1.14)

Heart and mind, emotion and reason are brought together here. In this section, we will explore the implications of thinking about capitalism as replete with emotion, looking particularly at emotion and (ordinary) consumption in order to develop some arguments about how emotions matter to the operation of contemporary capitalism. We'll see how public cultures and intimate feelings are influenced by capitalist processes and in turn affect the kinds of goods, services and experiences that people are interested in.

Emotion and the making of capitalism

Whilst economists position market action as inspired by rational preferences, distinct from emotion, we can make the argument that emotion matters to understanding markets. Hirschman ([1986]1992) (who we met in Chapter 2, 'Rival views of market society') suggests that 'passions and interests' were not inimical to Enlightenment thinkers, including early economists. Adam Smith (1723–1790), the father of contemporary economics, talked about emotions in *The Theory of Moral Sentiments* (1976[1759]). Smith considers the natural sympathy we feel for someone grieving to be a form of knowledge; he also says that we would only feel sympathy for an angry man if we felt his anger was just. In both cases he connects reason and emotion. Indeed Smith, like many of this era, thought that trade was an excellent way to manage the natural tensions between people. More recent thinking also traces connections between economics and feelings.

Eva Illouz, referring to the 20th century, suggests that

> the making of capitalism went hand in hand with the making of an intensely specialized emotional culture, and that when we focus on this dimension of capitalism – on its emotions so to speak – we may be in a position to uncover another order in the social organization of capitalism (Illouz, 2007: 4)

Illouz looks at the early 20th century to show how emotion and capitalism are entwined. Emotional capitalism is 'a culture in which emotional and economic discourses and practices mutually shape each other' (2007: 5). Emotional life looks to the logic of markets and economics, and this profoundly shapes even the most intimate parts of life, including finding love (Illouz, 2012). Illouz identifies twin processes that mark out emotional capitalism. First, the public sphere is rendered more emotional – that is, emotions become present in public life. Emotions are worked on and managed by emotional health service providers such as psychologists, counsellors and so on; workers are recruited for their competency in the management of feeling. Second, the private sphere becomes more rationalised, as when the search for love mimics the logic of exchange, or when we learn and apply self-management techniques when confronted with grief. Traditional discourses of gender that imply men are not comfortable with emotion ('Gender, reason and emotion') are now challenged as, for example, male workers need to understand the emotional compromises of team working, and women apply the same measurements and judgements to falling in love as men. Self-regulation, self-image and self-help become an ordinary part of life in emotional capitalism. The idea of emotional capitalism is productive for our consideration of consumerism, as it locates the desires and fantasies, the promises and seductions of consumer culture within the systems, processes and practices of markets and exchanges. Rationality and emotionality coincide; we are not different people when working to when consuming, but part of a broader emotional culture. This is not to say that all facets of feeling and emotional life are reducible to the market, but that market processes are significant in how they produce subjects. In the strictures of management texts, and in the performance of management, emotion is a resource. Contemporary business practices that advocate developing 'emotional intelligence' (e.g. Goleman, 1995), or that see 'emotional capital' as a form of human capital (e.g. Thomson, 1998) are manifestations of this. We might also see 'emotional labour' as an inevitable outcome of this operationalisation of emotion as a way of managing. In contemporary business practices, emotions appear cognitive, and therefore controllable.

Scientific management strategies, which were used to organise production in Fordism, can also be identified in the organisation of consumption. The emergent 'sciences' of the 'psy' (psychology, psychiatry, psychoanalysis) disciplines were particularly important. The most 'rationalised' way of selling, the new supermarkets of the mid-twentieth century, drew on this consumer psychology and new marketing strategies (Gabriel and Lang, 2006: 30–4). For some shoppers at the time, the new supermarkets were an exciting change; for others, the prospect of change and learning how to shop differently was scary (Bailey et al., 2010). The science of emotion and behaviour was harnessed by marketers to understand consumer habits and to influence consumers in what they bought and how they behaved. It was felt that irrational (emotional, female) customers needed careful handling (Deutsch, 2010). Edward Bernays' work, inspired by his uncle, the psychoanalyst Sigmund Freud, worked on co-opting repressed, subconscious desires and using them to sell by changing the feelings associated with goods. In the case of cigarettes, he and his associates worked to alter feelings and judgements about women who smoked; they became modern girls, not bad women. He also made use of the science of crowd psychology in early forays into what we would now understand as PR and marketing (Bernays, 1928). Understanding consumer psychology remains an enormous industry, although our earlier reconceptualisation of emotion as social, as well as individual, provides the means for a critique of such practices.

Everyday consumption

In this section, we consider how emotional capitalism is caught up in everyday life. In *The Purchase of Intimacy* (2005), Viviana Zelizer criticises the mistaken separation of economics (marked by rationality and calculation) and intimacy (made up of emotion, 'sentiment and solidarity' (2005: 22)). Western societies act as though these two spheres ought not to meet because rationality and calculation – the values of the market – will drive out feeling and replace it with efficiency, and intimacy might damage the rational workings of economy. Zelizer suggests that this kind of judgment is wrong, as intimate, social relations are often made through transactions. We are very careful to make distinctions between what is economic and what is intimate as we want to cherish the latter, but these spheres cannot help but blur into each other – as when parents legitimate the choices they make about paid childcare. Zelizer suggests that we see paying for services (such as sex or care) as breaking the boundary of what intimacy ought to be. It transgresses both because it is a short-term transaction and because payment is introduced.

The implications of Zelizer's work are that the boundaries of what is acceptable in the context of durable, caring and loving relations are moral boundaries, marked by what 'ought' to be. These boundaries of acceptability are not fixed, but change over time, as when new kinds of services are commodified. For example, lifestyle gurus and personal shoppers now do the labour of consuming on behalf of busy and wealthy executives, including buying family presents (Sherman, 2010). Other researchers have developed similar arguments in relation to how the 'economic' activity of consumption builds relationships through feeling. Miller (1998) suggests that ordinary consumption, that is, everyday practices like going to the supermarket, is extraordinarily important because of what it does to and tells us about family relationships and other sources of meaning and belonging. Careful decisions about good food and special treats are ways through which shoppers show love for family and for self. Using a different methodology to that of Zelizer (ethnographic observation and interviews, rather than documentary analysis), and using everyday language for emotion (love), Miller makes a comparable claim: that emotion is done through market exchanges, that consumption is about feeling as well as 'need'.

Emotion and consumption

We discussed in 'Beyond cognitive emotions' how emotions arise in relation to people and to things. These include consumer goods, services and experiences. Researchers interested in consumption have often reflected on customers' desires for goods. Consumption is a 'land of desire' says Leach (1993), and the search for new, better items of consumption that reflect the person we think we are, or would like to be, is seen as both an instigator of consumer capitalism and a project doomed to failure by the very instability of our desires. They are unreachable. Bauman, as we saw in Chapter 3, 'Chains, networks and global production', considers consumer societies to be volatile, as the objects of consumers' desires must be quickly available to bring instant satisfaction, and the satisfaction acquired in this way is likely to wane quickly. This means that 'consumers must be constantly exposed to new temptations in order to be kept in a state of constantly seething, never wilting excitation and, indeed, in a state of suspicion and disaffection' (Bauman, 1998: 26). The volatility of desires (Illouz, 2009: 378) is essential to a fashion system and hence to consumer culture.

Seduction might work through the emotional resonances implied by goods and services, or in the promotional materials of those consumer items. For example, using nostalgic emotion in marketing can generate attachments to goods (Stern, 1992, cited in Strickland et al., 2013), as when Australian wine marketing makes multiple references to the symbolic power of family (Smith Maguire et al., 2013). Mocking other advertising campaigns as part of a 'guerrilla marketing' strategy (Moore, 2007) may make us laugh. Customers engage in semiotic readings to make sense of such campaigns. That is, they look at the signs that are presented to them and identify what other themes and feelings these signs connote. Researchers who have spoken to consumers find that consumers can resist the seductions and blandishments of such attempts to make them feel, but they can also feel anxious, irritated and inadequate in response. For example, Rafferty (2011) describes a confident, privileged Irish woman's thrill at finding a designer skirt that counts as 'a bargain', and another's move between elation and despair as her income changed and she had to buy clothes differently; buying new underwear rearticulates women's gender identity (Jantzen et al., 2006); working-class Turkish shoppers see some global brands as infidels (Izberk-Bilgin, 2012). Feelings matter, and they are affected by the practice of shopping and the relationships to goods and services that we have.

These findings reflect Bauman's ideas that consumer markets are seductive, and rely on consumers who seek seduction. I'm a consumer, and I find this description of my feelings about goods and services too strong. Much of my consumption is mundane and gives rise to banal feelings, and for every advert or promotion that seduces there are many that I don't see, that leave me cold or irritated, or that are in the background of my life. Research into the relationship between emotion and things that does not assume that consumer culture matters produces different kinds of claims. For example, Jenkins et al. (2011) point out how when we imagine the future, with all the (positive) emotions that we would like to experience, consumer goods play a much smaller part than is assumed by consumer-culture-focused researchers. If you ask people about the goods they desire, then they say goods matter to them. But if you ask them to imagine their futures, consumer products do not matter as much. Sheller (2004) describes the feelings associated with cars and suggests that, whilst advertising campaigns try to generate emotional connection to cars, the emotional resonance of the car transcends its existence as a consumer good and draws in freedom, independence, family relationships, pleasure seeking, anxieties and fears. That is, the emotional culture of the car is linked to how we live, and how we think we should live. It is not separable from consumer capitalism, but nor is it reducible to a question of consumerism. So, whilst emotions are engendered through consumption, and whilst marketing seeks to influence emotions, emotions in everyday life and wider culture are part of – and simultaneously distinct from – global consumer capitalism. Affects matters too, as when consumers feel at home or out of place in some retail spaces (see Davila, 2010: 104–6, for a discussion of how Puerto Rican consumers move around high-status shopping malls even when they don't have much spare money).

Selling feeling

Consumer capitalism draws on feeling and works on producing feeling for our current possessions and for commodities we might desire. Not only are specific kinds of emotions attached to consumer goods, services and experiences, but feeling is used in selling strategies, including in retail spaces and brands. Things generate feeling long after they were commodities, and things we have taken for granted for some time may remind us of their nature as commodities, as when we start to think of them as old-fashioned and out of date. Parr (1999) shows how fridge designers incorporated 'emotional obsolescence' as well as the better-known technological obsolescence into their work, to encourage us to feel that we want and need something new, with a different style (cited in Zukin and Smith Maguire, 2004: 79).

An excellent example of the economy of emotion is how Disney theme parks, films, merchandise and other branded items are caught up in what corporate brand consultant Marc Gobé calls 'emotional branding' (Gobé, 2001). Gobé refers explicitly to the work of brand designers, and suggests that they have a clear effect on consumerism: 'at the end of the day, design creates emotions, sensory experiences, and, ultimately, sales' (2001: 107). Emotional branding has been found by brand researchers to be beneficial to corporations wanting to ensure customer engagement and loyalty (e.g. Rossiter and Bellman, 2012) whilst containing some risks (as when strong brands can be subverted by parody and by groups like Adbusters (Soar, 2000). Marketers explicitly try to generate ways of engaging customers on an emotional level by telling stories about brands in a way that makes the customer feel part of the brand, or even have a 'brand romance'. For example, the music playing in a shop is selected to reflect the symbolic character of the brand (DeNora and Belcher, 2000). Emotional attachment is explicitly worked on by these kinds of marketing. Disney and similar cross-platform entertainment businesses, provides a good case study for this discussion. Often presented as being about 'enchantment', these businesses are notable dimensions of the global cultural industry, where the Disney brand, and its specific sub-brands (such as the different films and the products associated with them) are themed to produce 'enchantment' and 'wonder' amongst target groups, often children. 'Disneyisation' renders other cultural forms – stories, aesthetic styles – into a recognisably 'Disney' form (Bryman, 2004) that promises safe fantasy and magic.

Critical accounts of the 'emotional brand' power of Disney, such as that by Bryman, find the seductions, enchantments, and 'magic' to be formulaic and limiting. Like other themed experiences, the Disney theme park generates emotional attachment through the aesthetics of the environment and through the emotional performances of workers in the 'smile factory' (as van Maanen, 1991, refers to Disney), including, but not limited to, those acting as Disney characters). It also provides an extraordinary range of opportunities to consume themed merchandise. Bryman refers to this as the dedifferentiation of consumption: different consumer products are sold using comparable techniques. The 'Disney Princesses' range is a good example: similar characters from different films are presented to consumers as having distinctive 'personalities'. Customers can buy comparable merchandise for their favourite. If you can get a consumer to love the film, then they might well line up to love the merchandise and the whole Disney aura.

Brakus et al., asked 25 US customers (and graduate students – a limited and partial sample) about different brands, asking open questions that were then coded to become amenable to statistical (factor) analysis. Disney was described in the following way:

> • Stimulates my senses. • I feel like a child; I feel warm and safe; I want to discover things; the brand reminds me to use my imagination. • I feel part of the magic. (Brakus et al., 2009: 56)

Distinguishing between the sensory, affective, behavioural and intellectual dimensions of a brand, the study found that Disney had a unique affective connection with customers, and also scored highly on the sensory dimensions. Graduate students, not so old as to have forgotten the 'magic' promised by Disney when they were children, felt warmly attached to the brand. However, as Pettigrew (2011) suggests, children's emotional responses to Disney are not quite as strong as either the marketing material or some of the critical sociology would suggest. Observing and interviewing her own children, she finds them decidedly less excited by the different theme parks than promotional material implies.

The production of emotional experiences for consumers in the case of Disney, as elsewhere, owes much to the controlled presentation of the experiences and retail spaces, as designed by brand-aware commercial workers of many kinds. Each has an understanding of what the Disney experience is and can be: its history, its multiple dimensions. This involves knowledge, monitoring and judging new possibilities and affects. Focus group analysts, brand valuers, mystery shoppers and futurologists may have a say. Comparable processes exist in other experiential spaces: Legoland; Guinness Ireland; Heineken Amsterdam; in boutique hotels and luxury retail outlets (Pine and Gilmore, 1999; Chadha and Husband, 2006); in tourist destinations and shopping spaces (and often the two combine) and in themed spaces (Fırat et al., 2011). Such grand experiences are interesting to consider because they combine multiple practices in one brand/space, but similar arguments apply elsewhere. Other kinds of consumer goods are produced by workers who have tried to 'design in' emotional attachment, trust, excitement and other feelings, through packaging, designs, changed functions and the like. Consider an ordinary object like a toothbrush. Avoiding the anxiety of poor dental hygiene and the exciting liberation of better teeth and more confidence have long been promised by dental marketing campaigns (Miskell, 2004). Recent innovations like integral tongue scrapers and bristles of different sizes are marketed by TV campaigns with happy, white-toothed people.

Affect and value

Until the 1960s, marketing tended to measure and compare customers on the grounds of socio-economic differences. From then they moved to using psychographic data that considered lifestyle. Now emotional branding and many other kinds of psychosocial marketing strategies (from advertising targeted to specific groups to corporate conversations with social media users) are common ways to generate and harness consumer feelings. These shifts, and the more recent transformation of public culture to bring 'private' feeling into the public domain through social media, contribute to an information economy that thrives on the flow and movement of affects (Arvidsson, 2011). Arvidsson is one of many writers using autonomist Marxist ideas to develop an understanding of how affect operates within consumer capitalism, that is, to understand work and consumption 'in the social factory'. The 'general sentiment' whereby 'values' become valuable is a significant feature of contemporary brand-focused capitalism, where values are generated through flows of affects. Jenkins (2006) describes the 'affective economy' as part of the 'convergence culture' of social media, where audience participation and brand communication are supported by the social media activity of ordinary consumers. Consumers contribute to the creation of such value as they use, adopt and adapt (branded) consumer goods, and distance themselves from other, undesirable goods.

'Affective labour' is a concept designed to help understand how value is produced in global capitalism. It is a dimension of 'immaterial labour' conceptualised by autonomist Marxist thinkers such as Lazzarato (1996), Hardt and Negri (2000). They argue that in post-Fordist capitalism, material production is not the main source of value. Instead, value is produced by 'immaterial labour', which creates meaning around products. Immaterial labour has three dimensions: the labour of production is 'informationalised', via computerisation and robotics; creative and routine symbolic-analytical services increase (such as management, problem-solving and symbol manipulation – through the work of advertising, for example); and affective labour is prevalent, directed at producing 'intangible feelings of ease, excitement, or passion' (Hardt and Negri, 2000: 292–3). Affect is captured by capitalism through a process conceptualised as 'the real subsumption of labour', whereby capitalism compels labour to submit to the wage relationship and transforms it to meet the requirements of capital. For immaterialists, value is produced not only in formal production (through the surplus value generated by wage labour, as Marx argued), but throughout life. Affective labour is the labour that produces and channels affect to create value. It can be paid or unpaid labour. It makes meaning, and through making meaning economic value is created. Demand for affective labour is driven by the service sector, but the accumulation of capital through and within the domain of affect is also influenced by how media modulate the circuit of emotion and affect and by the acquisition of information about the human body and its affective processes.

We can explore branding using the concept of immaterial value (Arvidsson, 2011). The economy of brands is not based on product A being better than product B according to some clearly defined criteria that all consumers comprehend. It is based on the meanings and signs that have come to be attached to product A that make it more appealing (perhaps trustworthy, perhaps sexy). The brand is therefore immaterial; its value is based not on the material product but its associations. Brands have meanings that are worked on by brand managers, advertisers, marketers and a whole panoply of paid workers. However, the theory of immaterial labour suggests that values are not just produced in production. Consumers contribute to the creation of value as they assign meanings to different brands, as they see themselves as suiting or not suiting a particular brand, as they tell their friends about what they bought or upload customer reviews of products online. Some kinds of customers are powerful; celebrity endorsements of branded goods draw on the 'value' of the celebrity to a target market and on the brand status (Seno and Lukas, 2007). From this point of view, we are all implicated in generating value, in working for the capitalist economy, in our everyday lives. We can't really help doing this as consumers. In Chapter 4, 'Consumption work', we discussed the idea of consumers as workers. Immaterial labour theories push this idea further. Arvidsson suggests that consumers engage in productive work through their consumption because they produce value as goods and services circulate. This is connected to the public, commercial work of advertising, marketing and particularly branding, which feed off consumers' immaterial labour (Carah, 2013). Arvidsson describes consumers' productive labour as an 'ethical' surplus of shared meaning that is appropriated from consumers (2005: 251).

In 'emotional capitalism' or an affective economy, feelings are worked on, developed and mobilised in the pursuit of sales; consumers are caught up in the selling of feeling, not as fools readily seduced by marketing blandishments, but as knowing participants. In the context of this book, emotions matter in contemporary consumer culture, as they influence how consumers act (and are imagined to act by those selling) in markets. They also matter because of the work directed at affecting feeling, and because of the emotional demands placed on workers. The promotional activities that sell feeling are developed by culture workers. For feeling to be sold, people have to work on its production and management; they understand and develop (new) ways of generating emotional responses. Delivering emotional experiences often rests on the frontline production of feeling, an area where there has been a great deal of research. In 'Work and emotion', we explore how commercial workers work with emotion.

Work and emotion

Having set out what is meant by emotion, and highlighted some of the ways in which emotion is particularly important to capitalism, the next question to ask is: what sorts of emotions are present in work? The emotional culture of the organisation and its brand (and all the manifestations of that brand in mission statements, company documents and the like) provide the context within which to understand employees', owners/shareholders' and directors' emotions (Fineman, 2003). Encounters with other organisations (as a client of an advertising agency, or as a regular customer) are full of feelings, although what sorts of emotion, what sorts of performance, and what happens when unpredictable emotions arise are worth discussing. In this section, we will look first at service work and then at culture work.

Emotional labour

Our encounters with, and purchases of, goods and services are often mediated by people employed to ensure that the transaction is smooth, and '[w]hen workers and customers meet... that relationship adds a new dimension to the pattern of human relations in industry' (Whyte, 1946: 123). Interactive service workers are customer-facing and are expected to draw on 'soft' and 'social' skills (see Chapter 5, 'Skill'), including in emotion management. The expectation that such workers manage their emotions to generate emotions in others has been extensively studied by researchers interested in understanding the experience of this kind of work. The concept 'emotional labour' has proved to be a captivating concept. It originated in Arlie Russell Hochschild's *The Managed Heart* (2003 [1983]) and refers to the compulsion for wage workers 'to induce or suppress feeling in order to sustain the outward countenance that produces the proper state of mind in others – in this case [flight attendants], the sense of being cared for in a convivial and safe place' (2003: 7). Emotional labour presumes a hierarchy between provider and recipient, where the recipient *deserves* to extract an emotional performance from the provider.

Customer/client-facing workers must monitor and control their own emotional performances as a condition of doing their work, that is, their emotion is commodified in the wage relationship. Hochschild suggests that there is a distinction between surface and deep acting. Surface acting involves pretending to feel, so to smile for as long as the customer can see you. *Fast Food, Fast Talk* (Leidner, 1993) explores routinisation in fast-food restaurants, where scripted encounters demand surface acting. Deep acting refers to the challenge of 'really' feeling what customers and managers expect you to feel, that is, to convince yourself to smile and feel happy regardless of your inclination. It is a disguise. Hochschild argues that flight attendants and debt collectors (the examples in *The Managed Heart*), like others selling personal services or managing transactions, risk losing track of their feelings. They get exhausted and burn out with the strain of emotional labour. Commodified emotion is thereby damaging. This is because feelings are transmuted so that private, even unconscious, feelings 'nowadays often fall under the sway of large organizations, social engineering, and the profit motive' (Hochschild, 2003: 19), although workers may struggle with and against the expectations that their feelings be managed in work. Some suggest the way Hochschild sees the private sphere as offering a safe, authentic place for emotion as a key limitation of Hochschild's idea of emotional labour (Weeks, 2007).

The concept of emotional labour has been used to explore all kinds of work that involves doing work on behalf of others, helpfully reviewed by Steinberg and Figart (1999) and Lopez (2010). There have been a number of studies of emotional labour in jobs that are not under consideration here, most obviously social care and medicine. We focus here on what emotional labour can contribute to our understanding of work in consumer culture. Whilst emotional labour researchers have focused on different occupations, the specificity of the occupation has not always been made relevant to the analysis. This means that there is little scholarly work comparing occupations, or locating an occupation within the context of the kind of consumer market it enacts. Emotional labour researchers vary in what they stress as the most significant part of this work: the employment relations which are the necessary pre-condition of emotional labour (Cohen, 2010), or what sorts of resistance are present (Paules, 1991; Gatta, 2009), or how racial and gendered abuse from customers generates particularly clear demands for emotional labour (Nath, 2011; Nixon et al., 2011).

For Hochschild and others, gender is significant to making sense of emotional labour. Women tend to be more numerous in the interactive service work jobs that demand emotional labour. Why is this? Earlier, we discussed how women have often been culturally associated with emotion, body and 'nature', so one explanation is the sex-stereotyping that grants women greater facility with emotion. Therefore, women are recruited into these jobs more readily than men and, as the gendered associations of occupations are sticky and gender segregation by job type is persistent, emotional labour jobs remain populated by women. Women in interactive service work are seen, and see themselves, as able to sense the needs of customers and respond accordingly because they are used to thinking of others. The naturalisation of this response is referred to by Tyler and Taylor as a 'gift' (1998). Shifts in gender norms and the heightened emotional culture that Illouz (2007) posits may contribute to greater numbers of men entering service work occupations where emotional labour is required; there are also national and regional differences about the gender of occupations that influence the gender and ethnicity of bartenders, waiters and other service staff. The feminisation of emotional labour jobs is connected to questions of whether emotional labour is a skill or not, or (more interestingly) under what conditions it is a routine requirement and when a skilled and contingent performance. Some writers are critical of how naturalised capabilities such as emotion management don't count as skill (Hampson et al., 2009; Bolton, 2004); others take issue with this viewpoint, arguing that routinised call centre work can scarcely be considered skilled (Lloyd and Payne, 2009). Where employees have little task discretion or control over the work process and the work is not complex, then jobs with emotional labour demands tend not to be seen as skilled. But, for example, in call centres where scripts are not standardised, workers may require greater skills, including skills at deceiving callers (Jenkins et al., 2010) or choreographing complex work processes (Whalen et al., 2002).

Developing 'emotional labour'

Bolton (2005) reconceptualises emotional labour. She criticises Hochschild's account for making a strong distinction between public and
private feelings, and criticises other researchers for applying the
concept to non-commercial workplaces. Bolton uses Goffman's work
on roles to get around Hochschild's problematic distinction between
public and private selves. For Goffman, actors acknowledge the different feeling rules demanded by different social roles (cited in Bolton,
2005: 83–5), and so the context matters. Labour process theory (LPT)
(introduced in Chapter 4, 'Work and the labour process') situates
work within structures of control, domination and exploitation and
also contributes to Bolton's advanced typology. Workers are managed
and controlled so as to extract the most surplus value from their
labour, and emotion is part of this commodified relationship. As
labour relations are characterised by conflict, and workers' creative
capacities cannot always or easily be captured, the capacity to use and
give emotional performances is uncertain and contingent. Where such
performances are extracted, emotion work has clear consequences, as
when unequal social relationships between customers and workers are
reinforced.

In *Emotion Management in the Workplace* (2005), Bolton presents
a typology of emotion in work that distinguishes between the emotional demands of different sorts of work. She delineates four types:
pecuniary, presentational, prescriptive and philanthropic. Pecuniary
emotion management is akin to Hochschild's emotional labour and is
common in commercial service work. Emotions, whether feeling rules
or display rules, are constrained so that 'good' customer service is
provided. Such emotion management is instrumental for the organisation, and potentially alienating for the employee. Prescriptive emotion
management is the sort of emotion work done by professionals who
may need to use feeling rules, in part in order to live up to ideals of
how professionals work. How an advertising executive or brand
designer produces enthusiasm when pitching to clients is a good
example, although, as Cronin notes, agencies are also concerned with
managing clients' own feelings of anxiety (Cronin, 2004b). Presentational emotion management refers to the social relations in the workplace. Colleagues support or bully each other, mess around, learn to
follow the norms of deference to seniority or success and such like; in
both culture work (Gottschall and Kroos, 2007; Hesmondhalgh and
Baker, 2010) and service work (Pettinger, 2005), friendships are
important to getting and keeping work. Philanthropic emotion

management is similarly social, and involves those occasions when a gift of care or effort is presented to another, either with the expectation of reciprocation, or in order to feel better about oneself (Bolton, 2005). This typology, based on an understanding of emotion as cognitive, disaggregates some of the complexities of emotion at work. It can encapsulate the constraints of emotion management as well as the pleasures of work, and can acknowledge the complexity of emotion labour in consumer capitalism. It also captures the and in some respects its ambiguity of emotional labour, where the most stressful part of work – clients – can also be a source of pleasure.

Whilst Bolton suggests that a worker is 'an emotive subject' (2005: 91) with private feelings as well as commodified ones, other labour process writers (Brook, 2009) suggest that there can be little space for non-commodified emotions at work. Such emotions are internalisations of what it takes to get the job done. Given our earlier discussion of the public culture of emotion and the emotionality of capitalism, I suggest that both are ignoring the way 'emotive subjects' at work are formed in relation to wider emotional cultures, including consumer capitalism. As David Harvey says:

> the experiential world, the physical presence, the subjectivity and the consciousness of that person are partially if not predominantly forged in the fiery crucible of the labor process, [in] the passionate pursuit of values and competitive advantage in the labor market, and in the perpetual desires and glittery frustrations of commodity culture (Harvey, 2000: 113).

The service triangle

One of the notable features about the service and cultural work that produces consumption is that thinking only about employer–employee relations means neglecting the complexity of this work. Rather, there is a 'service triangle' between employer, employee and customer. Customer-oriented workers are managed by customers in (at least) two ways. Those who face customers or clients are managed by the customers' demands and by the deference implicit and often explicit in that relationship. Further, management's interpretations of customer expectations may matter, as when an imagined customer is invoked to make work happen: if 'our lady hates viscose', to quote the title of a paper by Schultz (2008), then this fabric cannot be used. Workers and customers may collude against management. Perhaps a worker does an extra favour for a customer even though it's against the rules, or a customer helps the worker make money on the side (as in Monterrey, Mexico, where a bus driver's girlfriend blocked electronic sensors set to record how many passengers got on the bus, to help drivers skim bus fare from the company (Villarreal, 2010)). Workers and management may both benefit from managing customers (Bolton and Houlihan, 2010; Sloan, 2012), and neither 'worker' nor 'manager' is here a homogeneous category: shop-floor managers mediating between head offices, workers and customers have little power over stock, pricing and brand display (Bolton and Houlihan, 2010), but can seek to enact emotional performances from workers.

The 'service triangle' draws attention to the importance of thinking about customers. However, it's quite rare to see customers' voices and customers' opinions in studies done by those focused on work. Those interested in finding ways to sell more effectively do study customers, although often using survey methodologies that capture only that part of behaviour that can be made explicit. It's important to consider cultural understandings of the role of consumers (such as the discourse of customer sovereignty), as well as consumer behaviour and attitudes, to see how consumers are captured by consumption, marketing and services. Korczynski and Ott suggest that customers participate in an 'enchanting myth of customer sovereignty' (2004), whereby they seem to experience being in control, although they are subject to constraints imposed by management and workers. They contrast this 'irrational' feeling of power to 'rational' dimensions of exchange, such as the transfer of information. Considered in the light of our earlier critique of the rationality–emotion dualism, as well as instances where information 'enchants', or when customers knowingly refuse to be enchanted, the separation between seduction and reason doesn't quite work. Miliann Kang also recognises the importance of customers, and interviews customers and workers. What do customers get from visiting nail salons? 'From the customer's side, a weekly trip to the local nail salon can become a lesson in relating to a woman of a radically different social position, whom she would rarely encounter in her own milieu' (2003: 837). Differences of ethnicity as well as class and age mark out customers from workers here, and interactions are not merely conditioned by hierarchies between workers and customers, but by broader social dynamics.

It is well established that customer-facing work is demanding because of the expectations and obligations to manage feeling, although people-facing jobs do not have a monopoly on emotional exhaustion (Wharton, 1993). Some survey data problematises the common account of emotion in interactive service work. Sloan's (2004) analysis (again in the US) finds that those in people-facing jobs report facing more incidents of anger, and talk about this anger with others more often, as is expected from reading emotional labour research. Less expected is the finding that they are as likely to express anger directly (that is, not manage their emotions) as are workers in jobs with limited contact with others. Sloan finds also that status matters in a predictable way: low-status workers do not express direct anger (to the person who caused the incident) as often as high-status workers do. Anger is one common and specific emotion associated with emotional labour. Exploring another specific emotion, indignation, can also illustrate something about the dynamics within service encounters.

David Sims (2005) writes about indignation between colleagues, but his insights work well with customers. Indignation prompts us (willingly or reluctantly) to assess others as being in the wrong. These kinds of 'demonising' narratives work to shore up the demoniser's interpretation, to convey it to others, and thereby to make a moral claim. When we cannot find another way of understanding someone's behaviour, we dismiss the other as an innately bad person (Sims, 2005: 1626). We can use this idea of indignation in service work to make sense of encounters between customers and workers, understand their mutual misunderstandings and how they each claim their own responses as valid. Talking to colleagues to demonise customers for bad behaviour is common. But the ambiguity of the service encounter means that those same customers may feel entirely reasonable and engage in a similar demonising process, perhaps blaming the worker or perhaps the employer. Indignation when service appears to fail may be based in a customer's readings of their own status in relation to that of the worker. A worker who ends up as innately bad or 'just a bastard' (Sims, 2005) embodies a failure of broader economic processes to provide for and enchant the customer sufficiently. Indignation, anger and other negative feelings are common in service work and customer-facing commercial workers may resist the expectations that they provide emotional labour. Being rude and hostile to badly behaved customers is a way of acquiring some control over a situation, even when (as in the US) the waitresses rely on tips for their income and hence have an incentive to be subservient (Paules, 1991).

Service, feeling and emotional cultures

Those of you who have travelled outside your country of origin might have been surprised that you seem to be expected to behave differently in shops or cafés in other places and that you will be treated differently than in your home country. Not all sales assistants are enjoined to smile. Some will leave you alone, others will bring you just what you ask for, and others will suggest things you haven't requested. You're in a café: do you order at the bar, or sit at a table and wait for a waiter? How many times will customers and workers say please and thank you, if ever? These subtle cultural differences mean that the emotional labour expectations in a global consumer culture are not the same everywhere, although there is not very much research about this. McDowell et al. (2007) found that individual workers in a UK hotel chain were judged to embody national attributes which seemed to make them suitable or unsuitable for employment. For example, trainee hotel managers were recruited to the UK from India, because the recruiter thought that Indian workers had a naturally suitable personality (McDowell, 2009: 205). There are echoes here of our earlier discussion of gender stereotypes informing recruitment to service jobs: here, employers' judgements about ethnicity matter. As researchers we should be wary of making strong arguments that replicate national or ethnic stereotypes, given the extensive criticisms that have been made about the nation as an artificial construct, and given the risk of collapsing multiplicity and differences into stereotypes (such as Parisian waiters are rude, Thai waiters are subservient). But that does not mean we should not think about differences of place, class, ethnicity and status, as well as gender.

Much of the literature on emotional labour originates in the US. Hochschild studied American flight attendants working for American companies. She does not discuss their nationality, nor that of the customers. This absence is mirrored in subsequent studies of flight attendants (e.g. Tyler and Taylor, 1998), which explore and develop the concept in different national contexts without thinking through local culture and its impact on consumer norms. Kang's (2003) study of Korean-owned nail salons in the US is critical of simplistic applications of Hochschild's version of emotional labour: 'this kind of caring, attentive service has become a widely generalized definition, rather than being regarded as one particular form of emotional labor performed by mostly white, middle-class women largely for the benefit of white, middle- and upper-class men' (2003: 823). For Kang, emotional labour is also body labour and reproduces racial and class inequalities between women. We can develop this argument further by remembering the criticisms of presuming that emotions are universal and coherent, not formed in specific settings. So, emotional cultures and norms may differ. So too may expectations of what counts as good service.

A small study by Pollert (1995) revealed that Czech employees of a state-owned department store found it very challenging when the store was taken over by a private firm from the US. They were expected to work differently, with a flattened management structure, flexible working conditions and new training in customer service. Gottfried (2003) suggests that it is only in the West that emotion is opposed to rationality. Organisational life in Japan, she says, operates with a 'polite veneer' (2003: 262), where encoded, embodied etiquette norms stylise emotional engagement. Otis's (2008) study of a luxury hotel in Beijing catering predominantly to Western male travellers is also instructive. The female service workers were trained in an active and elaborate performance of deferential femininity, and to be extraordinarily aware of customers' preferences. This might seem like a standard story about luxury service, but Otis offers two significant and particular insights. The first is that customers are offered 'virtual personalism', that is, the hotel, via notes made by its workforce, records both stated customer preferences and customer habits on a database (Zwick and Denegri Knott, 2009). This means that services are personalised for the customer, but depersonalised for the worker. The second is that, workers claimed moral superiority for themselves for 'giving face' to these demanding customers and for bolstering the customers' low self-esteem. Otis suggests that, whilst this maintains dignity, it also maintains the subservient service relationship. In these cases, Western researchers have gone to study Asia, and it is worth reflecting on the nature of the knowledge that is produced by cultural outsiders.

Face-to-face/consumer services are very important for understanding emotion in consumer capitalism. Some service workers manage transactions, and others provide the very consumer good being paid for. Their bodies, their personalities and their labour are part of consumers' experiences. The employment relationship compels emotional labour: enacting feeling is the condition of getting and keeping work. But what of culture workers and how they produce the affective economy?

Culture work, emotion and affect

Our earlier discussion of emotions in consumer culture showed that it is obvious that the emotional work of consumption rests not only on the shoulders of interactive service workers, but is produced throughout consumers' wide, dynamic and diverse engagements in the world of goods, services and experiences. The emotional tone of consumer capitalism is affected by how material goods are made and provided, as when food in a restaurant takes a certain length of time to prepare and cook, or when a delay at a distribution centre prevents products getting through (as happens regularly with popular Christmas toys, or new technology products), and by the signs, symbols and feelings associated with (branded) goods, services and experiences. Culture workers thereby contribute to the generation of emotion in consumer capitalism. This section considers how culture workers do emotional labour, considers how they imagine and manipulate the emotions of customers and explores whether 'affect' provides a more comprehensive theory of the ways feelings matter in consumer capitalism.

Doing culture work

The longstanding recognition of how marketing speaks to emotions ('Emotion and consumption') is not matched by an understanding of how culture workers engender such emotions. The 'psy' disciplines and big data techniques such as sentiment analysis do make it possible for some information about consumer feelings to be picked up and analysed, within a limited methodology (sentiment analysis relies on feelings being translated into a set array of words that can be captured and analysed). As we saw in Chapter 5, the skill and craft of culture work does not rely on science alone, but on intuitions about what the market is currently like and how it might change, and these 'intuitions' may be performative, that is, serve to produce the market in that image. Entwistle (2009) refers to the 'gut feeling' of buyers when making decisions about what to stock: knowledge is felt, not articulated. Emotion here is part of how the job is done, and is important to understanding why the job gets done. Skov (2002) suggests that students and young designers in Hong Kong have a strong emotional involvement with fashion, and certainly this seems to be an inevitable result of a work culture that stresses 'loving' your work in order to be a successful and fulfilled individual, and where professional skills and creative self-expression are central to doing work.

   Direct uses of 'emotional labour' in the context of culture work research are less common than in service sector studies. Hesmondhalgh and Baker (2008) cite Grindstaff's (2002) study of culture workers producing 'confessional' television shows where ordinary people tell the stories of their lives. These shows rely on viewers being entranced by conflict and emotional outbursts, and researchers and producers on these shows work at managing these emotional outcomes. As for the TV talent show workers in Hesmondhalgh and Baker's own study, workers do emotional labour to manage the contestant and their own feelings. This is an example of how direct relationships with others tend to involve emotional labour. Most culture workers are involved in negotiations with clients who have commissioned services, rather than customers who will buy goods or services. What of the emotional demands of this part of work?

Clients

Marketing agencies developing new campaigns focus their attention on clients as much as on end customers. Clients need persuading that the agency has understood their company, their product and their needs, and can produce effective campaigns. Trust, anxiety, excitement and anticipation are all present. Moeran (2006) refers to the 'impression management' that advertising workers must do when presenting to clients. He draws on Goffman's dramaturgical understanding of front stage and back stage enactments of social roles (though he does not follow Hochschild in extending the dramaturgical model to recognise its emotional components). However, his descriptions of what he observes the presenter going through in the course of pitching his ideas – from the beads of sweat that appear to the exhaustion at the end of the pitch – suggest that emotion, felt in the body, is inescapable in this kind of work.

In the Japanese ad agency that Moeran (2006) observed, Japanese ad executives' vision of non-Japanese customers and clients influenced the kinds of campaigns they designed. For example, German and US customers were seen as similar enough (both Westerners) to be reached by comparable means; however, they might also be distinguished from each other – with Americans more open to a 'hard sell'. The agency's own understanding of target customers from overseas had to be set alongside their clients' feelings about how best to sell to Americans or Germans. Further, overseas clients or workers with experience in different business cultures who imported their habitual ways of doing business (such as an American firm which asked the agency to drop other clients) caused problems for the Japanese agency. Complex, charged conversations and negotiations between ad workers and managers and different client groups were common. Western 'dry' business relations were seen as different to Japanese 'emotionality' or 'wet' relations (Yano, a Japanese ad executive cited by Moeran, 2006: 109). Cultural difference, feelings and tensions within the agency–client relationship are part of how cultural intermediation operated through emotion. Feelings about how business should be done, about relationship building and economic efficiency, may differ across time and place and matter to understanding relations between culture workers and clients.

Affective labour

We've already considered the idea of affect and of immaterial labour. How does this matter to thinking about culture work? For affective labour theorists, there is no safe space outside of capitalism for feelings. We heard earlier that the concept of affect understands bodies as biological and social bodies, in contrast to how emotional labour stresses those conceptualisations of emotion that have explicit cognitive dimensions. We therefore expect affective labour to also recognise the importance of bodies to understanding feeling (see Chapter 5, 'Bodies', for a reminder about theories of bodies). So for forms of culture where bodies are clearly central, affective labour offers some insight.

Wissinger (2007) provides an account of modelling work designed to show the usefulness of 'affective labour'. This is one of a small number of empirical studies looking at affective labour; there is rather more theorising than exploration in this field. Good models are those who produce an 'affective flow', both during the photoshoot and when others see the image. That is, the flow of energies moving through models' bodies must be able to be manipulated and captured (by the camera and the viewer), but are not describable. Wissinger suggests that models are valued for their ability to transform, for the fluidity of their bodies and the work they can do with them, rather than for reaching an ideal of beauty. The model's body works to generate feeling, and this work is part of the circuit of images in contemporary capitalism, where value is created by flows of affect and all of social life is captured by the market. Wissenger mentions the other participants, from model bookers organising work, to stylists and photographers producing the atmosphere at photoshoots, to clients who want the right images to sell their products. She does not explicitly say that these too are involved in producing affect, but that is the implication. There is a raft of creative and knowledge workers involved in producing affects intended to enhance the flow of signs and values in consumer culture.

We saw earlier how affect moves through products (the example of the brand) and here have considered how affect is produced through affective labour in contemporary capitalism. The different formulations of emotional labour discussed previously can be seen as forms of affective labour within paid work. The concept of affective labour adds three insights to emotional labour. First, the most central differences between these concepts is how the body figures in affective labour so much more than in emotional labour; the latter very readily gives itself to an interpretation that stresses interaction and performance. In Hoschchild's understanding of emotional labour, deep acting challenges the worker's sense of self, but is not felt as corporeal. Second, it incorporates affects that are felt, rather than only emotions that can be named, and therefore reminds us to try to think about what is not spoken but matters. Third, it recognises that value is not just produced through wage labour, directly and inescapably commodified, but in nominally 'private' spheres too. However, we may question the explanatory power of a concept that considers everything part of the 'social factory' and contributing to value production.

Conclusion

In this chapter, we considered emotion to be critical to the operation of consumer capitalism. We developed a framework to understand emotion as a complex interplay of the biological, psychological and sociological elements. This gave us a comprehensive basis for exploring the ways emotion can be worked on, produced and generated in consumer capitalism, and how these differ between occupations and for different brands. Whilst some commercial workers play on fear and shame, others seek to generate wonder and excitement for consumers. Some work in occupations that expect them to use their feelings to generate value for clients and for customers, and we saw through our discussion of emotional labour that such practices can be hard on those who must do them. More research would help us to understand customers' responses to these blandishments, and might usefully include exploration of ugly feelings like boredom. More research is also needed to understand cultural differences in the experience of emotion in consumer capitalism. In the next chapter, we consider a different, but related, dimension of consumer capitalism by exploring the importance of the aesthetics of fashion, design and branding.

Research task

Consider the website of a major tourism experience (such as a theme park). Explore the ways consumer emotions are discussed and presented. Look at any job vacancies: what kind of worker do such theme parks look for?

OR

Interview a service worker to understand and assess doing emotional labour. What kinds of training in service did they have? Are they expected to manage their own emotions? Do they try to create feelings in others? What are the pleasures and pains of this work?

Discussion questions

1. To what extent do you think it makes sense to think of emotion as gendered?
2. How might emotional labour vary between different consumer markets? Consider either two different brands selling a similar kind of product to different market segments, or compare service norms in different places.
3. Consider a recent consumer experience: what does the idea of 'affect' add to your understanding of this experience?

Chapter 7

Aesthetics

This chapter argues that aesthetics are central to consumer capitalism and are worked on to generate particular sorts of consumer experience. Aesthetics, like emotion, are significant to the production of brand values and to the production of goods as desirable. Brand aesthetics are seen as important and 'all elements of a company's symbolic and material culture become subject to the same degree of analysis and design-intensivity as would previously be awarded to the product and its advertising' (Moor, 2007: 42). Fashion is a second important manifestation of this aesthetic focus, and this chapter pays attention to both phenomena.

The first section considers ways of theorising aesthetics. It explores why aesthetics is so important to understanding consumer capitalism, including the aesthetics of everyday consumption. 'An aesthetic economy' examines the role of multiple modes of marketing (advertising, product placement, celebrity endorsements) in producing this economy. It develops an account of how aesthetics relates to the sorts of complex materialities that have been presented elsewhere in the book: the materialities and atmospheres of selling spaces, of things for sale, and of the working bodies of those doing the selling. 'Brands' looks specifically at the science and practice of the branding of goods, objects, spaces and corporations, following Molotch's framing that 'branding [...] means design made corporate' (Molotch, 2003: 210), and hence privileging the production of aesthetics as central to understanding what a brand does. Fashion is considered in 'Fashion and aesthetics' in order to explore aesthetic change. The final section looks in detail at the usefulness of thinking about work as 'aesthetic labour', where working bodies are incorporated into processes of making value in consumer capitalism. It considers aesthetics in explicit relation to the working bodies of consumer capitalism, asking how bodies are included and excluded from commercial work, and how they produce aesthetic effects to contribute to value, both directly, through their bodies, and indirectly, through the creation of value in products and services.

Defining aesthetics

When we looked at ways of defining and conceptualising emotion, we had to look to many different intellectual disciplines to find our way through. In the case of aesthetics, the challenge is different. Aesthetics has been considered and debated mostly by philosophers and those in related humanities disciplines, such as art history. Understanding aesthetics therefore means looking back into the history of the idea. In its most general definition, aesthetics is 'the study of the feelings, concepts, and judgements arising from our appreciation of the arts or of the wider class of objects considered moving, or beautiful, or sublime' (Blackburn, 1994: 8). In this section, we will discuss how such conceptualisations help us to understand the aesthetics of commercial capitalism.

What is aesthetics?

The study of aesthetics began with the writings of Alexander Gottlieb Baumgarten in 1750. His *Aesthetica* argued for a 'science of sensual cognition' (cited in Highmore, 2011: 24). Baumgarten recognised that aesthetic experiences could not, and should not, be collapsed into science and reason, but that we could try to understand our sensuous and corporeal perceptions of the material world. The earliest writers on aesthetics focused on the beautiful and the tasteful. Immanuel Kant (1724–1804) wrote the most important works on this theme. In *Critique of Judgment* (1790), Kant argued that aesthetic judgement involves disinterested contemplation of the intrinsic properties of an art object. The disinterested viewer makes a judgement of the pleasure that this object provides and can hence judge its merits – as could any other equally disinterested viewer. These are not logical judgements based on reason, but aesthetic judgements of taste based on pleasure. This means that tastes can be taught; we can learn how to appreciate some things and find other things ugly. This idea of taste as learned is significant when we come to see how aesthetics affects how we see things as desirable and want to own them. Traditional approaches to aesthetics in the field of art consider what is beautiful or sublime, and art historians study how understandings of beauty change between times and places, how tastes are made and understood, whether there are universal standards of beauty and what role subjective judgements should play.

Various criticisms have been made of this traditional version of aesthetics, and these are important for making sense of aesthetics in consumer capitalism. The first criticism challenges the idea that judgements of beauty are universal, as implied by the idea of the disinterested contemplator. Instead, the subjectivity of the viewer (their sense of self, their history and social location) influences how beauty is seen. Different things count as beautiful in different contexts, as Saito's study (2007) of the clean lines and spaces of Japanese art objects shows. Removing universal judgement calls for more attention to individual experiences and subjectivities. You have probably had the experience of both sharing an understanding with others as to whether something was beautiful, and disagreeing. Tastes are not universally held, as the sociology of Pierre Bourdieu and those who followed him has found. In *Distinction* (see Chapter 3, 'Consumption and social status'), Bourdieu (1984) finds that different social classes (class fractions) find different kinds of paintings and other artworks beautiful. Cultural tastes for art, for leisure, for food and all kinds of consumption have been shown to vary between class groups, by gender, age, nation and colonial history (see for example, Katz-Gerro and Jaeger (2013) on Denmark; Lamont (1992) on France and the US; Bennett et al. (2008) on the UK, Bukodi (2007) on Hungary; Brosius (2010) on India's middle classes; Wong (2012) on Singapore). A further criticism challenges the restricted idea about what objects can be beautiful. In traditional aesthetics, neither nature nor everyday objects are art and therefore are not amenable to aesthetic judgement. However, a more open account of aesthetics makes it possible to think about non-art objects as generating the same kinds of aesthetic and non-rational pleasures as art objects do.

Judgement is important to thinking about aesthetics. But what is an aesthetic judgement? First, an aesthetic judgement is intersubjective (Brady, 2003) rather than individual. It arises in interaction with others. Second, contemporary accounts of aesthetics tend to stress the sensory dimensions of judgement: the importance of feelings and senses that inform our aesthetic tastes and preferences (Welsch, 1997). Here, aesthetic knowledge is derived from sensory experiences in specific situations. Still, some kinds of sensuality might be privileged over others: those of a 'higher order', those that are refined and not base. That is, whilst everything that is aesthetic is sensual, not everything sensual counts as 'aesthetic'. Aesthetics 'aims for the sensuous not as this ordinarily is, but for a higher and distinguished, an especially cultivated attitude towards the sensuous' (Welsch, 1997: 10). Despite the wider focus as to what might be aesthetic, only some experiences and encounters seem to count. Whilst 'people are primed to use sensory clues to recognize a clean toilet' (Senier et al., 2007: 305), Welsch and others would not consider this an aesthetic experience. So what kinds of aesthetic experiences do we have in our ordinary lives, and when do they count as 'aesthetic'?

Aesthetics and everyday experience

The American pragmatist philosopher, John Dewey (1859–1952) sees aesthetics as a mode of understanding, knowing and intelligence (Dewey, 1934). Aesthetics are part of experience and so are not distinct from everyday worlds. Experience may be intimate, but it is not private. Art and artists are firmly rooted in social life, and art takes ordinary experience and transcends it so that it stands out from the ordinary. The veneration of high art means that art objects tend to be treated as if they are detached from the social world in which they developed. They are remote. But for Dewey, multiple aesthetic experiences make up our everyday lives. 'High' art is part of ordinary experience and ordinary experience is in part aesthetic. Ordinary life is aesthetic because of the particular emotional experiences we each have when we encounter objects and events. We encounter the world as active agents, and so sensations are produced, not received (Dewey, 1967 [1887]:43).

Developing the idea that aesthetics involves a sensory knowledge of the world means, once again, thinking about the importance of bodies. When we understand the aesthetics of the world, we do so through our bodies, through our senses of sight, touch, taste and so on. Our bodies respond to these sensations, leading us to make judgements about ugliness, beauty, and other aesthetic sensibilities. As earlier discussions of taste suggest, we don't make such judgements on our own; we engage in a social world that is mediated by the presence of other people, objects and ideas, and the aesthetic norms that we are familiar with. Aesthetics are therefore social, and there is a great deal of scope for taste-makers to affect how we assess the sensory encounters we have with the world and so to call something beautiful or pleasant. This also means that judgements about taste can be political. Aesthetics is sometimes trivialised for being associated with sensory pleasure rather than understanding, but this denigration makes no sense if we accept that aesthetic experiences are present in many facets of life, and when technical function and image are recognised as being interconnected rather than belonging entirely to two different domains.

Aesthetics is an important part of global consumer capitalism and affects the goods, services and experiences that are sold and used in our everyday lives, whether as spectacular manifestations of self-identity, or as mundane and routine objects (see Chapter 3, 'Explaining consumption'). This has a long history: *Singer* sewing machines, common household items in Europe and the US in the late 19th and early 20th centuries, were designed to be beautiful as well as useful, reflecting idealisations of the home as a non-work space (Forty, 1986). Contemporary mass-market modernism reflected in *IKEA*-style furniture is quite a different aesthetic. Self-assembled flat-pack furniture is important, not only because it must be carefully designed to be assembled by the non-expert consumer (Glucksmann, 2013), but also because of the aesthetic work it does in reflecting and reconstructing understandings of an attractive home with clean lines and smooth-opening drawers (Molotch, 2003: 141). The familiarity of everyday objects and consumer practices may mean that their aesthetics pass without notice (Highmore, 2011). But as Venkatesh and Meamber (2008) show, consumers attend (in different ways) to the aesthetics of their consumption practices. Aesthetics informs consumer practices, as a source of identity and meaning making. When we shop for new jeans, we might be thinking about the rip in our current pair, or our bulging wardrobes, or what our friends will say, or how the jeans will look with what we already own. Venkatesh and Meamber (2008: 54–5) provide a typology of motives for aesthetic consumption: hedonism, immersion (in an experience), therapy, novelty and creativity. This shows how aesthetic judgements are important to why and how we consume, not only because of how products look, but because of what practices and experiences they relate to. Life practices are not *just* 'consumer choices' but sensual and ethical responses to a world that makes its own demands on us. But they *are* affected by consumption and 'consumer subjectivity is a vital element of an aesthetic framework' (Venkatesh and Meamber, 2008: 65).

Saito suggests, 'This power of the aesthetic is for the most part unrecognized when it comes to our everyday aesthetic judgements unless they lead to a standout aesthetic experience' (2007: 68). We don't always reflect on what is ordinary or routine and so we may not pay much attention to the implications of everyday aesthetics for our thoughts, beliefs and actions. For example, we rarely consider the 'type form' of everyday objects until we see a different version (for example, a bagless vacuum cleaner), or see what counts as normal in other places (overseas bathrooms often look strange to us and we treat our own style of bath, sink and toilet as the norm (Molotch, 2003: 97)). The sensory experience of everyday objects is thereby important to our use of them, and our (future) consumption of comparable things.

In the context of consumer capitalism, aesthetic knowledge also involves understanding corporate/organisational signs and symbols, including layout, architecture, design and decoration, brands and logos. The experiential knowledge of encountering a space, and the feelings and embodied experiences that emerge from this, inform our judgements and understanding. Global capitalism is made up of aesthetic experiences and knowledges which affect how consumer-oriented workers come to do and understand work, and how they relate to the products they sell and the customers they sell to. Sensuous elements cannot be separated from 'knowledge', as though the latter exists in a rational domain untouched by feeling. Extraordinary amounts of energy are devoted by designers, branders and other commercial workers to trying to manage that experience so it seduces us (if we are right for it). For example, colour is a significant dimension of sensory experience and so corporations may want to find a good colour and patent it. Green, for example, is readily understood as the colour of nature and eco companies usually use green – but avoid the 'repulsive' green that reminds us of bruises and reptiles (Sassoon, 1990: 177). This focus on the experiential is closer to the kind of understanding of aesthetics that Dewey offers us which helps us see how we 'sense' that a restaurant is not really our kind of place, or how we give up on navigating an online retailer's website.

Aesthetics and design

In Chapters 5 and 6 we mentioned how the dualisms common to the Western philosophical tradition have constrained imagination and understanding. There is a dualism within aesthetics too, one that builds on the privileging of reason over feelings and senses, and of mind over body. This is the separation between form (aesthetics, appearance) and function (usefulness, productivity) that guides conversations about need, desire and preference. We see use being privileged as the source of value, above and beyond any interest in aesthetics, in modernist design where 'form follows function', in critiques of fashion that consider the desire for something new as frivolous or silly, and in the practices of engineers who see innovation as only informed by utility (Petroski, 1992, cited in Molotch, 2003: 54). Does this chime with your personal experiences? Aesthetics affects how we desire, acquire and experience objects, including commercial goods, services and experiences. The experience of eating in a restaurant is an emotional-aesthetic composite informed by design and layout, the sensory experience of tasting food, the company around us, the temperature of the room and so on; things that are cheap and unfashionable might be nonetheless desirable because of their aesthetic benefits: a blanket made out of fleece has the sensory benefit of feeling soft and keeping us warm. Aesthetic value derives from these kinds of pleasures.

The form–function hierarchy may stem from how art is seen as, and claims to be, a world apart from everyday life. The aesthetic is thereby presented as non-essential. Mort describes the distinction between high art and useful design as 'cultural dualism' (Mort, 1996: 30) that which commercialised design has sought to resolve. He suggests that commercial design democratises art and design by applying it to mass-market products. Form and function are combined when objects and settings are designed and used so that 'the practical and the sensual merge' (Molotch, 2003: 70). We see the idea of the aesthetic as a powerful tool to produce feelings harnessed in the 'aesthetic economy' of consumer capitalism. Consumer capitalism makes use of the aesthetic, and builds aesthetic sensibilities in ways that are significant, and that take us some way from the traditional understanding of aesthetics as a reflection of the 'higher' attributes of beauty, truth and justice. But what does an 'aesthetic economy' look like?

An aesthetic economy

An aesthetic economy is one that is simultaneously concerned with what is beautiful or desirable and what is saleable and usable. Hancock and Tyler see the aesthetic economy as 'ultimately grounded in the manipulation of the desire for identification between the (working and consuming) subject and the objective realm of the organisation and its products and services' (2008: 212). It relies on workers able to locate themselves within, and generate, marketisable forms of sensibility that sit with consumers' desires. In this section, we'll consider consumer capitalism as an 'aesthetic economy', considering how aesthetics generate atmosphere in such a way as to encourage and facilitate consumption.

Defining the aesthetic economy

The 'aesthetic economy' is similar to other ways of schematising contemporary capitalism, such as the affective economy of 'hyperindus-
trial' capitalism that recruits the 'incalculable' of bodies and desires in
calculable economic flows (Stiegler, 2008, in Venn, 2009: 4). We will
focus here on the formulation developed by the German writer
Gernot Böhme that stresses how atmospheres and auras, symbols,
images and icons are produced by a capitalism that is adept at drawing
in and regenerating 'culture'. Böhme is strongly influenced by the
Marxist writings of the Frankfurt School (Chapter 3, 'Critics of mass'),
but attends to how the culture industries have changed since Adorno
and Horkheimer were writing. Now, 'art' and 'industry' are not distinct
and 'brand culture has dislodged art's hold on creativity' (Banet-
Weiser and Sturken, 2010: 266): designers and advertisers do art in
the course of doing creative work; artists like Shepard Fairey are
'cultural entrepreneurs' using marketing techniques (Banet-Weiser
and Sturken, 2010). Böhme describes the collapse of art and industry
as an aestheticisation 'of the real' (Böhme, 2003: 72). Everyday life
and everyday objects are offered to consumers with the aesthetic
attributes of high culture.

Böhme suggests that in addition to use value (the way a good meets
a human need, its qualitative value) and exchange value (the quantitative value of a commodity), a further category, staging value, matters
in an aesthetic economy. Staging value develops Baudrillard's ideas
about sign value: the value of a good within the system of objects
(Chapter 3, 'Consumption and identity'). Sign values matter when
understanding how commodities are made desirable and others
become undesirable. Whilst sign value sits alongside exchange value,
'staging value' is intended to increase exchange value: the 'aesthetic
qualities of the commodity then develop into an autonomous value,
because they play a role for the customer not just in the context of
exchange but also in that of use' (Böhme, 2003: 72). The key idea here
is that our desires for the aesthetic comprise part of use value. Aesthetics is not distinct from function, and the quest for new aesthetic
experiences drives the search to sate new, emerging desires and for us
to stage ourselves, to reveal our identity through our consumption.

In its original formation, the aesthetic economy is a stage in capitalist development, one that developed countries in Europe and North
America reached in the 1960s. With a shared understanding that a
good life is one where the pursuit of pleasure for all is morally appropriate (2003: 79), 'capitalism, having in principle satisfied primary

needs, must turn to desires' (Böhme, 2003: 78). It might, however, be useful for us to separate the idea of 'staging value' as significant to the aesthetic economy from this strong account of economic development occurring in stages. This would give us a tool to understand the aesthetics of desire for commodities amongst the wealthy of less-developed countries in the context of a global commodity culture. The wealthy classes in emerging economies look to global brands and corporations for luxury goods and services to generate self-identity, as in the case of the move in China from *Chengfen* (traditional markers of status) to *Shengjia* (a mediated value system that assigns contingent markers of worth and status through consumption) discussed by Li (2010), or the development of celebrities as national and global brand ambassadors. The complexity of the global production and consumption of aesthetic commodities is such that we cannot presume that staging value is a feature only of advanced capitalist consumer society, but is also a part of emergent consumer culture.

Atmosphere and the aesthetic economy

Böhme says that value is staged in the aesthetic economy through the production and consumption of 'atmospheres'. Sensory and aesthetic atmosphere is at the heart of our experience of a place or a thing. A kind of 'aesthetic labour' (we will use a different conceptualisation of aesthetic labour in 'Aesthetic labour') goes on in order that such atmospheres are made. Here 'aesthetic labour designates the totality of those activities which aim to give an appearance to things and people, cities and landscapes, to endow them with an aura, to lend them an atmosphere, or to generate an atmosphere in ensembles' (Böhme, 2003: 72). The audience works to make sense of such atmosphere. Atmospheres are experienced when we relate to objects – to other people and to things in spaces – in part because these objects have properties in their own right, distinct from our direct knowledge of them, and so generate aura and feeling. For Böhme, this is the basis of aesthetics, and by extension, the aesthetic economy. Tacit understandings and identifications exist when we consume (and critique) aesthetics.

Schroeder's (2012) account of the increasing use of 'snapshot' aesthetics helps us think through the aesthetic economy. Snapshot aesthetics are different from the drama and high production values of a film aesthetic and look more like the casual photographs ordinary people take and share on social media. They are used by organisations as part of their strategic imagery. Schroeder argues that snapshot 'can be harnessed to promote organisations as authentic, to invoke the "average consumer" as a credible product endorser, and to demonstrate how the brand might fit in with the regular consumer's or employee's lifestyle' (Schroeder, 2012: 129). The apparent realism of snapshot photographs 'articulates' a market segment, signalling informality and authenticity. The atmosphere of authenticity requires that target customers are sophisticated readers of images, comfortable with making sense of what images invite them to feel. Snapshot aesthetics are read in the context of a broader aesthetic economy in which consumers know that snapshots are used deliberately, and understand that informality and authenticity contribute to staging value, to the attachment with the product, to 'fit' with lifestyle.

Other examples of spectacular consumption that intends to create 'atmospheres' also illustrate the idea of the aesthetic economy. Joseph Hancock describes the merchandising and marketing concept of *Abercrombie & Fitch*, an American clothing company aimed at young people, as 'a nightclub that happens to sell clothes' (2009: 89), with stores using consistent styling, loud music, branded perfume and sexually attractive workers to create a branded store. In an aesthetic economy, such symbols and atmospheres are readily used by consumers in the quest for self-identity through consumption. Sports clothing brand *Nike* has several *Niketown* retail experiences, characterised by the multi-sensory stimulations that are supposed to encourage interaction with the brand, and to reinforce the brand meanings (competition, exceptional performance, style and recreation) as imaginable for the customers too (Peñaloza, 1999). As we saw in Chapter 3, 'Explaining consumption', consumers may respond quite differently to these urges, finding pleasure and self-identification with the aesthetic experience, or feeling overloaded and frustrated that buying trainers has been made so complicated. The point is that *Niketown* and comparable 'experiential' outlets use aesthetics to pull customers in, to create attachment and to make leisure time an ongoing encounter with commercialism. More generally, the aesthetics of the architecture and design of selling spaces matter. 'Flagship' retail stores and shopping centres are good examples, as in luxury brand retailing where expensive and renowned architect firms might be used to design new buildings. But more ordinary forms of retailing can also be considered here: 1960s shopping centres reflected the aesthetic fashions of the time; supermarkets are designed to encourage shopper movement whilst also persuading shoppers to stray from their intentions and their list (Thomas and Garland, 1993). The aesthetics of rationality are clearly present in the supermarket, and these aesthetics reveal key dynamics of consumer capitalism: branded products, fixed prices, rationalisation and enchantment combined in a brightly lit, smooth-floored, managed space.

The idea of the aesthetic economy forces us to explore how things are made consumable. 'Staging value' and the generation of 'atmosphere' are outcomes of particular kinds of workers operating within consumer markets. That is, they are the products of designers, marketers, branders, game programmers and all kinds of other commercial workers. Understanding the aesthetic economy means exploring staging value as a process and practice, and means paying attention to working subjectivities: how is knowledge of consumer markets gathered, understood and used? How do workers understand and present themselves as employable for their capacity to produce the aesthetic economy? In the rest of this chapter, we will consider three dimensions of commercial work in the aesthetic economy: branding, fashion and aesthetic labour, beginning with branding, because of its reliance on the combination of design and marketing.

Brands

When Bollywood film star Amitabh Bachchan promotes *Parker Pens* or tourism in Gujarat, when athlete Usain Bolt promotes *Hublot* watches, *Puma*, *Nissan* and *Soul Electronics* headphones, or when *L'Oréal* changes its list of 16 spokespeople to include a new celebrity, we see contemporary brand culture in action. The symbolic attributes of a brand are interlinked with the attributes and identity of a kind of promotional worker – the celebrity (themselves 'branded') – in globalised consumer capitalism in a way that is intended to encourage consumers to think well of those involved. Branding is a pervasive and economically significant part of consumer capitalism. In this section, we consider ways of conceptualising brands, what kinds of entities are branded, how brands are understood by those working on them through a consideration of the science of brands and of the status of brands, and how brands are affected by fakes.

What is a brand?

Although brands and branding have a long history, they became increasingly prominent in cultural life and to economic activity from the 1980s, when company accounts began to include the economic value of a brand on their balance sheet (Moor and Lury, 2011;

Aronczyk and Powers, 2010: 5). Later, 'brand equity' – how consumers valued the brand – was also considered. The cultural, the immaterial and the aesthetic are codified and measured by a new category of commercial workers and organisations devoted to knowing brands and measuring brand value and brand equity (e.g. *Interbrand*). Indeed, for some corporations 'brand value' exceeds the value of material assets such as factories. This is part of the vertical disintegration of post-Fordist production referred to in Chapter 2, 'Post-Fordism'. Brand agencies offering a comprehensive marketing package developed from the 1990s, later extending their remit when social media made 'always on' branding possible, adding a drip of branded messages to the established strategies of television ad spot, direct mail leaflet or sports team sponsorship. It is impossible to think of brands and branding – so much the emblem of contemporary commercial culture – without recognising their aesthetic dimensions and their aesthetic intrusions into everyday life. All dimensions of the aesthetic are relevant here: the sensory and the perceptual, knowledge and judgement.

A great deal of contemporary commercial work concerns brands, and our discussion of the aesthetic economy must extend the Chapter 6 discussion of emotions and brands to recognise this. Brands are aesthetic, in that they are intended to generate sensory responses in, and meanings for, potential and actual customers. The examples used to demonstrate this are often the big (American) brands like *Nike* and *Starbucks*. *Nike*'s brand is visible in its logo and slogan, in the *Nike-town* stores ('Atmosphere and the aesthetic economy') and especially in its advertising campaigns, which use globally recognisable sportsmen (and sometimes sportswomen). The majority of *Nike* employees work on the brand, as production is subcontracted. Consumer marketing research conceptualises such brands as contributing to a 'brandscape', whereby consumers derive personal meanings and create lifestyles from the symbolic resources of different brands (Sherry, 1998: 112); such meanings are produced by brand workers and consumers.

Branded what? Goods, spaces, organisations and people

From toothpaste and washing powder to computers and this book, you've made use of branded goods today. I suspect that this kind of branding of everyday consumer goods is very familiar to you; it certainly has a long history, as producers have long used branding to distinguish their product from that of their competitors and to give consumers reassurance (Moor, 2007). Branding is used to differentiate between products that are otherwise very similar, as when we choose between washing powders with different brand names, even though they might be made by the same company. Although the content of the product has only minor differences, the smells, colours, 'added science' and so on are all worked on in order to signal to customers the promises this product is making, and encourage them to choose this product over that one and then to keep on choosing it; brand loyalty is the aim. Attention to brand aesthetics tells us something about both the brand and the context of its consumption. For example, Davison (2012) discusses the 'iconography' of a British bank, *Bradford & Bingley*. In the 1970s, this brand was represented by cartoons of stereotypical British bankers in bowler hats and suits. Then the bowler hat and other signs of class difference disappeared, the cartoons were more comic and one of the characters became female, indicating a more friendly and casual relationship with the bank. More recently, the bowler hat alone signals the brands as this is thought of as a cultural object with clear enough associations to communicate the brand. How this kind of signalling work done by brands is developed needs articulating in order to see just how significant the work is that goes into creating such aesthetic values that are at the heart of the functioning of the brand.

As the banking example suggests, branded goods are only one dimension of the contemporary landscape of brands. Other objects are also branded: corporations (including not-for-profit ones), retail spaces, geographic places and even people. Globally powerful brands are good examples for considering the interrelated branding of objects, corporations, spaces and places. *Disney*, *McDonald's* and *Starbucks* are examples of companies that create similar aesthetic spaces in different places: Mickey Mouse or the red and yellow 'M' that signals a *McDonald's* restaurant are obvious examples of brand aesthetics. *McDonald's* and its customers refer to those M signs as the 'Golden Arches', a brand phrase that contains an aesthetic message. This company's products are globally similar but not identical, and its selling spaces are designed to be recognisable. *Disney* provides a more extensive set of branded relationships: shops sell only *Disney* products inspired by *Disney* films. Some of the products are bizarre to *Disney* outsiders like me, such as the *Disney*-branded potty. Here we have an example of brand extension where thinking aesthetically to keep the branded items 'on message' is important. Long discussions about product design and 'fit' with the existing brand are precursors to the launch of a new item, whether a new film and all the attendant marketing products, or a new range of potties.

Visual branding refers to the obvious and well-known dimensions of branding: the use of colour, style, layout, font, image and so on to generate a logo, advert or other promotional device. Indeed, language is central to branding and the production of spectacles of consumption, as when commercials use superlatives to describe branded products (Gottschalk, 2009). Sonic branding suggests that meanings can be generated using sound (there are also brand workers who concentrate on other sensory experiences, such as smell and touch). Jackson (2003) describes the work of the creative director in the process of sonic branding as being 'to identify the sounds that have been well received and interpret these in an ownable way' (2003: 124), in order to create a 'distinctive magic' (125). The sonic brander works by taking the client's brief and design and branding colleagues' moodboard and finding or creating sounds that fit; these are then translated into 'sonic guidelines' (129) so another composer would be able to understand the brand. In this way, the creativity of a knowledge worker is turned into a formula. Sonic branders draw on neuroscience, and see sonic branding as a way of easily accessing consumers; sound is inescapable and so customers are 'vulnerable' to its messages (Powers, 2010: 300). The sounds produced may be used in adverts, in shops or on websites to contribute to the promotion of the brand. Sonic branding has multiple dimensions: the *Nokia* ringtone or computer start-up sound are one kind of example, as is the sound a car's indicators make; elsewhere we see women's retail clothing companies creating ambience in stores and filtering their customers using music (DeNora and Belcher, 2000), as well as *Apple* using a series of cute and fey folk singers in its campaigns, a strategy that other retailers have also used (Powers, 2010). Sonic branding is an important, under-acknowledged part of the aesthetic economy.

The coffee shop chain *Starbucks* pays attention to the small details of aesthetics to create its branded spaces, even to the texture of the upholstery it uses. Design commentator Postrel (2004: 20) describes it as the 'touchstone' of branded success, as its 'design language' generates an all-encompassing retail aesthetics. She quotes *Starbucks* CEO Howard Schultz:

> All the sensory signals have to appeal to the same high standards. The artwork, the music, the aromas, the surfaces all have to send the same subliminal message as the flavor of the coffee: *Everything here is best-of-class* (cited in Postrel, 2004: 20, *emphasis* in original).

Starbucks is an example of how a branded space is intended to become an experience, and the company's global expansion suggests that customers like this control and familiarity. *Starbucks'* effect on American contemporary coffee shop culture is such that it is a reference point both for other kinds of coffee shops and for consumers, who are skilled at comparing the aesthetics of local cafés to that of *Starbucks*, considering ambiance, visual displays and music, layout, food menu, service style and such like (Thompson and Arsel, 2004). In Japan, however, global chains do not have such a homogenising effect; they appear as 'wrapped' cultural experiences where the West is exoticised for Japanese consumers, but they are not the only, nor the dominant, form of coffee consumption in Japan (Grinshpun, 2013). Two further points are worth noting about the apparent global reach of standardised, American brands. First, that origins matter: Italian café culture has not produced a brand like *Starbucks*, and the Northwest USA, where *Starbucks* originated, has produced few high-status clothing designers like the Italian firm *Armani* (Molotch, 2003: 161). That is to say that the environments in which design, aesthetics and branding emerge mediate the goods, services and experiences that are produced. Second, that it is easy to get caught up in the story of global brands and fail to give due weight to how local, national and regional cultures differentiate global consumer capitalism.

Brand cultures

Brand workers in different occupations seek knowledge about the brands they work on, about actual and potential customers and about how customers respond to different aesthetics. This makes them 'knowledge workers', as defined in Chapter 5, 'Knowledge work', and involves them doing creative work using cultural knowledge. Knowing customers involves studying consumer psychology, tracking sales data through data mining (Knox et al., 2010), talking to customers in focus groups or panel tests (Mallard, 2007), doing marketing ethnography (Boddy, 2011), measuring cognitive responses to different stimuli and targeting specific markets (for example, see Ottman, 2011, on green marketing). Such knowledge informs brand strategies. Naming a brand means understanding the associations consumers have with words and phrases. Xu Bai Yi (1991: 33) tells us that razor company *Gillette* uses the brand name 'Jili' in China, meaning lucky, and Electrolux refrigerators (which use Italian technology) are branded 'Zhongyi', which he says can mean 'Sino-Italian' and 'satisfactory', depending on pronunciation. There are many examples of brands getting this wrong.

Brands that dominate in Europe are not always those that dominate in Asia. And there is no reason to assume that brands that succeed in

Brazil will do so in Paraguay. That is, national and local cultures matter, as well as broad regional differences. Even in an 'aesthetic economy', the big global brands are only a part of our everyday consumption. We shop in national and local chains, or at market stalls; we buy some things because we're aware of the brand but not others. On holiday we might not recognise the brand name of the potato crisps in the supermarket but feel that the logo is familiar. A global marketing campaign is always different to work on a country-specific campaign, and requires different sensitivities, aesthetic competencies and knowledges. A simple example is the different meanings of the colour white in different cultures. In India this is the colour of mourning; in Europe it is a colour for marital celebration.

The material that commercial workers gather to use in a marketing campaign is often highly specific, and not readily translatable between cultures. Try looking on the internet for an ad campaign designed for another country, and identify the elements which specifically draw on national culture, or consider the sense of humour that the advert makers presume the audience shares (the series of adverts for *Brahma*, a Brazilian beer, is one to try, as is that for the Ajinomoto Stadium, Japan – use a search engine to find online versions). The 'creativity' of the work of the advertisers involves understanding where the advert is being shown. Knowledge of the customers is important to the production of an aesthetic experience.

Brand status

The apparently simple statement that brands are used to distinguish between products has many implications. Potential and actual consumers may not share the brand manager's estimation of what the brand means, and via 'co-creation' (see Chapter 4, 'Beyond paid work'), they may shift or subvert intended meanings. Attempts to create a coherent 'brand identity' through combinations of aesthetic artefacts may not be successful as it is hard to control meanings. For example, when an expensive brand creates a subsidiary line, perhaps for a mass-market retailer, both the high-status brand and the mass-market retailer are changed.

As an example of the importance of aesthetics and branding, consider the case of two 'fine fashion' luxury brands. Their brand identity is comprised of a collage of artefacts that include products, design and layout of the stores, logos, promotional materials like catalogues, runway shows and magazine shoots. Cappetta and Gioia (2006) compared how both tried to rebrand, although unfortunately, the precise details of the aesthetics of these brands are not discussed (because it is common for companies only to grant researchers access on conditions of anonymity). The brand that developed a more modern image and also offered staff discounts and made frontline staff as well as 'taste-makers' feel part of the change was more successful than the brand that worked only on image. Cappetta and Gioia conclude that:

> if you build a story that attends only your brand image (how your products are perceived by your customers) but not your identity (how your employees perceive who they are as an organization), then you will need at least two stories [...] and coherence will be difficult to achieve. (2006: 208)

This research reminds us of the kinds of objects that are worked on to produce a brand aesthetic, and of the relevance of generating enthusiasm and a sense of belonging amongst workers at different levels (see Chapter 6). In contrast, an expensive luxury hair salon in London directly incorporates the bodies of the hairdressers themselves into the aesthetics of the space. The pale architecture and design 'features' showcase the hairdressers themselves, dressed in black and white and with the kind of hairstyles clients might want (Chugh and Hancock, 2009).

That aesthetics matters is clear when we consider how branding and retail 'experts' talk. For example, Chadha and Husband (2006) contrast the experience of luxury shopping in Japan, where they were impressed by attention to aesthetic details, with that in other places: 'in India, the staff at some brands were poorly dressed and the stores felt cheap' (2006: 100). The *Chanel* flagship store in Ginza, Tokyo's shopping district, has a glass facade designed to echo the key brand identifier – *Chanel* tweed (2006: 75); one luxury brand, *Cartier*, employs five decorators in Tokyo and just one in Paris to check the quality of store displays. What others effects do questions of status have on brands and their customers?

Fake brands

Counterfeit goods, including fake brands, have a long history. Counterfeit goods may adapt established brand logos to look like the 'real thing'. Such goods violate the intellectual property rights that are the key to 'brand value' – perhaps because of their 'brand equity' with consumers. Expensive luxury items like watches, perfume and high fashion clothing are particular targets, and have been the subject of research (Chang, 2004; Crăciun, 2014) and media exposés. But ordinary consumer products (eggs, soy sauce, shampoo) can be faked, and damage consumer's trust as well as waste their money on inferior products (Gamble, 2011: 206). In some cases, the same factories that produce the 'genuine' articles also produce the fakes (Crăciun, 2014) and it takes someone knowledgeable about the aesthetics of the 'genuine' product to tell what's what. Lin (2011) shows the prevalence of fake brands and counterfeit goods that are produced and consumed in China and elsewhere. She suggests that consuming fakes is a way to 'resist and reclaim' the control of cultural meanings by large corporations, and can be a creative act. She also notes that fakes are not necessarily of worse quality. Fakes and counterfeits, as well as subversions and jokes, are part of an aesthetic economy where meaning is generated from brands. What a brand might mean to customers is complex and contingent, as people may be playful in their reference to fakes. Claims to 'brand identification' should be treated warily; how much customers care about brands is uncertain, especially when the reasons they give for preferring brand A are very similar to those for preferring brand B, and when preferences for brand C may not outlast brand D's discounting.

In this section, we've discussed some of the key dimensions of the aesthetics of brands and how they are worked on to affect the 'aesthetic economy'. Brands may try to know and manage how consumers engage with them, for example, by generating symbolic communication that speaks to specific social groups. Consumers in turn communicate with the brand, for example, when they promote it on social media, buy items with logos on, mock its customers and so on. Other dimensions of the dynamics of consumer preferences are not properly explained by thinking about the brand itself, as they require us to pay explicit attention to changes in fashions, and we will now turn our attention to this topic.

Fashion and aesthetics

So far the discussion appears to assume that most aesthetic work is done to generate a brand. We can understand something different about the aesthetic economy by considering fashion, although there are some overlapping themes. Thinking again about our daily experience of consumption will remind us that aesthetics, styles and brands change over time, and we can helpfully think of these as changes in fashion. That is to say that organisations do not just want to produce a distinct brand, but also want their products to be current. An early commentator on fashion, James Laver, describes fashion's movement as a 'mysterious satisfaction' that comes from 'being in harmony with the spirit of the age' (Laver, 1945: 197). For example, at the time of writing, craft production is being revived in several industries, including homeware and beverages. Hartmann and Ostberg (2013) show how craft production makes guitars seem desirable as they appear more authentic. The 'authenticity' of the 'vintage inspired' contrasts with how other products have been obviously mass produced and appears to 're-enchant' consumers.

Theories of fashion

Fashions change for complex reasons. Some commentators suggest that changes to fashion reflect social and political changes that affect patterns of thought and belief (e.g. Braun-Ronsdorf, 1964). More scholarship looks at fashion in relation to dress than at fashions in other goods, services and experiences, and so clothing provides many of the examples in this section. Fashion is often thought of as being motivated by a desire for status differentiation, as discussed in Chapter 3 (Simmel, 1904; Veblen, 1899). Class distinctions, for example, are signalled through tastes and preferences for different goods, and 'trickle down' as middle-class people mimic elite styles and are in turn copied. The driver for changes to fashion comes when elites seek to differentiate themselves from the wearers of newly popular styles.

Promotional, creative and cultural workers, however, do substantial work to influence fashion. The sociologist Herbert Blumer's explanation for fashion in all kinds of settings (from clothing, arts and entertainment, to academia and mortuary practices) is that it changes as a result of 'collective selection' (Blumer, 1969: 275–6). Blumer analysed the women's haute couture clothing industry in Paris, considering how competitive selection took place prior to publicity for the season's new fashion. This occurred in a process between designers and their representatives and buyers and their representatives, thus from over a hundred designs, six to eight would be selected. Designers and buyers from different areas tended to converge on key looks (much as fashion writers do today), selecting from the possibilities on behalf of the public. These commercial workers had common sensitivities as to what was appealing, beautiful and modern, and so had similar preferences about what would be this season's look. The designers themselves garnered ideas from past fashions, and recent developments in the fields of art, literature and the like, and tended to develop existing fashions, not recreate them anew each season, seeking 'to catch the proximate future as it is revealed in modern developments' (Blumer, 1969: 280).

In this account, fashion has its own motor for change. The continual 'progression' of taste, so that new fashions arrive to better reflect incipient tastes than the existing fashion perpetuates the fashion mechanism. How this process occurs is both mysterious and a result of the diversity of social experiences and interactions in a complex world (Blumer, 1969: 282). Tastes are formed, refined and disintegrate through social interactions between creators and adopters of fashion. For Blumer, new fashion permits a safe revolt; people feel they are being non-conformist, but have the security of knowing that others are also doing the same thing. The adoption of what is fashionable by an individual is not irrational (by which he means emotional). On the collective level, too, fashion is not about emotion, but may be a response to propriety and social distinction. Whilst Blumer's ideas have been adapted by others, there are some obvious omissions in his account, and contemporary media practices are somewhat different to those of the 1960s, meaning that new styles are rapidly judged by all kinds of actors. Further, new products emerge, not only in relation to the desire for something new, but because of weaknesses in earlier designs and/or innovations in fabric. Technological developments affect fashion, as when new tools like computer-aided design (CAD) or recent 'smart clothing' fabrics like *Gore-Tex* (McCann and Bryson, 2009) alter the possibilities of production.

How does fashion work?

Blumer developed his ideas by thinking through high fashion and they have been developed by others studying commercial work in this field (Entwistle, 2009, 2006; Mears, 2011; Godart and Mears, 2009). The clothing fashion industry has changed since Blumer was writing, as trends multiply and the Paris fashion houses compete with those of New York, London and Milan. Godart and Mears (2009) discuss how fashion models are chosen to appear in catwalk shows. Those interviewed because they are involved in producing fashion shows commonly say that it is their personal tastes that matter, but they are part of social networks that shape their taste. Whilst 'gut instinct' (2009: 679) as to whether a model was desirable counted, Godart and Mears show how socialisation into the industry and the consumption of fashion aesthetics (e.g. magazines) also influenced what casting directors thought of as a desirable look. They were influenced by the work of other commercial workers; agencies have models with very similar body types on their books and pre-select a 'show package' (2009: 681) of models. Only some in the show package are seen face-to-face by producers, who then negotiate with agents about who to book. Taking out an 'option' to book a model signals to others that model's desirability. This is a critical part of the taste network that affects which bodies are 'hot'. Homophily amongst high-fashion houses is likely: they agree on which models are 'this season'. New entrants to design use younger, cheaper models. Fashion producers tend to express their preferences with great certainty, and magnify small differences. What does this tell us about how fashions – in this case in model's bodies – are determined? Godart and Mears conclude that fashion producers' skills are intangible but strongly felt and protected by those involved. 'a "good eye" or a "strong vision", reflect socialisation into networks, status orderings, and strategic choices within the fashion world' (Godart and Mears, 2009: 688). The arguments they make are a refined version of collective selection, and they illustrate the complex interplay of different commercial workers in this field (see also Schultz, 2008, on the interactions between designers and buyers).

Consumers, too, play a part in the movement of fashion. For example, contemporary accounts of Islamic dress for women reveal new modes of subjectivity where fashion, consumerism and religious identity entwine (Gökarıksel and Secor, 2009, 2010; Sandıkcı and Ger, 2010). A more complex account of fashion, desirability and the social and cultural milieu in which people live is needed to explain changes to clothing fashion. Once stigmatised as backwards and against modernity, veiling in Turkey was rediscovered by urban middle-class women from the 1980s onwards. From interviews with Turkish women (those who did and did not wear a veil), Sandıkcı and Ger suggest a complex interplay between the politics of Islam, religiosity, an emergent fashion industry specialising in covering and self-identity. For Wilson (2003), the aesthetics of fashion provide a means through which individuals can make sense of their engagement in the social world.

Design, fashion and aesthetics

Aesthetics are produced in comparable ways outside of fashion and clothing design by comparably interconnected commercial workers negotiating with each other, and with clients. Fashion designers may have a greater public presence than do other product designers, but the web of social networks and collaborations between designer, specialist and mainstream media, retail buyers and the like also governs the way designs are adopted. Prior to adoption, engineers, marketers and clients have all had their say in what a design should include. Molotch says product designers 'turn cultural currents into economic goods' (2003: 20), that is, they engage in absorption and adaption of their broad experiences of living, as producers and as consumers of all kinds of goods, services and experiences, to generate aesthetic shifts. Key skills include intuitions as to what will work, how varying one dimension will affect others, what constraints emerge from production technologies and so on (Molotch, 2003: 29–50). Designers work using empathy for imagined consumers, rather than research into existing consumers, suggest Johansson and Holm (2006). They have intimate knowledge of the product, not the consumer, unlike brand workers.

The mediation of aesthetics in branding and fashion occurs both behind the scenes of design and in the public-facing world of promotion. Magazines and newspapers interpret trends and make judgements on the desirability of specific products and general aesthetics, and events are staged: a PR agent brings a celebrity sportsman to a shopping centre to promote an energy drink; a magazine has a 'get the look' feature that shows you where to buy cheaper equivalents to the clothes worn by a TV presenter at a brand party; a company's promotional offer for Mother's Day flowers appears in your social media stream. In each case a different range of social and technical mediation has contributed to a flow of aesthetic messages intended to subtly influence consumer behaviour, feeling and identity. As we saw in the discussion of co-creation in Chapter 4, 'Beyond paid work, mediation does not go in one direction, but consumers are part of the creation of meaning and value around aesthetic markers like brands and fashion: 'the boundary between culture making, cultural mediation and cultural consumption is increasingly blurred' (Molloy and Larner, 2010: 362). This idea is well illustrated by a consideration of the aesthetic work done by commercial workers.

Aesthetic labour

Many studies suggest that physical attractiveness leads to economic success, that is, that 'aesthetic capital' matters, defined as 'traits of beauty that are perceived as assets capable of yielding privilege, opportunity and wealth' (Anderson et al., 2010: 566). Aesthetic capital may encompass bodily features like symmetrical faces and body size, as well as body work, such as self-presentation through clothing, hairstyle and accessories. Anderson et al. (2010) found that good-looking people were seen as more credible and had better employment opportunities. Aesthetic labour is a term used to explain how workers dress and present their bodies in a way deemed acceptable by their employer.

Workers in many kinds of service jobs are expected to 'look good and sound right' (Warhurst and Nickson, 2001), and in doing so are part of the 'hardware' of the organisation: an embodiment of the organisation's values (Witz et al., 2003), service ethic and brand values. Early research into this concept stressed how 'style' outlets, that is, fashionable restaurants and bars, and designer retail stores, placed particular importance on the aesthetic. 'Aesthetic' in this sense (implicitly) is associated with 'beauty', rather than with our more expansive definition (sensory and perceptual experiences). This limited definition means that the concept of aesthetic labour could not easily be extended to commercial work occupations that were not offering some form of luxury. With an amended understanding of 'aesthetic' to encompass the sensory experiences within markets – that is, the aesthetic economy – we can use the 'aesthetic labour' concept more generally to understand commercial work, as involving both service and the production of atmosphere.

Body work and skills

Accent reduction or control is part of training in customer-facing work (Mirchandani, 2012; Eustace, 2012) and shows how much aesthetic labour (and training in it) goes beyond attention to physical appearance. Critical of a narrow definition of aesthetic labour, Entwistle and Wissinger (2006) develop the concept to emphasise its embodied nature, criticising Witz et al.'s (2003) treatment of the body as a façade upon which a corporate aesthetic is imposed (Entwistle and Wissinger, 2006: 776). In their case study, fashion modelling, the body is the tool of the trade and models produce their appearance, and thereby their working selves. Modelling involves a commitment to body maintenance beyond the working day, not least because fashions in bodies change. This relies on a considerable amount of body work: 'dieting, working-out, tanning, looking after one's skin, shaving, waxing, plucking bodily hair, paying regular trips to the hairdresser, the beauty salon, the gym' (Entwistle and Wissinger, 2006: 785). Note how this list of body work is also a list of consumer goods and services; being a model means being a consumer, and fashion models' bodies are commodified.

The social and technical body work skills involved in aesthetic labour may well be examples of the kinds of soft skills not easily measured by the usual markers of skill (see Chapter 5, 'Skill'). Attention might be paid to how those without work are trained to understand how to do aesthetic labour (Nickson et al., 2012). Seeing aesthetic labour as a dimension of body work makes it clear that gender matters.

Aesthetic labour involves the production of acceptable feminised or masculinised bodies, and relies on assumptions of acceptable gender performances being shared by managers, colleagues and customers, as when cosmetics sellers make up their own faces to show their work skills (Johnston and Sandberg, 2008; see also Wolkowitz, 2006). Ethnicity is also significant, as we'll discuss in the next section.

Being beautiful

Aesthetics and beauty have long been associated. Some commercial work occupations have explicit expectations that workers will be physically attractive, for example, models, some performers and some customer-facing salespeople. We'll consider three distinct examples of this. The first, modelling, shows how race and ethnicity are significant in aesthetic labour. Non-white models in the US are less likely to be recruited to modelling work and to find jobs. Models are treated as 'types', and '[t]ypes are often racially defined without clearly saying so' (Wissinger, 2012: 132). A client asking for an 'exotic' type uses code for a black or Asian model. Black models end up doing more body work on themselves on shoots, styling their own hair or bringing their own makeup when the paid stylists do not have appropriate skills and tools. Wissinger argues that 'the differential pressures felt by black models to be more fabulous, more beautiful, the tallest, the thinnest, and the most Caucasian-looking' (2012: 138) means that doing aesthetic labour involves deep and comprehensive body work, and emotional work. Whilst there is some evidence that more non-white models are now being used in the promotional activities of global brands, as a response to the development of new markets for luxury goods in Asia and elsewhere, casting agencies, clients and other commercial workers tend to share the idea that 'whiteness' is more attractive, so that the successful models in and from China are those with the palest skin and with 'Anglo–European' features (Xu and Feiner, 2007). That is to say, promotional work is conservative and reproduces gendered and racialised ideas of what is attractive.

Our second case looks at musicians as examples of cultural producers and draws attention to the semiotics of different elements of aesthetic labour. Clothing, hair, makeup, voice and instruments are part of the aesthetic labouring of musicians, and combine with stage design, instrument choices and set lists to make up the aural and visual aesthetics of performance. McDonald describes the practice, without using the concept, when discussing the spectacle offered to the audience by the pop boy band Take That:

areas of intimate flesh are offered to the viewer by the various states of underdress displayed by the boys. Additionally, lighting, colour and make-up, each contribute to presenting the flesh of these bodies as a smooth, firm surface (McDonald, 1997: 278).

Not all aesthetic labour in this context involves such an eroticised aesthetic. In other cases, aesthetic labour may signal genre member-ship, and hence is part of claiming a good, authentic performance. For example, country music audiences expect and respond to signifiers of 'country identity', which Peterson describes:

> establishing the right to speak involves knowing all the conventions of making the music…and the nuances of voice and gesture that make their work sound "country… ". Music and performances are vital to the audience, but signifiers are also vital. The boots, the hat, the outfit, a soft rural South-ern accent, as well as the sound and subjects of the songs, all help (Peterson, 1997: 218).

Physical recordings also contain these indicators, coming in designed packaging with graphics and photography to communicate with consumers.

The third example is Pei-Chia Lan's study of cosmetics saleswomen in Taiwan, an instance of a low-paid occupation that expects beauty. As one of the saleswomen Lan interviewed said, 'If you are able to work at a cosmetics counter, you've got to be pretty, right?' (Lan, 2003: 35). Like several of her colleagues, this sales worker enjoyed the feeling that others thought she was attractive. Lan uses the term 'bodily labour' to describe what we have been calling aesthetic labour. Bodily labour has three dimensions, encompassing: a disciplined body that is deferential, and has learned standardised gestures so well that they seem natural; a mirroring body that embodies the employer's specific messages, and wider consumerist ideas about beauty through con-sumption; and a communicating body that is professional and has expertise in the use of cosmetics (2003: 29). Cosmetics saleswomen 'do gender' both as consumers of beauty products and as employees selling such goods. Lan suggests that beauty cultures and concerns over body image are normalised. That this work is situated in branded selling spaces is, for many researchers, significant to how aesthetic labour happens.

Being branded

Pettinger (2004, 2008) argues that aesthetic labour contributes to how service brands are understood by customers. She compares clothing retail chain stores where shop-floor staff wear uniforms to those where they wear current stock, and suggests that this contrast is one manifestation of different brand propositions. Other researchers have taken this further, suggesting that aesthetic labour is a part of 'employee branding', intended to promote the brand to consumers, and to enhance workers' sense of belonging to 'the brand'. In the case of *Land Rover* cars, Harquail (2006) found that 'wearing the brand' was initially restricted to special customer-facing events. As more *Land Rover* branded products were made to be sold to customers, staff were expected to wear them more often. The idea is that 'each morning, the process of getting dressed for work activates the individual's brand schema and the individual's symbolic judgement, as he or she tries to assemble an outfit that expresses the brand' (2006: 168). The brand is here presented as consuming the lifeworld of the worker. We might well question whether the desire of the *Land Rover* brand to capture the minds of its employees like this is a good thing, and whether workers might resist the kind of colonisation implied here.

This kind of corporate branding reflects how marketers see front-of-house commercial workers as part of the aesthetic economy, or the 'brand-scape' of consumer capitalism. The differentiation and meanings that brands try to generate extend beyond the visual and sonic branding of artefacts like logos, adverts and design, and into the embodied form of other workers. A questionnaire study of Sydney clothing stores shows how aesthetic labour varies between outlets with different brand strategies (Hall and van den Broek, 2012). 96.9% of respondents ticked that 'right personality' was important or very important when recruiting staff, and 84.4% said 'right appearance' (78.1% thought previous experience counted most, and 43.8% said qualifications) (n=192). These results suggest appearance matters. Fitting the company image/brand was the most common response to explain why stores had a clothing policy (58.2%), closely followed by 'to display stock' at 57.7% and 'looking neat and presentable' at 46.6% of all with a clothing policy (in both cases, respondents were allowed to tick more than one category) (Hall and van den Broek, 2012: 91). Differentiating into three market segments, value, mass and boutique, the authors found that clothing policies were most common in value fashion and intended predominantly to make sure staff were 'neat and presentable'. In the high-fashion segment, policies were used to promote a specific style of appearance and presentation and to perform the brand. Workers were more likely to be pre-selected for having the right appearance in the high-fashion segment, and received more training (2012: 98–9). Overall, Hall and van den Broek suggest that aesthetic labour is a significant part of the workings of customer-facing retail.

Such workers, and those in comparable occupations, are managed by local managers, corporate guidelines and by customer expectations. Studying cosmetic sales workers in New Zealand, Johnston and Sandberg (2008) suggest that workers are recruited because they understand the store and its customers, that is, they are skilled because they are consumers. The New Zealand study found that sales workers resisted managerial demands for aesthetic labour, for example, by wearing makeup that was either too sombre or too edgy (2008: 402). They might, however, also resist customer attempts to manage them, playing on customers' fear of not belonging in high-end retail by telling them off, or by using their claim to professional expertise to justify being rude, as when young employees took revenge on superior customers by trying to lower their self-esteem by suggesting cosmetic surgery (2008: 410).

Studying the US, Williams and Connell (2010) show how being a consumer in a store can lead to getting a job there, as organisations want workers who understand the brand and its customers. Being an expert customer is also an entry point into other forms of specialist retailing: Sargent (2009) discusses men selling musical instruments and Baker (2012) considers retro retailing. Aesthetic labour relies on workers' consumption and leisure habits; a particular sort of consuming body is needed to produce the working body. The body doing aesthetic labour invests effort and resources to produce an acceptable working body, according to the norms of different occupations and different fields of consumption. Aesthetic labour, through its connection to consumption, means that these working bodies are part of the staging value of the aesthetic economy. Research from employers' perspective indicates why organisations are keen to ensure their norms are reached: Kim et al. (2009) found that customers used employee appearance to judge the store, and their own 'fit' with it.

Commercial workers who produce fashion (as Godart and Mears discussed) or who promote luxury brands (such as those interviewed by Chadha and Husband) may also be concerned by aesthetic labour:

> A female advertising executive in Tokyo told us: 'If you walk down the office, turning up the jacket collars to check the label, I bet 90 percent of the guys in client servicing will be in Armani suits'. How does she know? 'You hear the men talk about it in the office,' she explains (Chadha and Husband, 2006: 55).

Producing consumption involves specific kinds of consumption. Commercial workers' work spaces are also intended to convey messages through aesthetics, intended to boost 'creative' workers' sense of being skilled and to signal to clients and other visitors that this is a special kind of work. These commercial workers do not have their aesthetic labour directly managed, nor is it part of promotional culture. It is, however, often part of professional identity (as Nixon and Crewe, 2004, show in their discussion of when (male) creative workers wear a suit).

Mediating aesthetics

The configuration of service workers' bodies as part of the 'brand-scape', alongside other dimensions of design and spectacle, can be effectively understood using some of the STS ideas discussed in Chapter 2, 'Markets as moral projects', and by considering working bodies as mediating markets in the aesthetic economy. Sommerlund (2008) considers models, fairs, look-books and other elements of fashion as parts of the multiple mediations between production and consumption that produce a fashion brand. Using a new stylist or model in a photoshoot produces a new aesthetic for the look-book: meanings are co-constructed between human and non-human actors, here including models' bodies, fashion clothing and the setting of the shoot. Consumer marketing research does not use STS ideas, but does suggest that aesthetics in consumer culture has an embodied element, that is that aesthetics, fashion and bodies come together to produce the multiple meanings that clothing can have (Venkatesh et al., 2010).

Conclusion

This chapter suggests that the aesthetic economy goes 'all the way down' to the bodies of workers. Aesthetic labour is part of a commercial culture that is aesthetically aware. We see the importance of the aesthetic in how branding works, in the processes of fashion, and in the multifaceted mediations of products that occur in the intersections of commercial promotional activities. Aesthetic labour derives from the markets for both people and things and shows that for commercial workers to effectively sell labour, they must also be particular kinds of consumers. They do this in relation to other aesthetic practices. Lan, whose work on cosmetic saleswomen we discussed, observes the assemblage of the makeup counter, and the promise that the aesthetic economy makes to consumers:

> The shiny mirrors, stylish counters, and the displays of delicate product packages refer to a lifestyle of fashion, wealth, and taste. The super-sized

pictures of models and movie stars hanging over the counters deliver the promises of achieving beauty and preserving youth. This point is well made by a Revlon manager, who was quoted by an informant, "In factories we produce lipstick, in stores we sell hope!" (Lan, 2003: 31)

The attention paid to branding, fashion and aesthetics in consumer culture reflects an orientation to aesthetics and design that extends from art to spectacular consumption and to the consumption of mundane products. In a world with advertising campaigns that promote the advantages of a redesigned toilet roll inner tube, form, function and everyday aesthetics are inseparable. Whilst aesthetic experiences that once seemed astounding do become banal when encountered routinely, or even unpleasant (say, the bright strip lighting in super-markets), but it may be that the ordinary attention to aesthetics is one of the pleasures of consumerism. Welsch worries that 'Where every-thing becomes beautiful, nothing is beautiful anymore; contented excitement leads to indifference; aestheticization breaks into anaes-thetization' (Welsch, 1997: 25). Welsch draws our attention to what might be the negative implications of an obsessive focus on the aes-thetics of consumerism, which nicely foreshadows the discussion in Chapter 8, on the ethics of consumer capitalism.

Research task

Visit a consumption space – a restaurant, café or bar would be ideal. Sit there for a while, noticing what's going on around you. Write a summary of its aesthetic and sensory composition. Consider what part of the aesthetic experience has been managed by commercial workers, and what part is beyond their control. Does it make sense to write about the atmosphere conveyed by this aesthetic experience?

Discussion questions

1. What explains changes in fashion? Consider comparing fash-ions in two different sectors (for example, clothing, personal technology, food, leisure activities).
2. Do you buy fake brands? Why, or why not? What explains the popularity of fake brands?
3. What kinds of inequalities are (re)produced when aesthetic labour is the norm?

Chapter 8

Ethics

In this final chapter we pay explicit attention to the ethical questions that were often implicit in the preceding discussions. Earlier in the book, we discussed commodification: the way dimensions of social life might be brought into the sphere of markets and turned into a commodity to be bought and sold (see Chapter 3, 'Commodities, goods, services and experiences'). We also considered arguments about the extensive reach of capitalism as consumers 'worked' to produce value (Chapter 4, 'What is work?'). The ethical implications of these kinds of arguments are notable: social life is transformed when it is marketised. Questions as to the ethics of contemporary global consumerism are multiple and complex, and clear 'right' answers would be impossible to provide. Instead, the chapter considers on the most significant of these questions. We consider the ethics of commercial work in relation to the moralities of the market, asking how desires are made 'ethical'. We consider the rights and wrongs of consumption, what the limits to consumption should be, and the quality of commercial work for those who do it.

The first section considers how the different theories of markets introduced in Chapter 1 give rise to different understandings of the relation between markets and ethics. It argues for the importance of paying attention to how markets do moral work, through making some behaviours and beliefs possible and acceptable, and others not. It considers specifically environmental sustainability and ethical production initiatives as attempts to ameliorate some of the damages caused by a global capitalist system. The second section assesses the moral order of consumer capitalism, explores ethical arguments against consumerism, and considers the ethics of promotional culture's attempts to seduce consumers. The third section considers debates about the ethics of work in the light of arguments about how the materiality and subjectivity of commercial workers are co-opted into consumer capitalism. It asks about the pleasures and pains of such work for those who do it, and considers whether this work is decent and has dignity.

Capitalism and ethics

Students, scholars, consumers and workers should, I think, question the ethics of the market practices we've discussed in this book. We should be concerned with what's right and just, what's good and bad, what should and shouldn't be. Note that my statement itself is a normative one and advocates for there being a right way to think about the world. This claim has three dimensions: one, that in our everyday lives we should consider the ethics of the practices we engage in and how others understand what's right and wrong; two, that intellectuals should acknowledge and understand the moral and moralising nature of everyday life, as accounts of what is good and what is bad matter to the way that people experience and make sense of the world (Sayer, 2005); and three, that a value-free social science is impossible because the way we create knowledge and discuss it does not provide a true account of a real world, but a partial account of a world that is constantly in the process of being made and remade. In this section, we return to some of the ideas about the ethics of capitalism in general, and explore some of the implications of ethical understandings of capitalism for policies and consumer practices.

The ethics of capitalism

In Chapter 2, 'Theorising capitalism's values', I presented a typology of different accounts of capitalism that, following Hirschman ([1986] 1992) and Fourcade and Healy (2007), distinguished between theories of capitalism on the basis of their moral claims and assumptions about the effects of capitalism and markets. These rival views were: 'doux commerce', the idea that markets have civilising effects; 'destructive markets', where capitalism corrodes social life; 'feeble markets', where culture and social institutions intervene to alter the effects of capitalism; and 'markets as moral projects', the idea that economic discourses and activity create markets. The story of global consumer capitalism that subsequent chapters have told demands that further attention be paid to this question of the ethics of capitalism. In some chapters, ethics have been of obvious relevance (as in the Chapter 3 discussion of consumerism, or the Chapter 4 discussion of working conditions). In others, the ethical is implicit and it is time to make it more visible.

In the market economy, especially in its current formation as a neoliberal project, the logic of commodification has taken hold. From a 'doux commerce' position, via the discipline of economics, consumerism is legitimated if we accept that the free choices of individuals are at the heart of social life, and value the autonomous individual making rational choices – a kind of consumer democracy. Economic theory conceives of (and perhaps idealises) the rational individual who maximises utility, and this conceptualisation can seem to be both politically desirable and a true representation of how individuals act. Discourses of markets are critical in presenting the free individual as a moral actor. The primacy of the individual and the 'democracy' of the market support the idea that the customer is king. This kind of theory can be described as 'methodological individualism', a term that reflects the idea that we can best understand social phenomena by thinking about the actions of individual actors. From this point of view, changes to prices can explain consumer preferences, and the ethically right thing to do is to ensure there are few barriers or restrictions to consumers enacting their preferences. Actors' own moral positions become one variable amongst many that affect their rational consumption decisions. Political actors who subscribe to this view may support the progressive disembedding of markets, to use Polanyi's term, so that social life is expected to be attuned to the demands of capital accumulation.

In contrast, ideas derived from 'destructive markets' theories suggest that the ethical implications of consumer behaviours and consumer markets are far more negative. The writing of one contemporary critic of capitalism, David Harvey (a Marxist thinker, Harvey is firmly in the 'destructive markets' camp), contains strong attacks on contemporary capitalism for the harm it does. Harvey suggests that when we understand markets as operating through mysterious processes by which abstract capitalist firms seek new customers, develop new products and/or seek cheaper production in order to make profit, we miss out a fundamental dimension of how markets are situated in 'the web of life' (Harvey, 2006: 81). That is to say that institutional arrangements matter. Decisions to shift production to a new location, to financialise assets, to create tax incentives or to build new consumer spaces tend to be justified by abstract assessments of what markets are inevitably like, and what capital needs. But Harvey asks us to pay attention to how apparently abstract decisions like these are woven into social life. For example, a new product may be developed through marketing something previously not for sale; such commodification brings more dimensions of social life into the realm of the market. Another example, seeking cheaper production, often means finding cheaper workers to employ: women, children and citizens of poor countries who can be paid lower wages. In both instances, production and consumption do not emerge naturally, but are 'shaped by divisions of labor, the pursuit of product niches and the general evolution of discourses and ideologies that embody precepts of capitalism' (Harvey, 2006: 82). Such a way of organising social and market life seems legitimate to the extent that it effectively captures the feelings, identities and individual subjectivities of those caught up in it, and commercial work serves to engender such engagement. But Harvey questions whether it is right to accept the legitimacy of capitalism so readily.

The ethics of capitalism and regulation

There is a lot at stake in this contrast between competing views of the effects of capitalism. A political system that encourages capital looks different to one that restricts it, and applies different economic and social policies. Whilst in the 'doux commerce' theories the 'motors' of capitalism appear to come from within, they are facilitated by particular governance and institutional arrangements. The political and regulatory framework has an effect on what kinds of practices are promoted (for example, legislation that affects work and wages, or consumer rights, or measures of poverty that make reference to consumption), facilitated (for example, infrastructures that make production and consumption possible, such as transport systems and other public goods) and legitimated (thought to be morally acceptable in political and everyday discourses). Theories about how economic action operates, how decisions are made and how transactions are enacted all inform the policies and practices of global capitalism. There is therefore a political dimension to thinking about the ethics of capitalism. Do policymakers in the kinds of institutions mentioned in Chapter 2, 'Building contemporary global capitalism', think that global corporations need monitoring? Do people vote for politicians who believe that the 'free market' will produce an efficient and reasonable allocation of resources? Are there elements of life that shouldn't be opened to market competition? To put it another way, and drawing on the ideas of 'performativity' introduced in Chapter 2, 'Theorising capitalism's values', asking questions about how markets should work and could work affects how those same markets (and by extension, a system of global capitalism) do work. These are questions that need complex answers.

The ethics of capitalism and consumerism

In the late 20th century, scholars argued that consumption appeared to have eclipsed production as a source of identity and as a source of economic value (Sennett, 1998). Furthermore, flows of communication and financial capital – important parts of a 'weightless' economy – also seemed more powerful than before. In our current era, financial capitalism has an extraordinary reach. 'Financial capitalism' means that value is acquired by trading financial assets and through rents, rather than through production. It has produced an extraordinary group of rentier-consumers, and provides new work for commercial workers helping them to work out 'how to spend it' (Featherstone, 2012). In addition, new groups of consumers from elites and middle class social groups in countries with historically small numbers of consumers have joined the endless quest for satisfaction through marginally differentiated consumption of something new. The expansion of consumerism sits alongside financial capitalism. Comaroff and Comaroff describe the world like this:

> Here is the harsh underside of the culture of neoliberalism. It is a culture that ... re-visions persons not as producers from a particular community, but as consumers in a planetary marketplace: persons as ensembles of identity that owe less to history or society than to organically conceived human qualities (Comaroff and Comaroff, 2001: 13).

Consumerism seems distant from production because of the technologies, especially ICT, that enable economic globalisation and the importance of transnational corporations, including those producing consumer goods, services and experiences, to the global consumerism. For Comaroff and Comaroff, potential class conflicts are negated by the visibility of consumerism. Enormous income inequalities are somewhat occluded by the proliferation of things and targeting of lifestyle to class fractions; it is easy to forget that consumerism is *not* open to so many when it is so visible amongst the wealthy.

The changing lived experience of daily consumption is one reason why we might agree with Harvey that 'it is impossible [...] to sustain the view that capitalism has only a shadowy relation to daily life or that the adjustments and adaptations that occur in daily life are irrelevant for understanding how capital accumulation is working on the global stage' (Harvey, 2006: 80). That is to say that understanding abstract ideas about capitalism is important; understanding the macro-level flows of ideas, things and technologies and the power of institutions matters, so too does ordinary consumption, daily work and the regular achievements that produce social life, including consumption. In addition, we should consider and assess initiatives intended to intervene in the free flow of capital, to 'green' economic activity and to ameliorate working conditions.

The 'sustainability' challenge

Environmentalist thinkers question the sustainability of economic development plans that rely on promoting economic growth, including growth in consumption. Where consumerism promotes what is new and innovative as most desirable and encourages the turnover of goods, or where it promotes services that are energy-intensive, require the development of new land or generate harmful waste (for example, a large golf courses in a region where growing grass requires extensive irrigation and pesticide use), then it has negative impacts on the environment. If new was associated with waste, if green grass seemed aesthetically out of place in arid countries or if the environmental cost of travelling to see an 'unspoilt' landscape was clear, then consumption would be harder to legitimate: its bad effects would be more obvious to see.

One response to the environmentalist challenge has been the promotion of 'green consumption'. There is plenty of dispute over what counts as 'green', 'ethical' and 'sustainable' consumption, what it is reasonable to ask of consumers, and what companies will and will not do to alter their environmental impact. Dauvergne (2008) shows how corporations that make cars only support sustainability when it increases profit. Consumer preferences, such as for 'eco-chic' and other forms of green consumption, are presented as ways in which individuals can ameliorate threats to the environment (see Littler, 2009, for a critique of this). Such forms of consumption may reproduce existing class inequalities (Barendregt and Jaffe, 2014), as eco-chic is expensive. The environmental benefits of some forms of greened consumption, such as shifting from the purchase of goods to the purchase of services and experiences is illusory; golf courses and long plane flights to a holiday in a wilderness are environmentally damaging. We cannot fully understand sustainable consumption by focusing only on consumers. We must also consider the commercial cultures of global capitalism where individual consumption takes place, including the contributions of commercial workers to influencing what kinds of consumption are desirable.

Design work is part of this commercial culture. Green aesthetics indicate environmentally ethical goods. Green products may not be direct replications of 'non-green products', perhaps because they avoid glitter and shine, and use natural materials. Aesthetic markers of green products include minimal packaging, durability and longevity, the history of use (recycling) and the effects of the product (Saito, 2007: 84–95). The materiality of green products and the discourses of greenness are not incidental but are important components to consumer practices. The design and promotion of green consumption affects how consumers encounter green products, as when products with minimal packaging, fast decomposition, multipurpose uses or that will not wear out are sold, or when services are carbon neutralised or intended to promote environmental aims, as with national parks and comparable tourist sites. However, many instances of green promotional activities do not look virtuous when examined in detail. Green marketing, for example, has emerged alongside corporate discourses of sustainability and corporate social responsibility. Todd (2004) compares the strategies of different green brands to assess the extent to which ethical concerns are integrated into production and promotion. She finds instances of 'greenwashing', where promotional activities suggest a green commitment that is not, in fact, very deep. In the direct sales organisation in Brazil studied by Abílio (2012) (see Chapter 4, "Culture' and 'economy' revisited'), commitment to natural products and green ethics sat alongside poor conditions of employment for the sellers, indicating the complexity of making a claim to being an ethical organisation.

Whilst the quest for new consumer products drives capitalism, Molotch suggests not all new things are bad. The 'incessant zeal for innovation means there is also a chance to replace something nefarious with something more benign' (Molotch, 2003: 233). Molotch suggests that new consumer goods are not always bad: new white goods are more energy efficient than older models, even when the embedded energy use is accounted for (the energy used in production) and multipurpose machines require fewer materials. Whether such innovations or shifts add up to sustainability is another matter; the computer is a multipurpose machine, but it's neither green at the point of use (running a Google server farm takes as much energy as powering a medium-size city) nor in terms of the life cycle of each machine. Minimal packaging on food does not stop purchased food being thrown away whilst still edible, and putting motion-sensitive lighting in the toilets of an energy-consuming experience like a water theme park has little overall effect.

Ethical production for ethical consumption

Denim, considered in Chapter 1, contributes to the large global demand for cotton (48% of textile production, according to Skov (2009: 13)). Making cotton clothing requires enormous quantities of water, pesticides and poorly paid cotton workers using polluting chemicals to make the cotton sewable. Cotton becomes denim, and denim becomes jeans; each stage in production relies on a group of poorly paid workers linked by manufacturing subcontractors, as we saw in the discussion of global supply chains (Chapters 1 and 2). We saw how production is distanced from consumption, for example, when mainstream brands subcontract production and focus on creating symbolic meaning through marketing. Indeed, making production work invisible is one of the ways in which consumption seduces us. Shocking instances like the factory fire at Rana Plaza in Bangladesh make visible the impact of production on workers, and it becomes hard to deny the importance of this labour, the often unpleasant conditions under which production workers are employed, and the low wages they get. Women provide the majority of the garment production workforce, and for Dedeoğlu (2010), the twin effects of kinship ties and labour conditions serve to enforce gender inequalities in Turkey. *War on Want, Women Working Worldwide, Who Made Your Clothes?* and other campaigns to make conditions visible are intended to affect employers and consumers. Ethical codes have been implemented to improve working conditions but their success is limited by competitive pressures. Even in Sri Lanka, where compliance with ethical codes is comparatively strong, these codes are constantly under threat, not least because garment workers' voices are not heard (Ruwanpura, 2015). Consumers celebrating their easy access to cheap goods are not always keen to notice the costs of such goods to the health and wellbeing of production workers and may be unwilling to address solutions – including paying more for clothes.

Movements like Fairtrade seek to ameliorate the situation of production workers and ease the consciences of consumers. It is both an outcome of and a response to the current configuration of global consumer capitalism, and it relies on promotional work. The Fairtrade movement aims to achieve decent work and fair prices for commodities for farmers and farm workers. Products that meet the Fairtrade criteria have a logo on them to inform the consumer. Fairtrade is applied to cotton and to some foodstuffs exported from poor agricultural areas, often in Africa and South America. Where the Fairtrade mark is found on some cotton products it indicates the conditions under which cotton was produced, not the garments. The Fairtrade movement is itself often criticised for creating an illusion amongst consumers that the conditions of production are reasonable, that is, for being a marketing label that saves them worrying about the ethics and sustainability of their consumption practices (Wheeler and Glucksmann, 2013). The happy, smiling farmers printed on the packaging reinforce this positive message (Adams and Raisborough, 2010). Critics have suggested that, despite its good intentions, Fairtrade does not always deliver a better and more stable income to those involved. How, then, is it possible to do and be good in consumer capitalism? What kind of power do consumers have to consume well?

The ethics of consumption

The moral status of consumption is complex and disputed even in a consumer culture. Through being counterposed to creative acts of production, consumption has been thought of as wasteful, and this gives it lower moral standing (Campbell, 1987: 19; Firat and Dholakia, 1998). Miller (2001) suggests that academics who moralise about consumption are disengaged from everyday life, and refuse to recognise the complex and sometimes positive effects of consumption. He might agree with Schudson (1999) that

> there is dignity and rationality in people's desire for material goods. We should then seek to reconstruct an understanding of the moral and political value of consumption that we and others can decently live with. (Schudson, 1999: 354)

Isn't it, asks Schudson, good that people can access things that offer meaning? In this section, we explore how we think about multiple dimensions of the moral status of consumers and of consumerism, and might bear in mind that the scholarly knowledge presented here is produced by writers who may hold strong beliefs about the ethics of consumption.

The moral status of consumers

Different social groups, different kinds of consumers, may be judged differently, and the judgements they face are affected by the culture of consumption in which they operate. That is to say that the moral standing of consumption is always related to consumer practices, to the standing of different categories of consumers, and to the discourses that surround consumerism. Shifts in what is felt to be a luxury, decency or necessity involve a shift in the moral stories told about particular things, and in the moral judgements made about those who possess those things. Distinctions between needs and wants, decencies and luxuries, acceptable and excessive modes of consumption, are contingent and changeable. This means there are all kinds of ways in which people may be judged for the kinds of consumption they do. For example, those on low incomes may be condemned for consuming status brands or ready-made meals (Roper and La Niece, 2009); those who consume products that are seen as bad, such as cigarettes, end up managing their emotions against the judgements of others (Hamilton and Hassan, 2010). Some forms of consumption are legitimate at certain times, for example, more indulgent forms of consumption are permissible at festivals like Christmas. The struggles over recognition of legitimate and justifiable consumption reflect other power negotiations, for example of race, class, gender and age. We saw in Chapter 3 how the hedonism and frivolity of consumption were historically associated with women, and this seems quite different from the seriousness and technical competency displayed by, say, men who collected art and artefacts in 19th century France (Auslander, 1996) or antique tractors in contemporary USA (Nusbaumer, 2011).

In addition to considering the moral judgements made about individuals and social groups, it is important to consider the ethics of consumerism and consumer capitalism.

The ethics of a consumer culture

In response to the 'doux commerce' vision of consumer action as rational, scholars of different traditions provide arguments that indicate that the ethical and the emotional are significant forces to be considered when understanding consumers. Those working in consumer behaviour and marketing stress hedonism and pleasure in the formation of consumer subjectivity (Holbrook and Hirschman, 1982, and work as discussed in Chapter 3, 'Consumption and identity').

Others have discussed how the interplay between the governance of consumption and the selfhood of the consumer are significant to understanding how consumers think of the ethics of their own and others' consumption (Barnett et al., 2005; Caruana, 2007). Buying Fairtrade is thereby not a purely a calculative act, but one affected by moral dispositions formed in complex ways.

Historical analysis can give a nice insight into the specificities of ethical consumption. We saw in Chapter 3, 'Explaining consumption', how early department stores were new public spaces for middle-class female shoppers. This produced an array of moral anxieties about the seductive nature of consumer goods, and commentators struggled to understand why middle-class women shoppers would steal an item they could easily afford. The working-class shop-girls were also seen as being at risk from the temptations of consumption. Fears around gender were compounded by fears around class, in particular that shop-girls would develop ideas above their station, especially if they were to consume fashionable goods, start to dress like the customers they served and perhaps even be tempted to steal. Department stores often sought to control these risks by controlling working and living practices, for example directing leisure activities towards self-improvement not hedonism. Here, the effects of consumption are feared and the shop-girl is troubling because of her dual role: as an employee, she should know her place; as a woman encountering stylish and novel new goods, she is to be mistrusted.

Researchers have also considered multiple sources of the moral dispositions and sensibilities that might affect contemporary consumers, including political and religious identities. The figure of the 'citizen-consumer' signals desirable modernity, national belonging and – in the case of telephones in post-socialist Estonia – a new kind of freedom (Keller, 2005). Wealthy Kuwaiti women are careful about their desire for Western brands, playing with the tensions between revealing elegance and sexuality and the fear of seeming spendthrift (Al-Mutawa et al., 2014). In a detailed study of consumerism amongst practising Muslims in Turkey, Izberk-Bilgin indicates the complex ethical accounting done by respondents who reject 'infidel' brands and seek to 'moralise the marketplace' (2012: 664). Three moral discourses closely related to religious teachings were used by respondents discussing their ethical consumption practices: modesty, halal–haram and tyranny. Modesty, a strongly feminised ethics of consumption, refers to avoiding wasting time and energy in frivolous activities. Halal–haram refers to how consumption enables distinctions between good and bad Muslims to be drawn. Those who avoid films made in the West do so to promote Muslim values within their families. Tyranny refers to boycotts of Western brands, especially those associated with the political and economic dominance of Muslim regions by Western powers, as well as avoiding Turkish brands that seem to promote secular rather than Muslim values. Izberg-Bilgin indicates the complexity of moral reasoning about consumption, and reveals the limitations of thinking of consumerism as a practice that can be simply accepted or rejected.

The power of commercial work

Fears and anxieties as to the effects of advertising, marketing and other promotional activities are a further dimension of the ethics of consumption. Promotional work might be blamed for taking advantage of consumers' fears and inadequacies, for seducing consumers into spending more than they can afford, for encouraging waste (of things and of time), and for troubling well-established and clear status differentials. Let us consider the effects of commercial work on consumers, variously seen as passive dupes or active creators.

Persuasive advertising that tries to create feelings to make products desirable is not a new invention. McFall (2004: 178–85) refers to examples of adverts dating from the 1860s that played on feelings: often on fear (of ill-health, or of social shame). The mid-20th-century development of the new sciences of consumer psychology and such like saw promotional industries making explicit contributions to the success of the mass market. These drew on the 'psy' disciplines for insights into what consumers really felt. Like Freud's nephew, Edward Bernays, Ernest Dichter used Freudian psychoanalysis to develop marketing and promotional techniques to encourage consumption. Dichter saw his job as persuading consumers that the guilt they felt need not overwhelm their desire for pleasure, that it is morally acceptable to choose the pleasures of consumption. Not all were persuaded by Dichter's approaches, with British marketers worrying about importing American 'brainwashing' techniques (Schwarzkopf, 2007). Vance Packard, who we discussed in Chapter 3, 'Critics of mass', summarises some of these concerns: 'What does it mean for the national morality to have so many powerfully influential people taking a manipulative attitude toward our society?' (Packard, 1957: 255). Techniques emerging during Packard's time (1950s USA), such as motivational research, the mythical 'dark art' of subliminal marketing and other psychologically informed ways of understanding customers' subconscious desires, wants and frailties, were considered to be manipulative and to encourage 'irrationality' by consumers. For Packard, both the techniques and the irrationality that they produced were bad. In recent times, those who create experiences, especially mediated experiences such as reality TV shows, are the ones who are seen as causing harm. For example, TV production companies are criticised for how they manipulate image content, participants and audiences. Given the dubious ethics of persuasion, what should we think about the ethics of the persuaders who are willing to try out such techniques?

Contemporary critiques tend to avoid the idea that consumers are so readily duped by consumer goods and the actions of marketing, and suggest that consumers are skilled at understanding what advertising tries to do. Consumers are not passive, but active in the way they engage with consumption; they are cultural producers (although see Schroeder, 2002: 166 for an account of consumers' inability to decipher advertising messages). Indeed, we might reasonably doubt claims about both marketing's ability to creatively reconstitute the world, and consumers' abilities to creatively engage in the consumer landscape. Powers (2010) suggests that marketing dupes itself with self-plagiarism, as in the recent fashion for using folk singers in adverts; and we might also have reason to think that consumers do not so much actively create or resist, as be forced to tolerate the sensory experiences of retail spaces (see Bradshaw and Holbrook, 2008).

The new anxieties about marketing are not about glib sales people, but about the invisible processes through which software understands who we are (and the software workers who design the programs that gather, analyse and use such data). Internet marketing and promotional activity raises two particular sets of ethical questions. The first concerns the ease with which the web enables 'always on' promotional activity: pop-up ads and promotional feeds in social media are two obvious examples of promotion that are hard to avoid. Rather than generic advertising that might reach the target audience, digital promotion is personalised, even across devices and platforms (McStay, 2010), because consumer web activity can be captured and analysed. This brings us to a second ethical question raised by internet-based promotion. Web data scraped by search engine algorithms and from social media sites like Facebook and Twitter is then repackaged so as to target advertising to potential customers. Consumer purchase data of the kind generated by loyalty cards uses different tools and techniques, and tends to generate promotional offers targeted at current shoppers. But both these versions of big data raise ethical questions about privacy, consent and knowledge, and about the 'free work' done by consumers. Whilst consumers consent to having purchase data gathered when they sign up for a loyalty scheme and get discounts in return, it is less clear how consumers consent to how their web traces are tracked, and this raises real questions about privacy, given the ease with which internet footprints can be tracked to particular IP addresses. In both cases, consumers do not control how the data is used or to whom it is sold on, and produce an unthinking 'ethical surplus' (Arvidsson, 2009) of value that is gleefully seized by consumer brands.

The final section in this consideration of the ethics of consumerism involves addressing one of the central themes of the book: how commercial culture contributes to global reconfigurations. Kobayashi sees that an advertising and marketing campaign that draws on notions of national belonging 'confirms, reproduces and even reconstructs national consciousness' (2011: 727) for local consumers. Tourism provides a comparable instance: does your local tourist office recommend that visitors to your town go shopping? Mine does. It suggests I visit a nearby megamall or head into the city centre to see well-known brand names. It assumes that the tourist is a consumer, both of the place they're visiting and of the products that shopping centres and leisure complexes can offer. Tourism here becomes a multi-layered encounter with brands. In the case of a place like Macau, a city whose main industry is tourism, especially gambling tourism, 'place branding' and the marketing of the city have a strong effect on what life is like. Although the city is geographically close to China and most permanent residents (and hence service workers) are Chinese, visiting Macau means encountering a Latinised aesthetics that reflects the city's colonial history. The city is neither authentic nor inauthentic: tradition and customs are re-created for an audience of global consumers sensitised to spectacle in casinos, and in apparently public spaces that are privately managed (often by US-owned global gambling corporations) (Ho, 2013). Consumer capitalism in Macau involves presenting the place as a spectacle, drawing on a weird version of history. Should the people of Macau mind? Is this kind of commodification acceptable? In Dubai there are some enormous shopping malls; one has the world's largest *Starbucks,* others are themed to be like an Italian street market or souq (Elsheshtawy, 2008). The environmental impact of these is one ethical question; their reconfiguration of authenticity is another. Elsheshtawy (2008) raises a further ethical question: where do poor consumers go to engage in everyday consumption as Dubai promotes exclusivity and the global consumer? Tourists are taken on bus tours to see places that specialise in fakes; there are cafés and restaurants for the migrant workers, but the spectacle of the city and its brand involves hiding these ordinary practices. As in the case of the Epcot theme park in Florida (Houston and Meamber, 2011), the aesthetic configuration of tourist spaces produces a sanitised, fake, proxy version of the past or the present.

Ethics and work

There are several kinds of ethical questions that arise when considering the work that produces consumption. In Chapter 2, we saw that Weber's account of economic change suggested that explicit acceptance of the virtues of hard work were derived from religiously inspired moral ideas about being good, and contributed to economic growth. The moral virtue of hard and productive work can be seen in many historical and contemporary instances, from the idealisation of the labouring man in communist society to contemporary, if dubious, claims that use 'hard work' as a justification for paying extraordinarily high bonuses to city workers. Such cultural valorisation stands in contrast to how unpaid work, non-market work and consumption are seen, and so commercial workers who produce consumption may be readily thought of as engaging in frivolous and wasteful work. The moral status of hard work extends into the domain of consumption. Ulver-Sneistrup et al. (2011) suggest that an ethics of craft work permeates claims to moral consumption; bad brands are those produced and consumed without craft.

Work has a significant effect on workers' life chances, health, wellbeing and everyday experience. It is a central source of personal identity, and of citizenship and rights. The conditions that workers face vary greatly between occupations, industries and geographical locations, as hinted at in earlier discussions of the limits of consumerist campaigns such as Fairtrade to alleviate the poor conditions faced by production workers. Several different concepts have been used to think about the ethics of work, by para-state institutions, by academics and by political activists. In this section, we will consider the ethics of work in relation to debates on work identity, decent work, dignity and fit, and good and bad jobs.

Work identity

Asking people what work they do is in many places seen as a good starting point for conversation because people take a great deal of their sense of self, their identity, from the work that they do. Some sociologists have suggested that changes to the organisation of work in post-industrial society mean that work is now a less significant source of identity and belonging. We discussed these ideas in the Chapter 3 exploration of modernity (Bauman, 2000; Ransome, 2005). Whereas workers in industrial society may acquire a strong sense of work identity, embedded in communities where skills were recognised and where wages were sufficient to purchase new consumer goods, such strength of feeling has now been lost. The flexibilisation of work time and place, shifts from manufacturing to service, technological shifts to ICT and the flattening of organisational hierarchies combine to alter how work can and does provide belonging. Catherine Casey summarises the idea of the 'end of work identity':

> The industrial legacy of the centrality of production and work in social and self formation hovers precipitously with the post-industrial condition in which work is declining in social primacy. Social meaning and solidarity must, eventually, be found elsewhere (Casey, 1995: 2).

Note that Casey's (2012) recent work about the all-encompassing power of markets (see Chapter 5) suggests that she thinks differently now about the declining salience of work, although her observation about the loss of solidarity may still hold. Instead of work identity, lifestyle and consumer identities matter for Bauman and Ransome. For others, cultures of ethnicity, gender and sexuality, religion and such like are more significant sources of identity. Such claims go against some of the other ideas we have discussed about the all-consuming nature of work.

Work identity may be a significant part of feeling included in a society, community or other group, and we may feel that the work that we do both reflects and shapes the kind of person we are. He's sharp, assertive and smooth: he works in sales. She's empathetic and wants to help: she's a life coach. In these examples it's clear that work identity is not abstract, but draws on understandings of gender. Work identity is also marked by differences of ethnicity, class, sexuality and disability. In Chapters 6 and 7, we saw how people were recruited because their personalities and preferences were seen to suit the work that they did, and we saw that being a certain kind of consumer contributed to understanding them as a worker. People get important rewards from work, both pay and a sense of identity. Indeed, whilst sometimes work is assumed to be experienced as drudgery and not pleasurable, such assumptions deny workers' own accounts of their working lives. In the case of commercial work, where the boundaries between production and consumption are most blurred, the relationship between work identity and other sources of identity may be different. Here, knowledge about consumption, fashion and aesthetics, understandings of and feelings about consumers and consumption are integral to doing work and to identification with a career or occupation, or even with a brand: with a way of working that celebrates the search for the new.

Decent work

'Decent work' is the central principle of the ILO's (International Labour Organization) global agenda to improve paid work. It refers to

> opportunities for work that is productive and delivers a fair income, security in the workplace and social protection for families, better prospects for personal development and social integration, freedom for people to express their concerns, organize and participate in the decisions that affect their lives and equality of opportunity and treatment for all women and men. (http://www.ilo.org/global/topics/decent-work/lang--en/index.htm., accessed 4.2.15)

The agenda reflects the important idea that working conditions affect a person's chances for a decent life and is deliberately simple so as to be applicable to different contexts: to contribute to campaigns against conditions of work in garment factories in Morocco (Barrientos et al., 2011) or against casual and precarious work in South Africa (Webster et al., 2008). It is also possible to use the agenda to compare the quality of work in different sectors, regions and countries by measuring various indicators of the central tenets of decent work: the level of employment, social protection, working rights and dialogue (Ghai, 2003). There is great variation, some of it a result of how developed the economy is, some a result of political history – as when countries transitioning from socialism have far higher rates of union membership than otherwise similar places. This macro-level picture thus shows how complex and multiple are the possible indicators of 'decent work', and how the meaning of decent work differs between countries. There are differences between sectors, too. What kinds of dimensions might be used to assess the decency of commercial work?

A first reading may suggest that commercial workers already have the benefits of decent work: some have incomes that are more than fair; their work is fulfilling; their experiences are certainly better in comparison to those who work to produce the goods for sale in consumer capitalism. However, we have earlier discussed the impact of flexibilisation and contemporary work norms on commercial workers. For example, we saw in Chapter 5 that many researchers have found flexibilisation to be damaging to workers. I will use these arguments to suggest that there are several reasons to challenge the idea that commercial work is decent work: the excess of demands for personal development as workers must stay skilled and employable; the difficulties of separating work and non-work time and space; the lack of security, including how hard it is to express concerns about insecurity or overwork because of the competitiveness of the sectors and the importance of networks and reputation; and the way selfhood is co-opted into work through expectations that workers will support corporate and commercial culture.

We saw in Chapters 4 and 5 that the flexibilisation of labour markets makes work insecure and provides an impetus to lowering wages. It affects skills and 'employability'. As Casey says, 'many of the new jobs that have appeared in the highly competitive, information and knowledge-intensive economy and deregulated labour markets are found in an expanded lower-skilled, poorly paid and poorly protected service sector' (Casey, 2012: 117). This low-status work is easily disparaged when, as we saw in Chapter 4, knowledge work and creative work are valorised as 'good' kinds of work (Casey, 2012: 148). The flexibilisation of production and the labour market places new kinds of demands on workers, as it makes them responsible for finding and keeping work. Workers must gain new skills as they move from job to job and task to task. Work in the era of flexibility is intensified and demands new modes of self-regulation, such as workers accepting that they are expected to work long hours, identify with their employers and commit to a team. The justification for intensified work is often that it is satisfying to commit so thoroughly, a view that reflects the all-consuming nature of work: team bonding sessions, 'dress down Friday' and other consumerist managerial styles are intended to generate a stronger sense of belonging. Such intensification creates vulnerability for workers who cannot keep up, perhaps because they have care commitments at home. The collapse of 'life' into work through long working hours at physically, intellectually or emotionally draining jobs may have a bad effect on physical and mental health. As we saw in Chapter 5, 'Knowledge work', such challenges are worsened when a great deal of effort has to go into finding new contracts and maintaining networks.

Dignity

Personal development and equality of opportunity are dimensions of the decent work agenda that have been considered using the lens of 'dignity'. Attacks on dignity through bullying and harassment by colleagues and managers are obvious dimensions to thinking about dignity at work. Autonomy and self-reliance, being taken seriously, being recognised and trusted and being able to resist attacks on dignity in the context of the particular vulnerabilities of specific working relations (Sayer, 2007) are also important features for equality, dignity and respect in the workplace.

Michele Lamont (2000) shows how people's commitment to work and life and their self-identity as good workers are part of their moral landscape. For the workers she studied, holding to moral standards is a way of maintaining dignity, but also diminishes those who are different to them. Workers draw on class and racial differences to lay claim to their own moral status. Lamont's arguments suggest that feeling that you and those like you are good provides a resource for gaining and preserving dignity in the face of the denigrations of others. Dignity is claimed in relation to others (who may not be willing to grant us respect, perhaps because of their prejudices about our gender, class, ethnicity and age). Markers of social difference matter in this, but so do the hierarchies of work and employment relations, such as the demands of management. In the case of commercial work, there are multiple sources of pressure and threat to dignity, from customers and managers, from clients and competitors, which can make the quest for dignity fragile and unstable. Biggart, in her study of direct sales, shows that one response to this challenge is to form an occupational community that starts from the premise that the work they do is good:

> Committed distributors see their work as a superior way of life that embraces political values, social relations, and religious beliefs. It gives them not a job, but a worldview, a community of like-minded others, and a self-concept. (Biggart, 1989: 9)

Other writers, especially from the labour process tradition, show that resistance can maintain dignity at work (Hodson, 2001), as when resistance to the compulsions of management and the demands of customers provides workers with conscious awareness of what the hierarchies of work do. Where managerial control is tight, then frustrated workers can submit or rebel; where control is looser, then the shifting sands of dignity may be more capturable.

One source of dignity is the capacity to do work that seems important, and to do it well. Muirhead (2004) writes about this by considering 'fit' between worker and work. Does the worker do the job well and do they thrive by doing it? I suggest adding a third dimension: doing a job that seems socially useful. Muirhead tries to avoid implying that people have a natural and inevitable 'fit' in lower-status work, recognising that this is an unpleasant idea (and goes against decency and dignity). But he does suggest that some of the problems with our experience of work can be addressed by thinking about the multiple dimensions of fit. Fit with work can provide both internal goods (the sense of doing something that matters to you and doing it well) and external goods (recognition). To put it another way, a worker who understands what their work does, senses that it has social value and that they are suited for it, has work that is suited to them. They can be proud of their work. 'Fit' for a commercial worker involves accepting, even celebrating, the pleasures of consumerism, not its negatives. Some writers suggest that participation in even low-paid, low-status commercial work can offer satisfaction because it involves offering gifts to others that can be counted as 'internal goods'. Others might say that there are particular risks to dignity of doing this, given the tension, insincerity and insults that can make up a service relationship that involves subservience of worker to customer (Warren, 2005). Commercial workers are supposed to instrumentalise the multiple dimensions of their life into work: the brand executive gets an idea on holiday, and the sales worker spends his wages on new season clothes he'll wear at work. Fit for commercial workers is not just about doing important work well, but about consuming the right things, relating to others with suitable deference or confidence and so on. One of the limitations of using the idea of 'fit' is that it reduces people to their current work experiences and over-defines them through their work. It may be that Hesmondhalgh and Baker's (2010) idea of 'self-realisation', that is, the ability to develop talents and fulfil potential, is a rather less determining concept than 'fit'.

Good and bad jobs

This brings us nicely to a consideration of what in the content of the job makes it seem good or bad. What are the ethics of contemporary work that requires self-governance and self-management, working to stay employable, being 'always on' and ready to work, and that collapses the boundaries between work and leisure, work and home and production and consumption? Creative work is assumed to be good work, and Dean and Jones (2003) suggest that some kinds of creative work (like acting) are considered too pleasurable to be work! Being a 'creative worker' seems positive, particularly when compared to routine, repetitive, tightly managed and controlled work. Hesmondhalgh and Baker (2010) suggest that understanding the good and bad of creative work means exploring self-realisation, and the conditions of employment (both mentioned above), autonomy and outcomes. Autonomy can refer both to deciding what task to do next, and to the creative freedom to have and develop a novel idea; such a feature of good work may be shared with other knowledge workers (but not all service workers). In their empirical work with culture workers, they also found that making a 'good product' is an important dimension of good work (and is analogous in some respects with the idea of inter-active service workers feeling pleased when their work is acknowl-edged by consumers). Making a good product can be a source of pride and pleasure. This kind of idea, that the content of the work matters, is also present in discussions of the benefits of craft labour, thought to be fulfilling because the worker is part of the entire production process. Good craft work includes meeting an aesthetic standard (Becker, 1978: 864–5), with a demonstrable use of skill and judgement that calibrates an activity to the particular needs of what is being worked on at the moment. Care and commitment – and even passion – are affective components to the work, reflecting a requirement that the worker believe in what they're doing and in the value of doing a job well. In Hesmondhalgh and Baker's account, though, workers can experience the rewards of having worked on a good product that exceeds what they could have done alone as a craft worker. Both the outcome and the process can matter; a worthwhile cultural product and a good experience of collective working contribute to good work. And of course work can have both good and bad features. Interactive service work, for example, rarely offers workers creative autonomy but can invoke feelings of doing something good for others. Such benefits may not counterbalance the downsides of poor pay and treat-ment, but their presence points to the complexity of what counts as good and bad work.

Bad jobs are characterised not only by their lower status and poor pay and conditions, but also by the content of the work. The occupa-tions under discussion in this book have varied between routine, repetitive and sometimes dirty ones and those where the working day may comprise stimulating, interesting, autonomous tasks. Routine per se is not a reason to consider something as a bad job, unless there is nothing but repetitive action. Interactive service workers in consumer capitalism do routine work, and also deal with irregular and unpredict-able elements generated through interactions with customers. The unpredictable elements of these jobs are sometimes the reasons why service workers say they like their job. Certainly skilled work, though sometimes vulnerable to being deskilled, is more likely to count as a good job because it engages workers as knowing, thinking, feeling bodies. Creative responses to events, craft-style coordination of mind/body in the everyday doing of work, and the expectation of thoughtfulness are some markers of skilled work, and they contribute to the experience of work as positive.

What are the prospects for good work, dignity and identity in the commercial work that produces global consumer capitalism? The ambivalent moral status of consumption spills over into the moral standing of commercial work. It goes against the grain to see the work that produces consumption as laudable because of consumption's association with waste, luxury and hedonism.

Conclusion

This chapter has considered some of the complex moral questions raised by exploring the intersections of work and consumption in global consumer capitalism. The extensive scholarly and popular literature on the morality of consumption reflects longstanding fear of the seductive blandishments of consumer goods. When reading such critiques, it's sometimes hard to see what kind of consumption is acceptable, or what kind of life would be possible if we were to avoid consuming badly. But it is right to continually ask questions about the effects of mundane and spectacular practices. Understanding the ethics of consumption involves thinking through the social, cultural and economic context for consumption. We have framed this throughout as global consumer capitalism, which relies for its continued existence on successfully capturing the feelings, sensibilities, understandings and imaginations of those within it: consumers and also those workers who contribute to its effective maintenance. Commercial workers are in some way ethically committed to the maintenance of this way of living, and the settings that enable this are connected to the modes of economic organisation that influence their own experiences of paid work; the flexibility of their labour and of the productive work they do relies on and affects the consumer cultures they work with. The challenge in the case of commercial work is to think through whether (and why) this work does or does not seem important. On the one hand, consumer culture is a source of pleasure and self-actualisation, as well as an inescapable and ordinary part of life. On the other hand, as consumers we may be seduced into buying things that we don't need, or that are damaging to the environment or to the production workers.

Research task

Identify a consumer campaign you are interested in (e.g. Fairtrade, anti-consumerism, rights for production workers, greening consumption). Investigate the aims of the campaign and its reception by media and the relevant industries. Assess what counts as 'success' for this campaign, and identify what might support or interfere with the chances for success.

Discussion questions

1. Is 'ethical capitalism' possible? What would it look like? What would need to change?
2. What kinds of ethical judgements do you make about other consumers? What kinds of judgements have others made about you? Why is consumption such a significant object of ethical concern?
3. How would you assess whether commercial work was good or bad? Compare different occupations: are they 'decent' forms of work?

Chapter 9

Taking Seriously the Production of Consumption

In this book, I have taken consumer culture seriously as a structuring force, as a creator of subjectivities and as a manufacturer of bodies. I have considered how consumerism mediates between working and consuming bodies, and how the worlds of goods and services are made knowable, desirable and accessible through the activities of commercial work.

Reflections on the project

Commercial work is orientated towards the production of spectacular and ordinary consumption – whether by working out sales strategies, designing brands and advertising campaigns, making purchase possible or providing a service. It generates value in markets, which we have seen conceptualised as sign, symbolic and staging value. It makes consumption happen, whether by generating desire and enchantment, building brand values, or making consumption meaningful and possible. The umbrella term 'commercial work' is a device to think with, to help understand what relevant occupations have in common and what they contribute to global consumer capitalism. As do traditional categories of service or manufacturing, and concepts like 'culture work', 'cultural intermediary' and 'interactive service work', the phrase 'commercial work' draws attention to some features of this work and downplays others. It makes us notice the interconnections between forms of work that produce consumption, how they work on symbolic meanings and generate economic value. But it makes it harder to notice the different ways in which commercial work occupations are organised and the status that they have, and we must be wary of generalising about working conditions (although in the discussions of flexibility I have not avoided doing this). It is more reasonable to generalise about the way knowledge of and commitment to consumerism underpin this kind of work.

I have addressed the mismatch between studies of work and studies of consumption to consider the production of consumption. This means taking seriously, and making explicit, how this work relates to both labour markets and markets for goods, services and experiences, that is, in relation to commercial cultures. In this book, I used three dimensions of consumer capitalism to do this. I drew, on theories of emotion and affect which acknowledge the corporeal and cognitive as integrated, and on accounts of the aesthetics of bodies, of design and of how bodies produce aesthetics. I considered also what bodies do at work, and how bodies craft and create products and qualify value. We have seen also that in the context of work and consumption, ordinary moralising matters for how it affects our relations with others (who we may deem lazy or devious, wasteful or frivolous, or treat as subservient to us), for how it affects our responses to and journeys through consumer capitalism, and for what kinds of consumption are considered legitimate. We can see these elements interweave in the case of branded sportswear. *Nike,* for example, does not produce the highly engineered trainers, or high-tech running kit that it sells: its designers craft the products and the aesthetics of its own selling spaces; its creatives produce marketing, such as the tagline 'Just Do It', to generate feelings in potential consumers. Production is subcontracted, and distant supply chains may generate 'threats' to the *Nike* brand when the poor working conditions and low pay common to such ways of organising production are brought to public attention. It is a testament to the emotional and aesthetic appeal of the brand that many customers may be aware of the poor working conditions, but find the trainers themselves irresistible.

The 'commercial work' approach means we pay less attention to specific occupations, and less attention to the content of work per se than is usually the case in studies of work. In particular, this book is unusual in deliberately fuzzing the boundaries between high- and low-status commercial occupations. In my concept of commercial work, how an occupation relates to consumer markets determines its inclusion. This unusual approach provides a good understanding of the contribution of different forms of commercial work to global consumer capitalism, and an understanding of how consumption identities and practices matter to doing work and to work identity. It gives us an understanding of work that is grounded in its relationship to and effect on consumer capitalism. It prevents us falling into the trap of seeing work only as oppressive and consumption only as liberating and facilitating of self-identities and means we can understand, for example, the implications for a jobseeker whose consumer practices mark them as the 'wrong' class for some employers. It responds to Harvey's (2005) call for a holistic social science that synthesises diverse aspects of global capitalism, rather than one that explores disconnected hypotheses, and means we can see how, in David Harvey's words, 'the glittering frustrations of commodity culture' matter to the formation of subjectivities as much as the effects of 'the fiery crucible of the labor process' (Harvey, 2000: 113).

Five questions answered

In Chapter 1, I introduced the themes of the book by asking five questions. How might we answer these questions? Question 1, *Do you have a favourite pair of jeans?* asked about individual preferences as a way to begin to unpack the way consumerism speaks to us as individuals and asks us to think of ourselves in that way, and yet sells to us as types and as group members. Consumer culture emerged to celebrate and encourage desire for the 'world of goods' (and services) to provide a source of meaning. Within the abundant, competitive and uncompetitive markets for stuff, the sorcery of capitalism involves inviting us to move through life by possessing and using the products of the system to define ourselves. This takes mundane and spectacular forms, and sees us calculating and feeling. Individual preferences matter, as in the case of a favourite pair of jeans. But we can't understand much about consumerism if we stick at this individual level.

Question 2, *Are your jeans fashionable?* introduces one of the key ways in which individual consumption is marked and affected by group membership. Being fashionable involves an emotional and aesthetic engagement in consumer culture. It relates explicitly to others, both to other consumers (and their ideas about being fashionable and their judgements of us as dowdy or cool) and to the cultural intermediary occupations that contribute to defining and assessing fashion. Commercial work can shape what is fashionable, but it is also shaped by it. For example, 'street style' is co-opted by mainstream marketing as a means of generating symbolic values. Answering this second question means locating the individual within the flows of goods, knowledge and meanings that make up social life in a capitalist society.

Question 3, *Are your jeans branded?* takes us much further into the intricacies of the production of consumption. So what if your jeans (or bananas) are branded? What explains why brands matter? Brands are at the heart of contemporary global consumer capitalism, with economic value attached to their symbolic attributes. Brand workers consider the feelings and associations attached to sensory experiences when designing a brand; they try to indicate that a brand has worth because it connotes 'good value', or 'coolness', or 'reliability'. As cynical critics or as anti-consumerists, we could easily say that we are not affected by brands' attempts to seduce us; as consumers, though, we may well be persuaded that *Apple* computers are better than the alternative.

Question 4 asked *Why did you buy your jeans?* and focuses on the processes that consumers navigate in the course of everyday provisioning. When products are intended to ameliorate our insecurities, or to make us feel concerned that in some way, we are not quite right as we are (say, when skin-whitening products are marketed to women with darker skins), we see commercial work both drawing on existing understandings of gender and ethnicity, and contributing to the persistence of these inequalities. When data about consumer spending collected by loyalty cards is used to target the mix of cheaper 'basic' range and more expensive 'elite' range of comparable products on offer in a particular supermarket, then the possibilities of consumer choice are constrained. There are multiple ways in which commercial work affects how, what and why we consume. Promotional culture operates with typologies, abstractions and generalisations about 'the customer'. It seeks to imagine them and their life, and it seeks to know them as a type, as when lifestyle groups are identified, mapped and targeted. In so doing, it alters the fabric of consumption and hence of everyday life. It is predatory as it seeks new markets.

Question 5, *Where did your jeans come from?* was the first question we considered in Chapter 2, when we explored the chains and networks of production. We saw that contemporary capitalism relies on a complex division of labour and on ICT's ability to transmit information readily. In this book we have not considered the production of material goods in detail, but in Chapters 2 and 8, we saw how important this is to contemporary consumption. Capitalism's global reach affects how goods are made, how people work, and how they are persuaded to buy. A brand that keeps its distance from the production of the goods that carry its logo and a marketing team that tries to produce a global campaign are two sides of global contemporary capitalism.

These five questions are all linked. They are linked directly, as when the apparent ethical production of a good makes it attractive to some

consumers, and when cheaply produced 'fast fashion', or earlier decisions about what to grow, means others consumers can afford a new
pair of jeans, or choose bunches of gerberas rather than roses for
Mother's Day. Then individual and group preferences and how commerce is organised are interwoven. Doing commercial work means
breaking down the distinction between production and consumption
as separate spheres. It involves exploring the devices, spaces and activities that gather and produce knowledge about consumers and consumerism to 'reinject' (Moulier Boutang, 2012: 323) into production.
The skills needed to do this are multiple and embodied, and contingent both on learning as a worker and on being sensitive to what it is
to be a consumer. In many instances, from how the participation of
customers in sales and services is designed, to the extension of brand
identity into peripheral spaces, emotion and aesthetics are instrumen-
talised to produce market transactions. Emotion is comprehensively
worked on, operationalised, commodified and produced through consumerism. The commercial sphere is a significant site where emotion
draws 'the links between the body and the social world' (Lyon and
Barbalet, 1994: 48). Even in apparently depersonalised modes of consumption, emotion and aesthetics are critical to market practices.
Online consumption substitutes the labour of a paid checkout worker
for that of a paying customer, as when the customer fills in the payment
form. Repeat custom relies on a working technical system that doesn't
make you feel stupid, and design and branding work that does what
face-to-face encounters in stores are supposed to do: encourage loyalty
and ease your way.

Working in consumer capitalism

The production of consumption relies on the actions of specific kinds
of workers. Understanding the relationships between work and consumption demands a broad vision of what work is, one that does not
reduce work to factors that are mostly associated with employment –
like work identity and management practices and norms – and that
thereby seem to have no bearing on, nor to be affected by, the rest of
an individual's social life. Reimagining work as embedded in social
lives means that workers are not disconnected from consumer cultures
and patterns of consumption, even when doing work.

   A characteristic of doing commercial work is that it relies on participation in consumer capitalism. Consumption for work done outside
of work time is essential to labour market success, to being a good

employee and being able to mediate the consumption of strangers. Tools of the trade are necessary for many forms of work, and consumption of high-end equipment is one of the indicators of professional competency. Is commercial work different? Yes, in the sense that these workers' consumption is inescapably collapsed into their multiple commitments to consumer capitalism. As Williams and Connell say, 'From management's perspective, workers are ideally perceived as "brand representatives", chosen to personify the products on display; they are *not* supposed to look like or sound like low-wage workers struggling to make a living' (2010: 368). Sadly, this compulsion to consume in order to work sits uncomfortably alongside the lack of certainty and security in work itself (Comaroff and Comaroff, 2001: 8).

Commercial work is constituted as flexible work done by adaptable and emotionally competent employees who acquiesce to the implicit expectations to be measured, professional and effective. Work which leaves no time to do anything other than the work is troublesome, to say nothing of work that also demands that consumption be made useful to it. Gabriel sees the 'glass cage of work and glass palace of consumption' as sharing an expectation that work and consumption rely on the manipulation of images and signs, aesthetic and emotional displays (2005: 23). Working and consuming subjectivities are captured by consumer capitalism and, in the absence of (class) solidarity, the main solution is to keep consuming that which might make you a better employee in some future occupation: a training course, a mindfulness app, a haircut to give you confidence. It's hard to tell when you're producing and when you're consuming, and workers are commodified in the labour market and commodified through our consumption. The central theme in *Work, Consumption and Capitalism* is how work makes consumption, and the sad ending of the story is that markets seem inescapable.

Reflection questions

1. Return to the piece of reflective writing you did after Chapter 1. Consider how you would develop one of your answers in the light of your subsequent learning and reflection.
2. Is consumerism a global phenomenon? How does it differ between places? Does global capitalism produce homogeneity?

Bibliography

Abelson, E. S. (1989) *When Ladies Go A-Thieving: Middle-Class Shoplifters in the Victorian Department Store.* New York: Oxford University Press.

Abílio, L. C. (2012) 'Making Up Exploitation: Direct Selling, Cosmetics and Forms of Precarious Labour in Modern Brazil.' *International Journal of Management Concepts and Philosophy* 6(1), 59–70.

Abu-Lughod, A. and Lutz, C. A. (eds.) (1990) *Language and the Politics of Emotion.* Cambridge: Cambridge University Press.

Adams, M. and Raisborough, J. (2010). 'Making a Difference: Ethical Consumption and the Everyday.' *The British Journal of Sociology* 61(2), 256–74.

Addis, M. and Holbrook, M. B. (2001). 'On the Conceptual Link Between Mass Customisation and Experiential Consumption: An Explosion of Subjectivity.' *Journal of Consumer Behaviour* 1(1), 50–66.

Adkins, L. and Lury C. (1999) 'The Labour of Identity: Performing Identities, Performing Economies.' *Economy and Society* 28(4), 598–614.

Adorno, T. W. (1991 [1938]) 'On the Fetish Character in Music and the Regression of Listening.' In *The Culture Industry: Selected Essays on Mass Culture.* Edited and with an introduction by J. M. Bernstein. London and New York: Routledge.

Ahmad, A. (2013) *New Age Globalization: Meaning and Metaphors.* Basingstoke: Palgrave Macmillan.

Alexander, D. (1970) *Retailing in England during the Industrial Revolution.* London: Athlone Press.

Allen, J. and du Gay, P. (1994) 'Industry and the Rest: The Economic Identity of Services.' *Work, Employment and Society* 8(2), 255–71.

Al-Mutawa, F. S., Elliott, R., and Nuttall, P. (2014) 'Foreign Brands in Local Cultures: A Socio-Cultural Perspective of Postmodern Brandscapes.' *Journal of Consumer Behaviour* 14(2), 137–44.

Alozie, E. (2009) *Marketing in Developing Countries: Nigerian Advertising in a Global and Technological Economy.* New York: Routledge.

Alvesson, M. (2004) *Knowledge Work and Knowledge Intensive Firms.* Oxford: Oxford University Press.

Anderson, T. L., Grunert, C., Katz, A., and Lovascio, S. (2010). 'Aesthetic Capital: A Research Review on Beauty Perks and Penalties.' *Sociology Compass* 4(8), 564–75.

Appadurai, A. (1986) 'Introduction: Commodities and the Politics of Value.' In Appadurai, A. (ed.), *The Social Life of Things: Commodities in Cultural Perspective.* Cambridge: Cambridge University Press.

Araujo, L. (2007) 'Markets, Market-Making and Marketing.' *Marketing Theory* 7(3), 211–26.

Ariely, D. (2009) *Predictably Irrational: The Hidden Forces That Shape Our Decisions.* New York: Harper/Harper Collins.

Aronczyk, M. and Powers, D. (2010) 'Introduction: Blowing Up the Brand'. In Aronczyk, M. and Powers, D. (eds.), *Blowing Up the Brand. Critical Perspectives on Promotional Culture.* New York: Peter Laing Publishing.

Aronczyk, M. (2008) 'Living the Brand: Nationality, Globality and the Identity Strategies of Nation Branding Consultants'. *International Journal of Communication* 2(1), 41–65.

Arrighi, G. (1996) 'The Rise of East Asia: World Systemic and Regional Aspects'. *International Journal of Sociology and Social Policy* 16(7/8), 6–44.

Arvidsson, A. (2005) 'Brands: A Critical Perspective'. *Journal of Consumer Culture* 5(2), 235–58.

Arvidsson, A. (2009) 'The Ethical Economy: Towards a Post-Capitalist Theory of Value'. *Capital and Class* 33(1), 13–29.

Arvidsson, A. (2011) 'General Sentiment: How Value and Affect Converge in the Information Economy'. *The Sociological Review* 59(S2), 39–59.

Askegaard, S. (2006) 'Brands as a Global Ideoscape'. In Schroeder, J. and Salzer-Mörling, M. (eds.), *Brand Culture.* New York: Routledge, 91–102.

Aspers, P. (2009) 'Using Design for Upgrading in the Fashion Industry'. *Journal of Economic Geography* 10(2), 189–207.

Athique, A. and Hill, D. (2010) *The Multiplex in India: A Cultural Economy of Urban Leisure.* London: Routledge Contemporary South Asia Series.

Atkinson, J. (1984) *Flexibility, Uncertainty and Manpower Management*, IMS Report No. 89. Brighton: Institute of Manpower Studies.

Atkinson, J. and Meager, N. (1986) *Changing Working Patterns: How Companies Achieve Flexibility to Meet New Needs.* London: Institute of Manpower Studies, National Economic Development Office.

Auslander, L. (1996) 'The Gendering of Consumer Practices in Nineteenth Century France'. In de Grazia, V. and Furlough, E. (eds.), *The Sex of Things: Gender and Consumption in Historical Perspective.* Los Angeles, CA and London: University of California Press.

Azimont, F. and Araujo, L. (2007) 'Category Reviews as Market-Shaping Events'. *Industrial Marketing Management*, 36(7), 849–60.

Bailey, A. R., Shaw, G., Alexander, A., and Nell, D. (2010) 'Consumer Behaviour and the Life Course: Shopper Reactions to Self Service Grocery Shops and Supermarkets in England c.1947–1975'. *Environment and Planning A* 42, 1496–512.

Baker, S. E. (2012) 'Retailing Retro: Class, Cultural Capital and the Material Practices of the (Re)Valuation of Style'. *European Journal of Cultural Studies* 15(5), 621–41.

Banet-Weiser, S. (2012) *Authentic TM: The Politics of Ambivalence in a Brand Culture.* New York: New York University Press.

Banet-Weiser, S. and Sturken, M. (2010) 'The Politics of Commerce: Shepard Fairey and the New Cultural Entrepreneurship'. In Aronczyk, M. and Powers, D. (eds.), *Critical Perspectives on Promotional Culture.* New York:

Peter Lang Publishing Inc.

Barbalet, J. (2009). 'Consciousness, Emotions, and Science'. In Hopkins, D,, Kleres, J., Flam, H. and Kuzmics, H. (eds.), *Theorizing Emotions: Sociological Explorations and Applications*. Frankfurt/New York: Campus Verlag.

Barendregt, B. and Jaffe, R. (eds.) (2014) *Green Consumption: The Global Rise of Eco-Chic*. London: Bloomsbury Academic.

Barnett, C., Cloke, P., Clarke, N., and Malpass, A. (2005) 'Consuming Ethics: Articulating the Subjects and Spaces of Ethical Consumption'. *Antipode* 37(1), 23–45.

Barnett, D. (1998) *London, Hub of the Industrial Revolution: A Revisionary History 1775–1825*. London: IB Tauris.

Barrientos, S., Gereffi, G., and Arianna, R. (2011) 'Economic and Social Upgrading in Global Production Networks: A New Paradigm for a Changing World'. *International Labour Review* 150, 319–40.

Barroso, J. M./anonymous (2010) *EUROPE 2020 a Strategy for Smart, Sustainable and Inclusive Growth*. Brussels: European Commission.

Baudrillard, J. (1998) *The Consumer Society: Myths and Structures*. London: Sage.

Bauman, Z. (1998) *Work, Consumerism and the New Poor*. Buckingham: Open University Press.

Bauman, Z. (2000) *Liquid Modernity*. Cambridge: Polity.

Bauman, Z. (2005) *Liquid Life*. Cambridge: Polity Press.

Beck, A. (ed.) (2003) *Cultural Work: Understanding the Cultural Industries*. London: Routledge.

Beck, U. (2000) *The Brave New World of Work*. Cambridge: Polity Press.

Becker, G. S. (1962) 'Investment in Human Capital: A Theoretical Analysis'. *The Journal of Political Economy* 70(5), 9–49.

Becker, G. S. (1964) *Human Capital*. New York: National Bureau of Economic Research.

Becker, H. S. (1978) 'Arts and Crafts'. *American Journal of Sociology* 83, 862–89.

Becker, P. (2009) 'What Makes Us Modern(s)? The Place of Emotions in Contemporary Society'. In Hopkins, D., Kleres, J., Flam, H. and Kuzmics, H. (eds.), *Theorizing Emotions: Sociological Explorations and Applications*. Frankfurt/New York: Campus Verlag.

Beer, D. and Burrows, R. (2007) 'Sociology and, of and in Web 2.0: Some Initial Considerations'. *Sociological Research Online* 12(5). http://www.socresonline.org.uk/12/5/17.html

Bell, D. (1973) *The Coming of Post-Industrial Society*. New York: Basic Books.

Benner, C. (2002) *Work in the New Economy: Flexible Labor Markets in Silicon Valley*. Oxford: Blackwell.

Bennett, T., Savage, M., Silva, E., Warde, A., Gayo-Cal, M., and Wright, D. (2008) *Culture, Class, Distinction*. London: Routledge.

Berg, N. and Gigerenzer, G. (2010) 'As-If Behavioral Economics: Neoclassical Economics in Disguise?' *History of Economic Ideas* 18(1), 133–66.

Bernays, E. L. (1928) 'Manipulating Public Opinion: The Why and The How'. *American Journal of Sociology* 33(6) 958–71.

Biggart, N. W. (1989) *Charismatic Capitalism: Direct Selling Organizations in America*. Chicago, IL: University Press.

Blackburn, S. (1994) *Dictionary of Philosophy*. Oxford: Oxford University Press.

Blair, H., Grey, S., and Randle, K. (2001) 'Working in Film: Employment in a Project Based Industry'. *Personnel Review* 30(2), 170–85.

Bloomfield, B. P. and Best, A. (1992) 'Management Consultants: Systems Development, Power and the Translation of Problems'. *Sociological Review* 40(3), 533–60.

Blumer, H. (1969) 'Fashion: From Class Differentiation to Collective Selection'. *Sociological Quarterly* 10(3), 275–91.

Boddy, C. R. (2011) '"Hanging Around with People". Ethnography in Marketing Research and Intelligence Gathering'. *The Marketing Review* 11(2), 151–63.

Böhme, G. (2003) 'Contribution to the Critique of the Aesthetic Economy'. *Thesis Eleven* 73(1), 71–82.

Bolton, S. (2004) 'Conceptual Confusions: Emotion Work as Skilled Work'. In C. Warhurst et al. (eds.), *The Skills That Matter*. London: Palgrave.

Bolton, S. (2005) *Emotion Management in the Workplace*. London: Palgrave Macmillan.

Bolton, S. C. and Houlihan, M. (2010) 'Bermuda Revisited?'. *Work and Occupations* 37(3), 378–403.

Bone J. (2006) *The Hard Sell: An Ethnographic Study of the Direct Selling Industry*. Aldershot: Ashgate.

Boreham, N. (2004) 'A Theory of Collective Competence: Challenging the Neo-Liberal Individualisation of Performance at Work'. *British Journal of Educational Studies* 52(1), 5–17.

Bourdieu, P. (1984) *Distinction: A Social Critique of the Judgement of Taste*. Cambridge, MA: Harvard University Press.

Bowlby, R. (2000) *Carried Away: The Invention of Modern Shopping*. London: Faber and Faber.

Bradley, H., Erickson, M., Stephenson, C., and Williams, S. (2000) *Myths at Work*. London: Blackwell.

Bradshaw, A. and Holbrook, M. B. (2008) 'Must We Have Muzak Wherever We Go? A Critical Consideration of the Consumer Culture'. *Consumption Markets and Culture* 11(1), 25–43.

Brady, E. (2003) *Aesthetics of the Natural Environment*. Edinburgh: Edinburgh University Press.

Brakus, J., Schmitt, B., and Zarantonello, L. (2009) 'Brand Experience: What Is It? How Is It Measured? Does It Affect Loyalty?'. *Journal of Marketing* 73(3), 52–68.

Braudel, F. (1992) *The Wheels of Commerce (Civilization and Capitalism: 15th–18th Century - Volume 2)*. Berkeley, CA: University of California Press.

Braun-Ronsdorf, M. (1964) *The Wheel of Fashion: Costume since the French Revolution, 1789–1929*, trans. O. Coburn. London: Thames and Hudson.

Braverman, H. (1974) *Labor and Monopoly Capital*. New York: Monthly Review Press.

Brenner, R. (1977) 'The Origins of Capitalist Development: A Critique of Neo-Smithian Marxism'. *New Left Review* 104, 25–92.

Brockmann, M., Clarke, L., and Winch, C. (2009) 'Difficulties in Recognising Vocational Skills and Qualifications across Europe'. *Assessment in Education: Principles, Policy and Practice* 16(1): 97–109.

Brook, P. (2009) 'In Critical Defence of "Emotional Labour": Refuting Bolton's Critique of Hochschild's Concept'. *Work, Employment and Society* 23(3), 531–48.

Brosius, C. (2010) *India's Middle Class: New Forms of Urban Leisure, Consumption and Prosperity*. New Delhi: Routledge.

Brown, J. S. and Duguid, P. (2000). *The Social Life of Information*. Boston, MA: Harvard Business School Press.

Brown, P. (2001) 'Skill Formation in the 21st Century'. In P. Brown, A. Green and H. Lauder (eds.), *High Skills: Globalization, Competitiveness and Skill Formation*. Oxford and New York: Oxford University Press.

Brown, S. (2001) *Marketing – The Retro Revolution*. London: Sage.

Bryman, A. (2004) *The Disneyization of Society*. London: Sage.

Bryson, J. R. and Daniels, P. W. (2007) *The Handbook of Service Industries*. Cheltenham: Edward Elgar.

Bryson, J. R., Daniels, P. W., and Warf, B. (2004) *Service Worlds: People, Organisations and Technologies*. London: Routledge.

Bukodi, E. (2007) 'Social Stratification and Cultural Consumption in Hungary: Book Readership'. *Poetics* 35: 112–31.

Burawoy, M. (1979) *Manufacturing Consent: Changes in the Labor Process Under Monopoly Capitalism*. Chicago, IL: University of Chicago Press.

Burke, T. and Shackleton, J. R. (1996) 'Trouble in Store: UK Retailing in the 1990s'. In *Hobart Paper* no. 130. London: Institute of Economic Affairs.

Çalışkan, K. and Callon, M. (2009) 'Economization, Part 1: Shifting Attention from the Economy Towards Processes of Economization'. *Economy and Society* 38(3), 369–98.

Callon, M. (1998) *The Laws of the Markets*. Oxford: Wiley Blackwell.

Campbell, C. (1987) *The Romantic Ethic and the Spirit of Modern Consumerism*. Oxford: Basil Blackwell.

Campbell, C. (1997). 'Romanticism, Introspection and Consumption: A Response to Professor Holbrook'. *Consumption Markets & Culture*, 1(2), 165–173.

Campbell, C. (2005) 'The Craft Consumer: Culture, Craft and Consumption in a Postmodern Society'. *Journal of Consumer Culture* 5(1), 23–42.

Candy, F. (2005) '"The Fabric of Society": An Investigation of the Emotional and Sensory Experience of Wearing Denim Clothing'. *Sociological Research Online* 10(1). http://www.socresonline.org.uk/10/1/candy.html.

Cappetta, R. and Gioia, D. (2006) 'Fine Fashion: Using Symbolic Artifacts, Sensemaking, and Sensegiving to Construct Identity and Image'. In Rafaeli,

A. and Pratt, M. (eds.), *Artifacts and Organizations: Beyond Mere Symbolism*. Mahwah, NJ: Lawrence Erlbaum Associates.

Carah, N. (2013) 'Brand Value: How Affective Labour Helps Create Brands' *Consumption Markets and Culture* 17(4), 1–21.

Caruana, R. (2007) 'A Sociological Perspective of Consumption Morality' *Journal of Consumer Behaviour* 6(5), 287–304.

Casey, C. (1995) *Work, Self and Society after Industrialism*. London: Routledge

Casey, C. (2012) *Economy, Work and Education: Critical Connections*. New York: Routledge.

Castells, M. (1996) *The Rise of the Network Society: The Information Age: Economy, Society and Culture Vol. I*. Cambridge, MA: Blackwell Publishers

Castells, M. (1997) *The Power of Identity: The Information Age: Economy, Society and Culture Vol. II*. Cambridge, MA and Oxford: Blackwell.

Castells, M. (1998) *End of Millennium: The Information Age: Economy, Society and Culture Vol. III*. Cambridge, MA and Oxford: Blackwell.

Centeno, M. A. and Cohen, J. N. (2010) *Global Capitalism: A Sociological Perspective*. Cambridge: Polity.

Chadha, R. and Husband, P. (2006) *The Cult of the Luxury Brand: Inside Asia's Love Affair with Luxury*. London and Boston, MA: Nicholas Brealey International.

Chan, A. and Siu, K. (2010) 'Analyzing Exploitation: The Mechanisms Underpinning Low Wages and Excessive Overtime in Chinese Export Factories.' *Critical Asian Studies* 42(2), 167–90.

Chan, A. H. N. (2000) 'Middle Class Formation and Consumption in Hong Kong'. In Chua, B. H. (ed.), *Consumption in Asia: Lifestyles and Identities*. London: Routledge.

Chang, H. (2004) 'Fake Logos, Fake Theory, Fake Globalization'. *Inter-Asia Cultural Studies* 5(2), 222–36. Trans. Y.-C. Liao.

Chaudhuri, K. N. (2006) *The Trading World of Asia and the English East India Company, 1660–1760*. New York: Cambridge University Press.

Cheng, H. (2012) 'Cheap Capitalism: A Sociological Study of Food Crime in China'. *British Journal of Criminology* 52(2), 254–73.

Chin, E. (2001) *Purchasing Power: Black Kids and American Consumer Culture*. Minneapolis: University of Minnesota Press.

Christopherson, S. (2008) 'Beyond the Self-Expressive Creative Worker: An Industry Perspective on Entertainment Media'. *Theory, Culture and Society* 25(7–8), 73–95.

Chua B. H. (2003) *Life Is Not Complete Without Shopping: Consumer Culture in Singapore*. Singapore: Singapore University Press.

Chugh, S. and Hancock, P. (2009) 'Networks of Aestheticization: The Architecture, Artefacts and Embodiment of Hairdressing Salons.' *Work, Employment and Society* 23(3), 460–76.

Ciravegna, L. (2011) 'Outsourcing of New Product Development and the Opening of Innovation in Mature Industries: A Longitudinal Study of Fiat During Crisis and Recovery'. *International Journal of Innovation Management* 15(1), 69–93.

Clough, P. T., Goldberg, G., Schiff, R., Weeks, A., and Willse, C. (2007) 'Notes Towards a Theory of Affect-Itself'. *Ephemera: Theory and Politics in Organization* 7(1), 60–77.

Cobble, D. S. (1991) 'Organizing the Postindustrial Workforce: Lessons from the History of Waitress Unionism'. *Industrial and Labor Relations Review* 44(3), 419–36.

Cochoy, F. (2007) 'A Sociology of Market-Things: On Tending the Garden of Choices in Mass Retailing'. *The Sociological Review* 55(s2), 109–29.

Cochoy, F. (2008) 'Calculation, Qualculation, Calqulation: Shopping Cart Arithmetic, Equipped Cognition and the Clustered Consumer'. *Marketing Theory* 8(1), 15–44.

Cochoy, F. (2009) 'Driving a Shopping Cart from STS to Business, and the Other Way Round: On the Introduction of Shopping Carts in American Grocery Stores (1936–1959)'. *Organization* 16(1), 31–55.

Cockburn, C. (1983) *Brothers: Male Dominance and Technological Change*. London: Pluto.

Cohen, R. L. (2010) 'When It Pays to be Friendly: Employment Relationships and Emotional Labour in Hairstyling'. *The Sociological Review* 58(2): 197–218.

Collins, H. (2010) *Tacit and Explicit Knowledge*. Chicago, IL and London: University of Chicago Press.

Comaroff, J. and Comaroff, J. L. (eds.) (2001) *Millennial Capitalism and the Culture of Neoliberalism*. Durham and London: Duke University Press.

Conor, B. (2014) *Screenwriting: Creative Work and Professional Practice*. London: Routledge.

Cook, D. T. (2004). 'Beyond Either/Or'. *Journal of Consumer Culture* 4(2), 147–53.

Corley, T. A. B. (1987) 'Consumer Marketing in Britain 1914–1960'. *Business History* 29(4), 65–83.

Courtois, C., Mechant, P., Paulussen, S., and De Marez, L. (2012) 'The Triple Articulation of Media Technologies in Teenage Media Consumption'. *New Media and Society* 14(3), 401–20.

Crăciun, E. M. (2014) *Material Culture and Authenticity: Fake Branded Fashion in Europe*. London: Bloomsbury.

Cremin, C. (2011) *Capitalism's New Clothes: Enterprise, Ethics and Enjoyment in Times of Crisis*. London: Pluto.

Crewe, B. (2003) *Representing Men: Cultural Production and Producers in the Men's Magazine Market*. Oxford: Berg.

Cronin, A. M. (2004a) 'Currencies of Commercial Exchange: Advertising Agencies and the Promotional Imperative'. *Journal of Consumer Culture* 4(3), 339–60.

Cronin, A. M. (2004b) 'Regimes of Mediation: Advertising Practitioners as Cultural Intermediaries?'. *Consumption Markets and Culture* 7(4), 349–69.

Cross, G. S. (1993) *Time and Money: The Making of Consumer Culture*. London: Routledge.

Damasio, A. (2006) *Descartes' Error: Emotion, Reason and the Human Brain*. New York: Vintage.

Daniel, R. and Daniel, L. (2013) 'Enhancing the Transition from Study to Work: Reflections on the Value and Impact of Internships in the Creative and Performing Arts'. *Arts and Humanities in Higher Education* 12(2–3), 138–53.

Daniels, P. W. and Bryson, J. R. (2002) 'Manufacturing Services or Servicing Manufacturing?: New Forms of Production in Advanced Capitalist Economies'. *Urban Studies* 39, 977–91.

Dant, T. (2010) 'The Work of Repair: Gesture, Emotion and Sensual Knowledge. *Sociological Research Online* 15(3), 7.

Dauvergne, P. (2008). *The Shadows of Consumption: Consequences for the Global Environment*. Cambridge, MA: MIT Press.

Davidoff, L. (1995) *Worlds Between: Historical Perspectives on Gender and Class*. Cambridge: Polity Press.

Davila, A. (2010) 'A Nation of "Shop 'til you Drop" Consumers? On the Overspent Puerto Rican Consumer and the Business of Shopping Malls'. In Aronczyk, M. and Powers, D. (eds.), *Blowing up the Brand. Critical Perspectives on Promotional Culture*. New York: Peter Laing Publishing, 93–114.

Davis, A. (2013) *Promotional Cultures: The Rise and Spread of Advertising, Public Relations, Marketing and Branding*. Cambridge: Polity Press.

Davison, J. (2012) 'Icon, Iconography, Iconology: Banking, Branding and the Bowler Hat'. In Puyou, F. R., Quattrone, P., McLean, C. and Thrift, N., *Imagining Organizations: Performative Imagery in Business and Beyond*. New York and London: Routledge, 152–72.

Dawson, A. and Holmes, S. P. (2012) *Working in the Global Film and Television Industries: Creativity, Systems, Space, Patronage*. London: Bloomsbury.

Dean, D. and Jones, C. (2003) 'If Women Actors Were Working …'. *Media, Culture and Society* 25(4), 527–41.

Dean, J. (2009) *Democracy and Other Neoliberal Fantasies*. Durham: Duke University Press.

de Certeau, M. (1984) *The Practice of Everyday Life*. Berkeley: University of California Press.

Dedeoğlu, S. (2010) 'Visible Hands – Invisible Women: Garment Production in Turkey'. *Feminist Economics* 16(4), 1–32.

De Grazia, V. (1998) 'Changing Consumption Regimes in Europe, 1930–1970: Comparative Perspectives on the Distribution Problem'. In Strasser, S., McGovern, C. and Judt, M. (eds.), *Getting and Spending: European and American Consumer Societies in the Twentieth Century*. Washington, DC: German Historical Institute and Cambridge University Press.

DeNora, T. and Belcher, S. (2000) '"When You're Trying Something on You Picture Yourself in a Place Where They Are Playing This Kind of Music" – Musically Sponsored Agency in the British Clothing Retail Sector', *Sociological Review* 48(1), 80–101.

Despret, V. (2004 [1999]) *Our Emotional Makeup: Ethnopsychology and Selfhood*, trans. M. de Jager. New York: Other Press.

Deutsch, T. (2010) *Building a Housewife's Paradise: Gender, Politics and American Grocery Stores in the Twentieth Century.* Chapel Hill, NC, University of North Carolina Press.

Deuze, M. (2005) 'What Is Journalism?: Professional Identity and Ideology of Journalists Reconsidered'. *Journalism* 6(4), 442–464, http://doi.org/10.1177/1464884905056815

Devasahayam, T. W. (2005) 'Power and Pleasure Around the Stove'. *Women's Studies International Forum* 28, 1–20.

Dewey, J. (1934) *Art As Experience.* New York: Berkeley Publishing Group.

Dewey, J. (1967 [1887]) *Psychology in John Dewey: The Early Works 1882-1898 Volume 2,* edited by H. W. Schneider. Carbondale: Southern Illinois University Press.

Dickinson, K. (2008) *Off Key: When Film and Music Won't Work Together.* Oxford: Oxford University Press.

Diprose, R. and Reynolds, J. (eds.) (2008) *Merleau-Ponty: Key Concepts.* Stocksfield: Acumen.

Donkin, R. (2001) *Blood, Sweat and Tears: The Evolution of Work.* New York: Texere.

Doogan, K. (2009) *New Capitalism? The Transformation of Work.* Cambridge: Polity Press.

Douglas, M. and Isherwood, B. (1996) *The World of Goods.* 2nd Edition. London, Routledge.

du Gay, P. (1996) *Consumption and Identity at Work.* London: Sage.

du Gay, P., Hall, S., Janes, L., Mackay, H., and Negus, K. (1997) *Doing Cultural Studies: The Story of the Sony Walkman.* London: Sage.

du Gay, P. and Nixon, S. (2002) 'Who Needs Cultural Intermediaries?'. *Cultural Studies* 16(4), 495–500.

du Gay, P. and Pryke, M. (eds.) (2002) *Cultural Economy: Cultural Analysis and Commercial Life.* London: Sage.

Edwards, L. (2011) 'Public Relations and Society: A Bourdieuvian Perspective'. In Edwards, L. and Hodges, C. M. (eds.), *Public Relations, Society and Culture Theoretical and Empirical Explorations.* Abingdon and New York: Routledge.

Elias, P. and Davies, R. (2004) 'Employer Provided Training Within the European Union: A Comparative Perspective'. In Sofer, C. (ed.), *Human Capital Over the Lifecycle.* Cheltenham and Northhampton, MA: Edward Elgar, 137–53.

Elsheshtawy, Y. (2008) 'Navigating the Spectacle: Landscapes of Consumption in Dubai'. *Architectural Theory Review* 13(2), 164–87.

Elvins, S. (2004) *Sales and Celebrations – Retailing and Regional Identity in Western New York State 1920–1940.* Athens: Ohio University Press.

Entwistle, J. (2006) 'The Cultural Economy of Fashion Buying'. *Current Sociology* 54(5), 704–24.

Entwistle, J. (2009) *The Aesthetic Economy of Fashion: Markets and Value in Clothing and Modelling.* Oxford: Berg.

Entwistle, J. and Wissinger, E. (2006) 'Keeping Up Appearances: Aesthetic Labour in the Fashion Modelling Industries of London and New York'. *The Sociological Review* 54(4), 774–94.

Euromonitor International. (n.d.) *Consumer Expenditure Data*. Euromonitor. com (accessed 4 Feb. 2015).

Eustace, E. (2012) 'Speaking Allowed? Workplace Regulation of Regional Dialect'. *Work, Employment and Society*, 26(2), 331–48.

Evans, G. (2009) 'Creative Cities, Creative Spaces and Urban Policy'. *Urban Studies* 46(5–6), 1003–40.

Ewen, S. and Ewen, E. (1982) *Channels of Desire: Mass Images and the Shaping of American Consciousness*. New York: McGraw-Hill.

Featherstone, M. (2012) 'Super-Rich Lifestyles'. In Birtchnell, T. and Caletrío, J. (eds.), *Elite Mobilities*. London: Routledge.

Fehérváry, K. (2002) 'American Kitchens, Luxury Bathrooms, and the Search for a "Normal" Life in Postsocialist Hungary'. *Ethnos* 67(3), 369–400.

Felker, G. and Jomo, K. S. (2013) *Technology, Competitiveness and the State: Malaysia's Industrial Technology*. London: Routledge.

Fernandes, L. (2000) 'Restructuring the New Middle Class in Liberalizing India'. *Comparative Studies of South Asia, Africa and the Middle East* 20(1), 88–104.

Fine, B. and Leopold, E. (1993) *The World of Consumption*. London: Routledge.

Fineman, S. (2003) *Understanding Emotion at Work*. London: SAGE Publications.

Firat, A. F. and Dholakia, N. (1998) *Consuming People: From Political Economy to Theaters of Consumption*. London: Routledge.

Fırat, A. F., Pettigrew, S., and Belk, R. W. (2011) 'Themed Experiences and Spaces'. *Consumption Markets and Culture* 14(2), 123–4.

Fischer, E. and Bristor, J. (1994) 'A Feminist Poststructuralist Analysis of the Rhetoric of Marketing Relationships'. *International Journal of Research in Marketing* 11(4), 317–31.

Fiske, J. (1989) *Understanding Popular Culture*. London and New York: Routledge.

Fligstein, N. (1996) 'Markets as Politics: A Political-Cultural Approach to Market Institutions'. *American Sociological Review* 61, 656–73.

Fligstein, N. (2001) *The Architecture of Markets: An Economic Sociology of Twenty-First Century Capitalist Societies*. Princeton, NJ: Princeton University Press.

Florida, R. (2002) *The Rise of the Creative Class*. New York: Basic Books.

Fortunati, L. (2007) 'Immaterial Labor and Its Machinization'. *Ephemera: Theory and Politics in Organization* 7(1), 139–57.

Forty, A. (1986) *Objects of Desire: Design and Society, 1750–1980*. London: Thames and Hudson.

Fourcade, M. and Healy, K. (2007) 'Moral Views of Market Society'. *Annual Review of Sociology*, 33, 285–311.

Frank, A. (1997) *The Wounded Storyteller: Body, Illness and Ethics*. Chicago, IL: University of Chicago Press.

Frank, A. G. (1998) *ReOrient: Global Economy in the Asian Age*. Berkeley, CA: University of California Press.

Fraser, M. (2009) 'Experiencing Sociology'. *European Journal of Social Theory* 12(1): 63–81.

Fraser, W. H. (1981) *The Coming of the Mass Market, 1850–1914.* London: Macmillan.

Freeman, C. (2000) *High Tech and High Heels in the Global Economy: Women, Work and Pink-Collar Identities in the Caribbean.* Durham and London: Duke University Press.

Frosh, S. (2011) *Feelings (Short Cuts).* Abingdon: Routledge.

Fuchs, C. (2010) 'Labor in Informational Capitalism and on the Internet'. *The Information Society* 26(3): 179–96.

Fuchs, C. (2013) 'Capitalism or Information Society? The Fundamental Question of the Present Structure of Society'. *European Journal of Social Theory* 16(4), 413–34.

Fuchs, V. (1968) *The Service Economy.* New York: National Bureau of Economic Research; distributed by Columbia University Press.

Fuller, M. and Goffey, A. (2012) *Evil Media.* Cambridge, MA: MIT Press.

Gabriel, Y. (2005) 'Glass Cages and Glass Palaces: Images of Organization in Image-Conscious Times'. *Organization* 12(1), 9–27.

Gabriel, Y. and Lang, T. (2006) *The Unmanageable Consumer.* 2nd Edition. London: Sage.

Galbraith, J. K. (1998 [1958]) *The Affluent Society.* 40th Anniversary Edition. New York, Mariner Books.

Gallie, D. (2007) *Employment Regimes and the Quality of Work.* Oxford: Oxford University Press.

Gallie, D., White, M., Cheng, Y., and Tomlinson, M. (1998) *Restructuring the Employment Relationship.* Oxford: Oxford University Press.

Gamble, J. (2011) *Multinational Retailers and Consumers in China.* Basingstoke: Palgrave Macmillan.

Gardner, C. and Sheppard, J. (1989) *Consuming Passion: The Rise of Retail Culture.* London: Unwin Hyman.

Garnham, N. (1990) *Capitalism and Communication: Global Culture and the Economics of Information.* London: Sage.

Garnham, N. (2005) 'From Cultural to Creative Industries'. *International Journal of Cultural Policy* 11(1), 15–29.

Gatta, M. (2009) 'Restaurant Servers, Tipping, and Resistance'. *Qualitative Research in Accounting and Management* 6(1/2), 70–82.

Gautié, J. and Schmitt, J. (eds.) (2010) *Low-Wage Work in the Wealthy World.* New York: Russell Sage Foundation.

Gentilcore, D. (2010) *Pomodoro! A History of the Tomato in Italy.* New York: Columbia University Press.

Gereffi, G. (2005) 'The Global Economy: Organization, Governance, and Development'. In Smelser, N. J. and Swedberg, R. (eds.), *The Global Economy: Organization, Governance, and Development.* Princeton: Princeton University Press and Russell Sage Foundation.

Gereffi, G. (1994) 'The Organization of Buyer-Driven Global Commodity Chains: How US Retailers Shape Overseas Production Networks'. In Gereffi, G. and Korzeniewick, M. (eds.), *Commodity Chains and Global Capitalism*. Westport, CT: Greenwood.

Gereffi, G. and Korzeniewicz, M. (eds.) (1994) *Commodity Chains and Global Capitalism*. Westport, CT: Praeger.

Gesterland, R. and Seyk, G. (2002) *Marketing across Cultures in Asia*. Copenhagen: Copenhagen Business School Press.

Ghai, D. (2003) 'Decent Work: Concept and Indicators'. *International Labour Review*, 142 (2), 113–45.

Gibson-Graham, J. K. (1996) *The End of Capitalism (As We Knew It): A Feminist Critique of Political Economy*. Malden, MA: Blackwell.

Gill, R. (2002) 'Cool, Creative and Egalitarian?: Exploring Gender in Project-Based New Media Work in Europe'. *Information, Communication and Society* 5(1), 70–89.

Gill, R. (2007) *Technobohemians or the New Cybertariat? New Media Work in Amsterdam a Decade after the Web*. Amsterdam: Institute of Network Cultures.

Gill, R. and Pratt, A. (2008) 'In the Social Factory?: Immaterial Labour, Precariousness and Cultural Work'. *Theory, Culture and Society* 25(7–8), 1–30.

Gimlin, D. (2007) 'What Is "Body Work"? A Review of the Literature'. *Sociology Compass* 1(1), 353–70.

Glucksmann, M. A. (2013) 'Working to Consume: Consumers as the Missing Link in the Division of Labour'. *Centre for Research in Economic Sociology and Innovation (CRESI)* Working Paper 2013–03. Colchester: University of Essex.

Gobé, M. (2001) *Emotional Branding*. New York: Allworth Press.

Godart, F. C. and Mears, A. (2009) 'How Do Cultural Producers Make Creative Decisions? Lessons from the Catwalk'. *Social Forces* 88(2), 671–92.

Godlovitch, S. (1998) *Musical Performance: A Philosophical Study*. London: Routledge.

Goffman, E. (1990) *The Presentation of Self in Everyday Life*. London: Penguin.

Gökarıksel, B. and Secor, A. (2009) 'New Transnational Geographies of Islamism, Capitalism and Subjectivity: The Veiling-Fashion Industry in Turkey'. *Area* 41(1), 6–18.

Gökarıksel, B. and Secor, A. (2010) 'Between Fashion and Tesettür: Marketing and Consuming Women's Islamic Dress'. *Journal of Middle East Women's Studies* 6(3), 118–48.

Goldie, P. (2010) *The Oxford Handbook of Philosophy of Emotion*. Oxford and New York: Oxford University Press.

Goleman, D. (1995) *Emotional Intelligence*. New York: Bantam Books.

Gottdiener, M. (1997) *The Theming of America: Dreams, Visions, and Commercial Spaces*. Boulder, CO: Westview Press.

Gottfried, H. (2003) 'Temp(t)ing Bodies: Shaping Gender at Work in Japan'. *Sociology* 37(2), 257–76.

Gottschalk, S. (2009) 'Hypermodern Consumption and Megalomania: Superlatives in Commercials'. *Journal of Consumer Culture* 9(3), 307–27.

Gottschall, K. and Kroos, D. (2007) 'Self-Employment in Comparative Perspective: General Trends and the Case of New Media'. In Walby, S., Gottfried, H., Gottschall, K. and Osawa, M. (eds.), *Gendering the Knowledge Economy: Comparative Perspectives*. Basingstoke, Hampshire and New York: Palgrave Macmillan.

Graham, S. (2011) 'Disruptions'. In Gandy, M. (ed.), *Urban Constellations*. Berlin: Jovis.

Granovetter, M. (1985) 'Economic Action and Social Structure: The Problem of Embeddedness'. *American Journal of Sociology* 91, 481–510.

Green, F. (2011) *What is Skill? An Inter-Disciplinary Synthesis*. London: Centre for Learning and Life Chances in Knowledge Economies and Societies (LLAKES), IOE, University of London.

Green, A. with Akiko, S. (2001) 'Models of High Skills in National Competition Strategies'. In P. Brown, A. Green, and H. Lauder (eds.), *High Skills: Globalization, Competitiveness band Skill Formation*. Oxford, New York: Oxford University Press, 56–130.

Gregson, N., Crewe, L., and Brooks, K. (2003) 'The Discursivities of Difference: Retro Retailers and the Ambiguities of the Alternative'. *Journal of Consumer Culture* 3(1), 61–82.

Grinshpun, H. (2013) 'Deconstructing a Global Commodity: Coffee, Culture, and Consumption in Japan'. *Journal of Consumer Culture* 14(3), 343–64.

Gronow, J. and Warde, A. (eds) (2001) *Ordinary Consumption*. London: Harwood.

Guerrier, Y. and Adib, A. (2000) '"No, We Don't Provide That Service": The Harassment of Hotel Employees by Customers'. *Work, Employment and Society* 14(4), 689–705.

Guillén, M. F. and García-Canal, E. (2009) 'The American Model of the Multinational Firm and the "New" Multinationals from Emerging Economies'. *The Academy of Management Perspectives* 23(2), 23–35.

Gunelius, S. (2008) *Harry Potter: The Story of a Global Business Phenomenon*. Basingstoke: Palgrave Macmillan.

Hale, A. (2000) 'What Hope for "Ethical" Trade in the Globalised Garment Industry?'. *Antipode* 32, 349–56.

Hall, P. and Soskice, D. (eds.) (2001) *Varieties of Capitalism: The Institutional Foundations of Comparative Advantage*. Oxford: Oxford University Press.

Hall, R. and van den Broek, D. (2012) 'Aestheticising Retail Workers: Orientations of Aesthetic Labour in Australian Fashion Retail'. *Economic and Industrial Democracy*, 33(1), 85–102.

Hall, S. (1992) 'The West and the Rest: Discourse and Power'. In Hall, S. and Bram, B. (eds.), *Formations of Modernity*. Cambridge: Polity Press and Open University.

Hamilton, K. and Hassan, L. (2010) 'Self-Concept, Emotions and Consumer Coping: Smoking Across Europe'. *European Journal of Marketing* 44(7/8), 1101–20.

Hampson, I., Junor, A., and Barnes, A. (2009) 'Articulation Work Skills and the Recognition of Call Centre Competence in Australia'. *Journal of Industrial Relations* 51(1), 45–58.

Hancock, J. (2009) *Brand/Story: Ralph, Vera, Johnny, Billy, and Other Adventures in Fashion Branding.* New York: Fairchild.

Hancock, P. and Tyler, M. (2008) 'It's All Too Beautiful: Emotion and Organization in the Aesthetic Economy'. In Fineman, S. (ed.), *The Emotional Organization: Passions and Power.* Malden, MA: Blackwell Publishing.

Hardt, M. and Negri, A. (2000) *Empire.* Cambridge, MA: Harvard University Press.

Harquail, C. (2006) 'Employees as Animate Artifacts: Employee Branding by "Wearing the Brand"'. In Rafaeli, A. and Pratt, M. (eds.), *Artifacts and Organizations: Beyond Mere Symbolism.* Mahwah, NJ: Lawrence Erlbaum Associates.

Hartmann, B. J. and Ostberg, J. (2013) 'Authenticating by Re-Enchantment: The Discursive Making of Craft Production'. *Journal of Marketing Management* 29(7–8), 882–91.

Harvey, D. (1990) *The Condition of Postmodernity: An Enquiry into the Origins of Cultural Change.* Cambridge, MA: Blackwell.

Harvey, D. (2000) 'The Work of Postmodernity: The Laboring Body in Global Space'. In Davis, J. E. (ed.), *Identity and Social Change.* New Brunswick: Transaction Publishers.

Harvey, D. (2005) *A Brief History of Neoliberalism.* Oxford: Oxford University Press.

Harvey, D. (2006) *Spaces of Global Capitalism: Towards a Theory of Uneven Geographical Development.* London and New York: Verso.

Harvey, M. (2012) 'Drinking-Water and Drinking Water: Trajectories of Provision and Consumption in the UK, Taiwan and Delhi'. *Centre for Research in Economic Sociology and Innovation (CRESI) Working Paper,* 2, 2. Colchester: University of Essex.

Harvey, M. and McMeekin, A. (2007) *Public or Private Economies of Knowledge?: Turbulence in the Biological Sciences.* Cheltenham and Northampton, MA: Edward Elgar.

Harvey, M., Quilley, S., and Beynon, H. (2002) *Exploring the Tomato: Transformations in Nature, Economy and Society.* Cheltenham: Edward Elgar.

Held, D., McGrew, A., Goldblatt, D., and Perraton, J. (1999) *Global Transformations: Politics, Economics and Culture.* Stanford: Stanford University Press.

Herzenberg S., Alic, J. and Wial, H. (1998) *New Rules for a New Economy.* Ithaca, NY: Cornell University Press.

Hesmondhalgh, D. (2007) *The Cultural Industries.* 2nd Edition. London: SAGE.

Hesmondhalgh, D. and Baker, S. (2008) 'Creative Work and Emotional Labour in the Television Industry'. *Theory, Culture and Society* 25(7–8), 97–118.

Hesmondhalgh, D. and Baker, S. (2010) *Creative Labour: Media Work in Three Cultural Industries.* New York: Routledge.

Highmore, B. (2011) *Ordinary Lives: Studies in the Everyday.* New York and London: Routledge.

Hirschman, A. O. (1992) *Rival Views of Market Society and Other Recent Essays*. New York: Viking Penguin.

Hirst, P. and Zeitlin, J. (1991) 'Flexible Specialisation Versus Post-Fordism: Theory, Evidence and Policy Implications'. *Economy and Society* 20(1): 1–56.

Hirst, P. Q. and Thompson, G. F. (1999) *Globalization in Question: The International Economy and the Possibilities of Governance*. 2nd Edition. Cambridge: Polity Press.

Ho, V. W. K. (2013) 'Casino Multiculturalism and the Reinvention of Heritage, Macau and Singapore'. Paper presented at *Inter-Asia Cultural Studies Society (IACS) Conference 2013: Beyond The Culture Industry* 3–5 July, Singapore.

Hochschild, A. R. (2003) *The Managed Heart: Commercialization of Human Feeling*. Berkeley: University of California Press.

Hodson, R. (2001) *Dignity at Work*. Cambridge: Cambridge University Press.

Holbrook, M. B. (1997) 'Romanticism, Introspection, and the Roots of Experiential Consumption: Morris the Epicurean'. *Consumption Markets and Culture*, 1(2), 97–163.

Holbrook, M. B. and Hirschman, E. C. (1982) 'The Experiential Aspects of Consumption: Consumer Fantasies, Feelings, and Fun'. *The Journal of Consumer Research* 9(2), 132–40.

Horkheimer, M. and Adorno, T. W. (2006 [1944]) 'The Culture Industry: Enlightenment as Mass Deception'. In Durham, M. G. and Kellner, D., *Media and Cultural Studies: Keywords*. Malden, MA: Blackwell.

Horne, J. (2006) *Sport in Consumer Culture*. Basingstoke: Palgrave Macmillan.

Houston, H. R. and Meamber, L. A. (2011) 'Consuming the "World": Reflexivity, Aesthetics, and Authenticity at Disney World's EPCOT Center'. *Consumption Markets and Culture* 14(2), 177–91.

Huang, Y. (2008) *Capitalism with Chinese Characteristics: Entrepreneurship and the State*. Cambridge: Cambridge University Press.

Hughes, A. (2000) 'Retailers, Knowledges and Changing Commodity Networks: The Case of the Cut Flower Trade'. *Geoforum* 31(2). 175–90.

Humphrey, K. (1998) *Shelf Life*. Cambridge: Cambridge University Press.

Hutton, T.A. (2007) 'Service Industries, Global City Formation and New Policy Discourses within the Asia-Pacific'. In Bryson, J. R. and Daniels, P. W. (eds.), *The Handbook of Service Industries*. Cambridge: Edward Elgar.

Ibroscheva, E. (2013) 'The Unbearable Lightness of Advertising: Culture, Media and the Rise of Advertising in Socialist Bulgaria'. *Consumption Markets and Culture* 16(3), 290–310.

Illeris, S. (2007) 'The Nature of Services'. In Bryson, J. R. and Daniels, P. W. (eds.), *The Handbook of Service Industries*. Cambridge: Edward Elgar.

Illouz, E. (2007) *Cold Intimacies: The Making of Emotional Capitalism*. Cambridge: Polity Press.

Illouz, E. (2009) 'Emotions, Imagination and Consumption: A New Research Agenda'. *Journal of Consumer Culture* 9(3), 377–413.

Illouz, E. (2012) *Why Love Hurts: A Sociological Explanation*. London: Polity Press.

Izberk-Bilgin, E. (2012) 'Infidel Brands: Unveiling Alternative Meanings of Global Brands at the Nexus of Globalization, Consumer Culture, and Islamism'. *Journal of Consumer Research* 39(4), 663–87.

Jackson, D. (2003) *Sonic Branding: An Introduction*. London: Palgrave Macmillan.

Jagannathan, S. and Geronimo, D. (2013) *Skills for Competitiveness, Jobs, and Employability in Developing Asia-Pacific*. Manila: Asian Development Bank.

Jansson, J. O. (2006) *The Economics of Services*. Cheltenham and Northampton, MA: Edward Elgar.

Jantzen, C., Fitchett, J., Ostergaard, P., and Vetner, M. (2012) 'Just for Fun? The Emotional Regime of Experiential Consumption'. *Marketing Theory* 12(2), 137–54.

Jantzen, C., Ostergaard, P., and Sucena Viera, C. M. (2006) 'Becoming a "Woman to the Backbone": Lingerie Consumption and the Experience of Feminine Identity'. *Journal of Consumer Culture* 6(2), 177–202.

Jenkins, H. (2006) *Convergence Culture*. New York: New York University Press.

Jenkins, R., Nixon, E., and Molesworth, M. (2011) '"Just Normal and Homely": The Presence, Absence and Othering of Consumer Culture in Everyday Imagining'. *Journal of Consumer Culture* 11(2), 261–81.

Jenkins, S., Delbridge, R., and Roberts, A. (2010) 'Emotional Management in a Mass Customised Call Centre: Examining Skill and Knowledgeability in Interactive Service Work'. *Work, Employment and Society* 24(3), 546–64.

Johansson, U. and Holm, L. S. (2006) 'Design and Branding – A Nice Couple of False Friends?'. In Schroeder, J. and Salzer-Mörling M. (eds.), *Brand Culture*. New York: Routledge, 136–151.

Johnston, A. and Sandberg, J. (2008) 'Controlling Service Work: An Ambiguous Accomplishment between Employees, Management and Customers'. *Journal of Consumer Culture* 8(3), 389–417.

Jordan, L. K. (2011) 'Avoiding the "Trap": Discursive Framing as a Means of Coping with Working Poverty'. In Grugulis, I. and Bozkurt, Ö. (eds.), *Retail Work*. Basingstoke: Palgrave Macmillan.

Jordanova, L. (1991) *Sexual Visions: Images of Gender in Science and Medicine between the Eighteenth and Twentieth Centuries*. Hemel Hempstead: Harvester/Wheatsheaf and Madison: University of Wisconsin Press.

Joy, A., Hui, M., Kim, C., and Laroche, M. (1995) 'The Cultural Past in the Present: The Meaning of Homes of Working Class Italian Immigrants in Montreal'. In: Costa, J. and Bamossy, G. (eds.), *Marketing in a Multicultural World*. Thousand Oaks, CA: Sage.

Joy, A. and Venkatesh, A. (1994) 'Postmodernism, Feminism, and the Body: The Visible and the Invisible in Consumer Research'. *International Journal of Research in Marketing* 11(4), 333–57.

Kalleberg, A. L. (2012) 'Job Quality and Precarious Work: Clarifications, Controversies, and Challenges'. *Work and Occupations* 39(4), 427–48.

Kang, M. (2003) 'The Managed Hand: The Commercialization of Bodies and Emotions in Korean Immigrant–Owned Nail Salons'. *Gender and Society* 17(6), 820–39.

Kant, I. (1987 [1790]) *Critique of Judgment*, trans. W. S. Pluhar. Indianapolis: Hackett.

Karababa, E. and Ger, G. (2011) 'Early Modern Ottoman Coffeehouse Culture and the Formation of the Consumer Subject'. *The Journal of Consumer Research* 37(5), 737–60.

Katz-Gerro, T. and Jaeger, M. M. (2013) 'Top of the Pops, Ascend of the Omnivores, Defeat of the Couch Potatoes: Cultural Consumption Profiles in Denmark 1975–2004'. *European Sociological Review* 29(2), 243–60.

Kauppinen-Räisänen, H. and Luomala, H. T. (2010) 'Exploring Consumers' Product-Specific Colour Meanings' *Qualitative Market Research: An International Journal*, 13(3), 287-308.

Kawamura, Y. (2012) *Fashioning Japanese Subcultures*. London and New York: Berg.

Keep, E. and Mayhew, K. (2010) 'Moving Beyond Skills as a Social and Economic Panacea'. *Work, Employment and Society* 24(3), 565–77.

Keller, M. (2005) 'Freedom Calling: Telephony, Mobility and Consumption in Post-Socialist Estonia'. *European Journal of Cultural Studies*, 8(2), 217–38.

Kemper, S. (2003) 'How Advertising Makes Its Object'. In deWaal Malefyt, T. and Moeran, B. (eds.), *Advertising Cultures*. Oxford and New York: Berg.

Kim, J. E., Ju, H. W., and Johnson, K. K. P. (2009) 'Sales Associate's Appearance: Links to Consumers' Emotions, Store Image, and Purchases'. *Journal of Retailing and Consumer Services* 16(5), 407–13.

Kim, Y. (2013) 'Media Work of the Youth'. Paper presented at *Inter-Asia Cultural Studies Society (IACS) Conference 2013: Beyond The Culture Industry* 3–5 July, Singapore.

Kinsey, D. C. (2009) 'Koh-i-Noor: Empire, Diamonds, and the Performance of British Material Culture'. *The Journal of British Studies* 48(02), 391–419.

Kline, S. (1998) 'Toys, Socialization, and the Commodification of Play'. In Strasser, S., McGovern, C. and Judt, M. (eds.), *Getting and Spending: European and American Consumer Societies in the Twentieth Century*. Washington, DC: German Historical Institute and Cambridge University Press.

Kniazeva, M. and Belk, R. W. (2007) 'Packaging as Vehicle for Mythologizing the Brand'. *Consumption Markets and Culture* 10(1), 51–69.

Knox, H., O'Doherty, D., Vurdubakis, T., and Westrup, C. (2010) 'The Devil and Customer Relationship Management: Informational Capitalism and the Performativity of the Sign'. *Journal of Cultural Economy* 3(3), 339–59.

Kobayashi, K. (2011) 'Globalization, Corporate Nationalism and Japanese Cultural Intermediaries: Representation of Bukatsu Through Nike Advertising at the Global-Local Nexus'. *International Review for the Sociology of Sport* 47(6), 724–42.

Kochuyt, T. (2004) 'Giving Away One's Poverty. On the Consumption of Scarce Resources within the Family'. *Sociological Review* 52(2), 139–61.

Koeber, C. (2011) 'Consumptive Labor: The Increasing Importance of Consumers in the Labor Process'. *Humanity and Society* 35(3), 205–32.

Koller, V. (2007) '"The World's Local Bank": Glocalisation as a Strategy in Corporate Branding Discourse'. *Social Semiotics* 17(1), 111–31.

Kong, L. and O'Connor, J. (2009) *Creative Economies, Creative Cities: Asian-European Perspectives* (Vol. 98). Heidelberg, Springer Verlag.

Korczynski, M. and Ott, U. (2004) 'When Production and Consumption Meet: Cultural Contradictions and the Enchanting Myth of Customer Sovereignty'. *Journal of Management Studies* 41(4), 575–99.

Kritzer, H. M. (2007) 'Toward a Theorization of Craft'. *Social and Legal Studies* 16(3), 321–40.

Kuipers, G. (2012) 'The Cosmopolitan Tribe of Television Buyers: Professional Ethos, Personal Taste and Cosmopolitan Capital in Transnational Cultural Mediation'. *European Journal of Cultural Studies* 15(5), 581–603.

Kumar, K. (2005) *From Post-Industrial to Post-Modern Society: New Theories of the Contemporary World*. Oxford: Blackwell Publishers.

Lamont, M. (1992) *Money, Morals, and Manners: The Culture of the French and the American Upper-Middle Class*. Chicago, IL: University of Chicago Press.

Lamont, M. (2000) *The Dignity of Working Men*. Cambridge, MA: Harvard University Press.

Lan, P. C. (2003) 'Working in a Neon Cage: Bodily Labor of Cosmetics Saleswomen in Taiwan'. *Feminist Studies* 29(1), 21–45.

Land, C. and Taylor, S. (2010) 'Surf's Up: Work, Life, Balance and Brand in a New Age Capitalist Organization'. *Sociology* 44(3), 395–413.

Lande, B. (2007) 'Breathing Like a Soldier: Culture Incarnate'. *Sociological Review* 55, 95–108.

Larner, W. and Molloy, M. (2009) 'Globalization, the "New Economy" and Working Women: Theorizing from the New Zealand Designer Fashion Industry'. *Feminist Theory* 10(1), 35–59.

Lash, S. and Lury, C. (2007) *Global Culture Industry: The Mediation of Things*. Cambridge: Polity Press.

Latour, B. (1992) 'Where are the Missing Masses? The Sociology of a Few Mundane Artifacts'. In Bijker, W. E. and Law, J., *Shaping Technology/Building Society: Studies in Sociotechnical Change*. Cambridge, MA: MIT Press.

Latour, B. (1994) 'On Technical Mediation'. *Common Knowledge* 3(2), 29–64.

Lave, J. and Wenger, E. (1990) *Situated Learning: Legitimate Peripheral Participation*. Cambridge: Cambridge University Press.

Laver, J. (1945) *Taste and Fashion from the French Revolution to the Present Day*. London: G. G. Harrap.

Lazarus, R. S. and Lazarus, B. N. (1994) *Passion and Reason: Making Sense of Our Emotions*. New York: Oxford University Press.

Lazzarato, M. (1996) 'Immaterial Labor'. In Virno, P. and Hardt, M. (eds.), *Radical Thought in Italy: A Potential Politics*. Minneapolis: University of Minnesota Press.

Leach, W. R. (1993) *Land of Desire: Merchants, Power, and the Rise of a New American Culture*. New York: Pantheon.

Leadbeater, C. (1999) *Living on Thin Air: The New Economy*. Harmondsworth: Viking.

Leder, D. (1990) *The Absent Body*. Chicago, IL: Chicago University Press.

Lee, H. K. (2012) 'Cultural Consumers as "New Cultural Intermediaries": Manga Scanlators'. *Arts Marketing: An International Journal* 2(2), 131–43.

Lee, M. J. (2000) *The Consumer Society Reader*. Malden, MA: Blackwell.

Lefresne, F. (2012) *Youth Unemployment and Youth Employment Policy: Lessons from France*. Berlin: Friedrich-Ebert-Stiftung.

Leidner, R. (1993) *Fast Food, Fast Talk: Service Work and the Routinization of Everyday Life*. Berkeley: University of California Press.

Lewis, M., Haviland-Jones, J. M., and Feldman Barrett, L. (eds.) (2010) *Handbook of Emotions*. 3rd Edition. New York: The Guilford Press.

Li, H. (2010) 'From *Chengfen* to *Shenjia*. Branding and Promotional Culture in China'. In Aronczyk, M. and Powers, D. (eds.), *Blowing up the Brand. Critical Perspectives on Promotional Culture*. New York: Peter Laing Publishing.

Lin, G. C. S. (2005) 'Service Industries and Transformation of City-Regions in Globalizing China: New Testing Ground for Theoretical Reconstruction'. In Daniels, P. W., Ho, K. C. and Hutton, T. A. (eds.), *Service Industries and Asia-Pacific Cities: New Development Trajectories*. London and New York: Routledge.

Lin, Y.-C. J. (2011) '*Fake Stuff: China and the Rise of Counterfeit Goods*. London and New York: Routledge.

Littler, J. (2009). *Radical Consumption: Shopping for Change in Contemporary Culture*. Maidenhead: Open University Press.

Liu, X. (2010) *The Silk Road in World History*. Oxford and New York: Oxford University Press.

Lloyd, C. and Payne, J. (2009) '"Full of Sound and Fury, Signifying Nothing": Interrogating New Skill Concepts in Service Work – The View from Two UK Call Centres'. *Work, Employment and Society* 23(4), 617–34.

London, T. and Hart, S. L. (2004) 'Reinventing Strategies for Emerging Markets: Beyond the Transnational Model'. *Journal of International Business Studies* 35, 350–70.

Lopez, S. H. (2010) 'Workers, Managers, and Customers: Triangles of Power in Work Communities'. *Work and Occupations* 37(3), 251–71.

Lupton, D. (1998) *The Emotional Self: A Sociocultural Exploration*. London: Sage.

Lury, C. (2004) *Brands: The Logos of the Global Economy*. London and New York: Routledge.

Lury, C. (2009) 'Brand as Assemblage'. *Journal of Cultural Economy* 2(1–2), 67–82.

Lyon, D. (2010) 'Intersections and Boundaries of Work and Non-Work'. *European Societies* 12(2), 163–85.

Lyon, M. and Barbalet, J. (1994) 'Society's Body: Emotion and the Somatization of Social Theory'. In Csordas, T. (ed.), *Embodiment and Experience: The Existential Ground of Culture and Self*. Cambridge: Cambridge University Press.

Lyotard, F. (1984 [1979]) *The Postmodern Condition*. Manchester: Manchester University Press.

McCann, J. and Bryson, D. (eds.) (2009) *Smart Clothes and Wearable Technology*. Cambridge: Woodhead Publishing.

McCracken, G. D. (2005) *Culture and Consumption II: Markets, Meaning, and Brand Management*. Bloomington: Indiana University Press.

McDonald, P. (1997) 'Feeling and Fun: Romance, Dance and the Performing Male Body in the Take That Videos'. In Whiteley, S. (ed.), *Sexing the Groove*. New York and London: Routledge.

McDowell, L. (2009) *Working Bodies: Interactive Service Employment and Workplace Identities*. Chichester: Wiley-Blackwell.

McDowell, L., Batnitzky, A., and Dyer, S. (2007) 'Division, Segmentation, and Interpellation: The Embodied Labors of Migrant Workers in a Greater London Hotel'. *Economic Geography* 83(1), 1–25.

McFadden, D. (1999) 'Rationality for Economists'. *Journal of Risk and Uncertainty* 19(1/3), 73–105.

McFall, L. (2002) 'Who Were the Old Cultural Intermediaries?: An Historical Review of Advertising Producers'. *Cultural Studies* 16, 532–52.

McFall, L. (2004) *Advertising: A Cultural Economy*. London: Sage.

McKendrick, N. (1982) 'Part 1: Commercialization and the Economy'. In McKendrick, N., Brewer, J. and Plumb, J. H., *The Birth of a Consumer Society: The Commercialization of Eighteenth-Century England*. London: Europa Publications, 9–195.

McKendrick, N., Brewer, J., and Plumb, J. H. (1982) *The Birth of a Consumer Society: The Commercialization of Eighteenth-Century England*. London: Europa Publications.

McKercher, C. and Mosco, V. (eds.) (2008) *Knowledge Workers in the Information Society*. Lanham, MD: Lexington Books.

McKinlay, A. and Smith, C. (2009) *Creative Labour: Working in the Creative Industries*. London: Palgrave Macmillan.

McRobbie, A. (1998) *British Fashion Design: Rag Trade or Image Industry?* London: Routledge.

McRobbie, A. (2002) 'From Holloway to Hollywood: Happiness at Work in the New Cultural Economy?'. In du Gay, P. and Pryke, M. (eds.), *Cultural Economy: Cultural Analysis and Commercial Life*. London: Sage.

McStay, A. (2010) *Digital Advertising*. Basingstoke: Palgrave Macmillan.

Malär, L., Krohmer, H., Hoyer, W. D., and Nyffenegger, B. (2011) 'Emotional Brand Attachment and Brand Personality: The Relative Importance of the Actual and the Ideal Self'. *Journal of Marketing* 75(4), 35–52.

Malos, E. (ed.) (1980) *The Politics of Housework*. London: Allison and Busby.

Mallard, A. (2007) 'Performance Testing: Dissection of a Consumerist Experiment'. In Callon, M., Millo, Y. and Muniesa, F. (eds.), *Market Devices*. Oxford: Blackwell.

Manovich, L. (2011) 'Inside Photoshop'. *Computational Culture*. 1 (n.p.) Web. http://computationalculture.net/article/inside-photoshop.

Marchington, M., Grimshaw, D., Rubery, J., and Willmott, H. (2005) *Fragmenting Work: Blurring Organizational Boundaries and Disordering Hierarchies*. Oxford: Oxford University Press.

Martin, H. P. and Schumann, H. (1997) *The Global Trap: Globalization and the Assault on Democracy and Prosperity*. London: Zed Books.

Marx, K. (1976) *Capital: A Critique of Political Economy*, Vol. 1, trans. B. Fowkes. London: Penguin.

Marx, K. (1997) 'The Economic and Philosophical Manuscripts'. In Pierson, C. (ed.), *The Marx Reader*. Cambridge: Polity Press.

Masi de Casanova, E. (2011) `Multiplying Themselves: Women Cosmetics Sellers in Ecuador'. *Feminist Economics* 17(2), 1 -29, http://doi.org/10.1080/13545701.2011.568419

May, E. T. (1999) 'The Commodity Gap: Consumerism and the Modern Home'. In Glickman, L. B. (ed.), *Consumer Society in American History: A Reader*. Ithaca, NY: Cornell University Press.

Mayer, K. U. and Solga, S. (eds.) (2008) *Skill Formation: Interdisciplinary and Cross-National Perspectives*. New York: Cambridge University Press.

Mears, A. (2011) *Pricing Beauty: The Making of a Fashion Model*. Berkeley: University of California Press.

Miege, B. (1987) 'The Logics at Work in the New Cultural Industries'. *Media, Culture and Society* 9(3), 273–89.

Miller, D. (1998a) *A Theory of Shopping*. Cambridge: Polity Press.

Miller, D. (1998b) 'Coca-Cola, a Black, Sweet Drink from Trinidad'. In D. Miller (ed.), *Why Some Things Matter*. Chicago, IL: Chicago University Press, 169–87.

Miller, D. (2001) 'The Poverty of Morality'. *Journal of Consumer Culture* 1(2): 225–43.

Miller, D. (2009) *Stuff*. Cambridge and Maldon MA: Polity Press.

Miller, D. and Slater, D. (2000) *The Internet: An Ethnographic Approach*. Oxford: Berg.

Miller, D. and Woodward, S. (eds.) (2011) *Global Denim*. Oxford: Berg.

Miller, M. B. (1981) *The Bon Marché: Bourgeois Culture and the Department Store, 1869–1920*. Princeton, NJ: Princeton University Press.

Miller, P. and Rose, N. (1990) 'Governing Economic Life.' *Economy and Society* 19, 1– 31.

Mills, C. W. (1956) *White Collar*. New York: Oxford University Press.

Mintz, S. (1985) *Sweetness and Power: The Place of Sugar in Modern History*. Harmondsworth: Penguin.

Mirchandani, K. (2012) *Phone Clones: Authenticity Work in the Transnational Service Economy*. Ithaca, NY: ILR Press.

Miskell, P. (2004) 'Cavity Protection or Cosmetic Perfection? Innovation and Marketing of Toothpaste Brands in the United States and Western Europe, 1955–1985'. *Business History Review* 78(01), 29–60.

Moeran, B. (2006) *Ethnography at Work*. New York: Berg.

Molé, N. J. (2012) *Labor Disorders in Neoliberal Italy: Mobbing, Well-Being, and the Workplace*. Bloomington: Indiana University Press.

Molloy, M. and Larner, W. (2010) 'Who Needs Cultural Intermediaries Indeed?'. *Journal of Cultural Economy* 3(3), 361–77.

Molnár, V. and Lamont, M. (2002) 'Social Categorisation and Group Identification: How African-Americans Shape Their Collective Identity Through
Consumption'. In Mcmeekin, A., Green, K., Tomlinson, M. and Walsh, V.
(eds.), *Innovation by Demand: An Interdisciplinary Approach to the Study
of Demand and Its Role in Innovation.* Manchester and New York: Manchester University Press.

Molotch, H. (2003) *Where Stuff Comes From.* London and New York:
Routledge.

Moor, L. (2007) *The Rise of Brands.* Oxford: Berg.

Moor, L. (2008) 'Branding Consultants as Cultural Intermediaries'. *The Sociological Review* 56(3), 408–28.

Moor, L. (2012) 'Beyond Cultural Intermediaries? A Socio-Technical Perspective on the Market for Social Interventions'. *European Journal of Cultural
Studies* 15(5), 563–80.

Moor, L. and Lury, C. (2011) 'Making and Measuring Value: Comparison,
Singularity and Agency in Brand Valuation Practice'. *Journal of Cultural
Economy* 4(4), 439–54.

Moore, A. M. (2007) *Unmarketable: Brandalism, Copyfighting, Mocketing, and
the Erosion of Integrity.* New York: New Press.

Morais, R. J. (2007) 'Conflict and Confluence in Advertising Meetings'. *Human
Organization* 66(2), 150–9.

Morgan, D., Brandth, B., and Kvande, E. (eds.) (2005) *Gender, Bodies, and
Work.* Aldershot: Ashgate.

Morgan, G., Wood, J., and Nelligan, P. (2013) 'Beyond the Vocational Frag-
ments: Creative Work, Precarious Labour and the Idea of "Flexploitation"'.
The Economic and Labour Relations Review 24, 397–415.

Morshidi, S. (2000) 'Globalising Kuala Lumpur and the Strategic Role of the
Producer Services Sector'. *Urban Studies* 37(12), 2217–40.

Mort, F. (1989) 'The Politics of Consumption'. In Hall, S. and Jacques, M. (eds.),
New Times: The Changing Face of Politics in the 1990s. London: Lawrence
and Wishart in Association with Marxism Today.

Mort, F. (1996) *Cultures of Consumption.* London: Routledge.

Moulier Boutang, Y. (2010) 'Cognitive Capitalism and Education: New Fron-
tiers'. In de Bary (ed.), *Trace 5, University in Translation,* trans. P. Bonin.
Cambridge and Malden, MA: Polity Press.

Moulier Boutang, Y. (2012) *Cognitive Capitalism.* Cambridge: Polity Press.

Moynagh, M. and Worsley, R. (2005) *Working in the Twenty-First Century.*
Leeds: ESRC Future of Work Programme.

Muirhead, R. (2004) *Just Work.* Cambridge, MA: Harvard University Press.

Mukerji, C. (1983) *From Graven Images: Patterns of Modern Materialism.* New
York: Columbia University Press.

Muller, L. (2005) 'Localizing International Business Services Invest-
ment: The Advertising Industry in Southeast Asia'. In Daniels, P. W.,
Ho, K. C. and Hutton, T. A. (eds.), *Service Industries and Asia-Pacific
Cities: New Development Trajectories.* London and New York:
Routledge.

Nath, V. (2011) 'Aesthetic and Emotional Labour through Stigma: National Identity Management and Racial Abuse in Offshored Indian Call Centres'. *Work Employment and Society* 25(4), 709–25.

Neal, D. (1995) 'Industry Specific Human Capital: Evidence from Displaced Workers'. *Journal of Labour Economics* 13(4) 653–77.

Neal, D. (1999) 'The Complexity of Job Mobility among Young Men'. *Journal of Labour Economics* 17(2), 237–61.

Negus, K. (2002) 'The Work of Cultural Intermediaries and the Enduring Distance Between Production and Consumption'. *Cultural Studies* 16(4): 501–15.

Nenga, S. K. (2003) 'Social Class and Structures of Feeling in Women's Childhood Memories of Clothing, Food, and Leisure'. *Journal of Contemporary Ethnography* 32(2), 167–99.

Ngai, S. (2005) *Ugly Feelings.* Cambridge, MA: Harvard University Press.

Nickson, D., Warhurst, C., Commander, J., Hurrell, S. A., and Cullen, A. M. (2012) 'Soft Skills and Employability: Evidence from UK Retail'. *Economic and Industrial Democracy* 33(1), 65–84.

Nippert-Eng, C. E. (2010) *Islands of Privacy.* Chicago, IL: University of Chicago Press.

Nixon, A. E., Yang, L. Q., Spector, P. E., and Zhang, X. (2011) 'Emotional Labor in China: Do Perceived Organizational Support and Gender Moderate the Process?'. *Stress and Health* 27(4), 289–305.

Nixon, S. (2003) *Advertising Cultures: Gender, Commerce, Creativity.* London: Sage.

Nixon, S. and Crewe, B. (2004) 'Pleasure at Work? Gender, Consumption and Work-Based Identities in the Creative Industries'. *Consumption Markets and Culture* 7(2), 129–47.

Nixon, S. and du Gay, P. (2002) 'Who Needs Cultural Intermediaries?'. *Cultural Studies* 16(4), 495–500.

Nonaka, I. and Takeuchi, H. (1995) *The Knowledge-Creating Company.* Oxford: Oxford University Press.

Nusbaumer, M. (2011) 'Rural Masculinity and Antique Tractors: Reliving the Men in the Machines'. *Journal of Rural Social Sciences* 26(2): 101–25.

Nussbaum, M. C. (2001) *Upheavals of Thought: The Intelligence of Emotions.* Cambridge: Cambridge University Press.

Ocejo, R. E. (2012) 'At Your Service: The Meanings and Practices of Contemporary Bartenders'. *European Journal of Cultural Studies* 15(5), 642–58.

O'Dougherty, M. (2002) *Consumption Intensified: The Politics of Middle-Class Daily Life in Brazil.* Durham and London: Duke University Press.

Ohmae, K. (1995) *The End of the Nation State.* New York: Free Press.

Otis, E. M. (2008) 'Beyond the Industrial Paradigm: Market-Embedded Labor and the Gender Organization of Global Service Work in China'. *American Sociological Review* 73(1), 15–36.

Ottman, J. (2011) *The New Rules of Green Marketing: Strategies, Tools, and Inspiration for Sustainable Branding.* San Francisco, CA: Berrett-Koehler Publishers, Inc.

Packard, V. (1957) *The Hidden Persuaders*. New York: Pocket Books.

Park, S. O. and Choi, J. S. (2005) 'IT Service Industries and the Transformation of Seoul'. In Daniels, P. W., Ho, K. C. and Hutton, T. A. (eds.), *Service Industries and Asia-Pacific Cities: New Development Trajectories*. London and New York: Routledge.

Parr, J. (1999) *Domestic Goods: The Material, the Moral, and the Economic in the Postwar Years*. Toronto: University of Toronto Press.

Paules, G. F. (1991) *Dishing It Out: Power and Resistance among Waitresses in a New Jersey Restaurant*. Philadelphia: Temple University Press.

Payne, J. (2009) 'Emotional Labour and Skill: A Reappraisal'. *Gender, Work and Organization* 16(3), 348–67.

Peck, J. (2005) 'Struggling with the Creative Class'. *International Journal of Urban and Regional Research*, 20(4), 740 -770.

Peñaloza, L. (1999) 'Just Doing It: A Visual Ethnographic Study of Spectacular Consumption Behavior at Nike Town'. *Consumption, Markets and Culture* 2(4), 337–400.

Perrons, D. (2003) 'The New Economy and the Work Life Balance: A Case Study of the New Media Sector in Brighton and Hove'. *Gender, Work and Organization* 10(1), 65–93.

Peterson, R. A. (1997) *Creating Country Music: Fabricating Authenticity*. Chicago, IL and London: University of Chicago Press.

Pettigrew, S. (2011) 'Hearts and Minds: Children's Experiences of Disney World'. *Consumption Markets and Culture* 14(2), 145–61.

Pettinger, L. (2004) 'Brand Culture and Branded Workers: Service Work and Aesthetic Labour in Fashion Retail'. *Consumption, Markets and Culture* 7, 165–84.

Pettinger, L. (2005) 'Friends, Relations and Colleagues: The Blurred Boundaries of the Workplace'. *The Sociological Review* 53, 37–55.

Pettinger, L. (2006) 'On the Materiality of Service Work'. *The Sociological Review* 54(1), 48–65.

Pettinger, L. (2008) 'Developing Aesthetic Labour: The Importance of Consumption'. *International Journal of Work Organisation and Emotion* 2(4), 327–43.

Pettinger, L., Parry, J., Taylor, R., and Glucksmann, M. (2006) *A New Sociology of Work?* Oxford: Wiley-Blackwell.

Pinch, T. and Swedberg, R. (eds.) (2008) *Living in a Material World: Economic Sociology Meets Science and Technology Studies*. Cambridge, MA: MIT Press.

Pine, B. J. and Gilmore, J. H. (1999) *The Experience Economy*. Boston, MA: Harvard Business Review Press.

Piore, M. and Sabel, C. (1984) *The Second Industrial Divide: Possibilities for Prosperity*. New York: Basic Books.

Polanyi, K. (1957 [1944]) *The Great Transformation: The Political and Economic Origins of Our Time*. Boston, MA: Beacon Press.

Polanyi, M. (1967) *The Tacit Dimension*. New York: Anchor Books.

Polhemus, T. (1994) *Street Style: from Sidewalk to Catwalk*. London, Thames and Hudson Ltd.

Pollert, A. (1988) 'The Flexible Firm: Fixation or Fact?'. *Work, Employment and Society* 2(3), 281–316.

Pollert, A. (1995) 'Women's Employment and Service Sector Transformation in Central Eastern Europe: Case Studies in Retail in the Czech Republic'. *Work, Employment and Society* 9(4), 629–55.

Postrel, V. (2004) *The Substance of Style: How the Rise of Aesthetic Value is Remaking Commerce, Culture and Consciousness*. New York: Harper Perennial.

Powers, D. (2010) 'Strange Powers: The Branded Sensorium and the Intrigue of Musical Sound'. In Aronczyk, M. and Powers, D. (eds.), *Blowing up the Brand. Critical Perspectives on Promotional Culture*. New York: Peter Laing Publishing.

Prahalad, C. K. and Ramaswamy, V. (2004) *The Future of Competition: Co-creating Unique Value with Customers*. Boston, MA: Harvard Business School.

Pye, D. (1968) *The Nature and Art of Workmanship*. Cambridge: Cambridge University Press.

Quinn, J. B. (1992) *Intelligent Enterprise: A Knowledge and Service-Based Paradigm for Industry*. New York: Free Press.

Rafferty, K. (2011) 'Class-Based Emotions and the Allure of Fashion Consumption'. *Journal of Consumer Culture* 11(2), 239–60.

Ransome, P. (2005) *Work, Consumption and Culture: Affluence and Social Change in the Twenty-First Century*. London: Sage.

Rappaport, E. (2000) *Shopping for Pleasure: Women in the Making of London's West End*. Princeton, NJ: Princeton University Press.

Reekie, G. (1993) *Temptations: Sex and Selling in the Department Store*. St Leonards: Allen and Unwin.

Reidl, S., Schiffbanker, H., and Eichmann, H. (2006) 'Creating a Sustainable Future: The Working Life of Creative Workers in Vienna'. *Work, Organization, Labour and Globalization* 1(1), 48–58.

Ritzer, G. (1998) *The McDonaldization Thesis: Explorations and Extensions*. London: Sage.

Ritzer, G. (2004) *The Globalization of Nothing*. 2nd Edition. Thousand Oaks, CA: Pine Forge Press.

Ritzer, G. and Jurgenson, N. (2010) 'Production, Consumption, Prosumption: The Nature of Capitalism in the Age of the Digital "Prosumer"'. *Journal of Consumer Culture* 10(1), 13–36.

Roper, S. and La Niece, C. (2009) 'The Importance of Brands in the Lunch-Box Choices of Low-Income British School Children'. *Journal of Consumer Behaviour* 8(2–3), 84–99.

Ross, A. (2001) No-Collar Labor in America's 'New Economy'. *Socialist Register* 37: 76-87.

Ross, A. (2003) *No Collar: The Humane Workplace and Its Hidden Costs*. New York: Basic Books.

Ross, A. (2004) *Low Pay, High Profile: The Global Push for Fair Labor*. New York: New Press.

Ross, A. (2009) *Nice Work If You Can Get It: Life and Labor in Precarious Times*. New York: New York University Press.

Rossiter, J. and Bellman, S. (2012) 'Emotional Branding Pays Off: How Brands Meet Share of Requirements Through Bonding, Companionship, and Love'. *Journal of Advertising Research* 52(3): 291–6.

Roth, T. P. (1989) *The Present State of Consumer Theory*. Lanham, MD: University Press of America.

Rust, R. T., Moorman, C., and Bhalla, G. (2010) 'Rethinking Marketing'. *Harvard Business Review* 88(1/2), 94–101.

Ruwanpura, K. N. (2015) 'Garments Without Guilt? Uneven Labour Geographies and Ethical Trading – Sri Lankan Labour Perspectives'. *Journal of Economic Geography*, http://joeg.oxfordjournals.org/content/early/2015/05/13/jeg.lbu059

Saffu, K. and Walker, J. (2006) 'The Country-of-Origin Effect and Consumer Attitudes to "Buy Local" Campaign'. *Journal of African Business* 7(1–2), 183–99.

Saito, Y. (2007) *Everyday Aesthetics*. Oxford and New York: Oxford University Press.

Sandel, M. (2012) *What Money Can't Buy: The Moral Limits of Markets*. London: Allen Lane.

Sandıkcı, Ö. and Ger, G. (2010) 'Veiling in Style: How Does a Stigmatized Practice Become Fashionable?'. *Journal of Consumer Research* 37, 15–36.

Sargent, C. (2009) 'Playing, Shopping, and Working as Rock Musicians: Masculinities in "De-Skilled" and "Re-Skilled" Organizations'. *Gender and Society* 23(5), 665–87.

Sassatelli, R. (2007) *Consumer Culture: History, Theory and Politics*. Los Angeles, CA: Sage.

Sassoon, J. (1990) 'Colors, Artifacts, and Ideologies'. In Gagliardi, P. (ed.), *Symbols and Artifacts: Views of the Corporate Landscape*. New York: Aldine de Gruyter.

Sayer, A. (2005) *The Moral Significance of Class*. Cambridge: Cambridge University Press.

Sayer, A. (2007) 'Dignity at Work: Broadening the Agenda'. *Organization* 14(4), 565–81.

Sayer, A. and Walker. R. (1992) *The New Social Economy: Reworking the Division of Labor*. London: Blackwell.

Scheff, T. J. (1990) *Microsociology: Discourse, Emotion, and Social Structure*. Chicago, IL: University of Chicago Press.

Schivelbusch, W. (1992) *Tastes of Paradise: A Social History of Spices, Stimulants and Intoxicants*. New York: Pantheon Books.

Schor, J. (1998) *The Overspent American: Why We Want What We Don't Need*. New York: Basic Books.

Schroeder J. E. (2002) *Visual Consumption*. Routledge: London.

Schroeder, J. (2012) 'Style and Strategy: Snapshot Aesthetics in Brand Culture'. In Puyou, F. R., Quattrone, P., McLean, C. and Thrift, N. (eds.), *Imagining*

Organizations: Performative Imagery in Business and Beyond. New York and London: Routledge.

Schudson, M. (1999). 'Delectable Materialism: Second Thoughts on Consumer Culture'. In L. B. Glickman (ed.), *Consumer Society in American History: A Reader.* Ithaca, NY: Cornell University Press.

Schultz, S. (2008) 'Our Lady Hates Viscose: The Role of the Customer Image in High Street Fashion Production'. *Cultural Sociology* 2(3): 385–405.

Schwarzkopf, S. (2007) '"Culture" and the Limits of Innovation in Marketing: Ernest Dichter, Motivation Studies and Psychoanalytic Consumer Research in Great Britain, 1950s–1970s'. *Management and Organizational History* 2(3), 219–36.

Schweingruber, D. (2006) 'Success Through a Positive Mental Attitude?: The Role of Positive Thinking in Door-to-Door Sales'. *The Sociological Quarterly* 47(1), 41–68.

Schweingruber, D. and Berns, N. (2003) 'Doing Money Work in a Door-to-Door Sales Organization'. *Symbolic Interaction,* 26(3), 447–71.

Sechele, L. (2011) 'Youth Unemployment and Self-Employment in Botswana'. Unpublished PhD Thesis, University of Essex.

Sedgewick, E. K. and Frank, A. (eds.) (1995) *Shame and Its Sisters: A Silvan Tomkins Reader.* Durham, NC: Duke University Press.

Senier, L., Mayer, B., Brown, P., and Morello-Frosch, R. (2007) 'School Custodians and Green Cleaners: New Approaches to Labor Environment Coalitions'. *Organization and Environment* 20(3), 304–24.

Sennett, R. (1998) *The Corrosion of Character: The Personal Consequences of Work in the New Capitalism.* New York: Norton.

Sennett, R. (2008) *The Craftsman.* London: Allen Lane.

Seno, D. and Lukas, B. A. (2007) 'The Equity Effect of Product Endorsement by Celebrities: A Conceptual Framework from a Co-Branding Perspective'. *European Journal of Marketing* 41(1/2), 121–34.

Sheller, M. (2004) 'Automotive Emotions: Feeling the Car'. *Theory, Culture and Society* 21(4/5): 221–42.

Sherman, R. (2010) 'The Production of Distinctions: Class, Gender, and Taste Work in the Lifestyle Management Industry'. *Qualitative Sociology,* 34(1), 201–19.

Sherry, Jr., J. F. (1998) 'The Soul of the Company Store: Nike Town Chicago and the Emplaced Brand-Scape'. In J. F. Sherry Jr. (ed.), *Servicescapes.* Lincolnwood, IL: NTC Business Books.

Shin, K.-H. and Timberlake, M. (2000) 'World Cities in Asia: Cliques, Centrality and Connectedness'. *Urban Studies,* 37(12), 2257–85.

Siebert, S. and Wilson, F. (2013) 'All Work and No Pay: Consequences of Unpaid Work in the Creative Industries'. *Work, Employment and Society* 27(4), 711–21.

Simmel, G. (1957 [1904]) 'Fashion'. *The American Journal of Sociology* LXII 6, 541–58.

Simmel, G. (1997 [1903]) 'The Metropolis and Mental Life'. In Frisby, D. and Featherstone, M. (eds.) *Simmel on Culture,* London: Sage.

Bibliography

Simms, C. D. and Trott, P. (2006) 'The Perceptions of the BMW Mini Brand: The Importance of Historical Associations and the Development of a Model'. *Journal of Product and Brand Management* 15(4), 228–38.

Sims, D. (2005) 'You Bastard: A Narrative Exploration of the Experience of Indignation within Organizations'. *Organization Studies* 26(11), 1625–40.

Skov, L. (2002) 'Hong Kong Fashion Designers as Cultural Intermediaries: Out of Global Garment Production'. *Cultural Studies* 16(4), 553–69.

Skov, L. (2009) 'Ethics and the Fashion Industry in West Europe'. Creative Encounters Working Paper, CBS, Copenhagen. Retrieved from http://openarchive.cbs.dk/handle/10398/7770 4 Sept. 14.

Slater, D. (1997) *Consumer Culture and Modernity*. Cambridge: Polity.

Slater, D. (2011) 'Marketing as a Monstrosity: The Impossible Place between Culture and Economy'. In Zwick, D. and Cayla, J. (eds.), *Inside Marketing: Practices, Ideologies, Devices*. Oxford: Oxford University Press.

Slavishak, E. (2010) 'Made by the Work'. In Moore, L. J and Kosut, M. *The Body Reader: Essential Social and Cultural Readings*. New York, NYU Press, 147–163.

Sloan, M. (2004) 'The Effects of Occupational Characteristics on the Experience and Expression of Anger in the Workplace'. *Work and Occupations*, 31(1), 38–72.

Sloan, M. M. (2012) 'Unfair Treatment in the Workplace and Worker Well-Being: The Role of Coworker Support in a Service Work Environment'. *Work and Occupations* 39(1), 3–34.

Smith, A. (1976 [1759]) *The Theory of Moral Sentiments*, edited by D. D. Raphael and A. L. Macfie. Oxford: Clarendon Press.

Smith, A. (1999 [1796]) *The Wealth of Nations*. Harmondsworth: Penguin Books.

Smith, C. and McKinlay, A. (2009) 'Creative Industries and Labour Process Analysis'. In McKinlay, A. and Smith, C. (eds.), *Creative Labour: Working in the Creative Industries*. London: Palgrave Macmillan.

Smith Maguire, J. (2008) 'Leisure and the Obligation of Self-Work: An Examination of the Fitness Field'. *Leisure Studies* 27(1), 59–75.

Smith Maguire, J., Strickland, P., and Frost, W. (2013) 'Familiness as a Form of Value for Wineries: A Preliminary Account'. *Journal of Wine Research* 24(2), 112–27.

Soar, M. (2000) 'The Politics of Culture Jamming: Adbusters on the Web and in Print'. *M/C Reviews* 12 Apr. 2000. http://www.uq.edu.au/mc/reviews/features/politics/jamming.html (accessed Oct. 2014).

Soar M. (2002) 'The First Things First Manifesto and the Politics of Culture Jamming: Towards a Cultural Economy of Graphic Design and Advertising'. *Cultural Studies* 16(4): 570–92.

Sohn-Rethel, A. (1977) *Intellectual and Manual Labour: A Critique of Epistemology*. London: Macmillan.

Sombart, W. (1922 [1913]) *Luxury and Capitalism*. Ann Arbor: University of Michigan Press.

Sommerlund, J. (2008) 'Mediations in Fashion'. *Journal of Cultural Economy* 1(2), 165–80.

Sosteric, M. (1996) 'Subjectivity and the Labour Process: A Case Study in the Restaurant Industry'. *Work, Employment and Society* 10(2), 297–318.

Stare, M. (2007) 'Service Development in Transition Economies: Achievements and Missing Links'. In Bryson, J. R. and Daniels, P. W. (eds.), *The Handbook of Service Industries*, Cambridge: Edward Elgar.

Steinberg, R. J. and Figart, D. M. (1999) 'Emotional Labor since the Managed Heart'. *Annals of the American Academy of Political and Social Science* 561, 8–26.

Stewart, K. (2007) *Ordinary Affects*. Durham, NC: Duke University Press.

Stranger, M. (2011) *Surfing Life: Surface, Substructure and the Commodification of the Sublime*. Farnham Surrey and Burlington, VT: Ashgate Publishing Ltd.

Strangleman, T. and Warren, T. (2008) *Work and Society: Sociological Approaches, Themes and Methods*. London: Routledge.

Strasser, S., McGovern, C., and Judt, M. (eds.) (1998) *Getting and Spending: European and American Consumer Societies in the Twentieth Century*. New York: German Historical Institute, Washington DC and Cambridge University Press.

Strasser, S. (ed.) (2003) *Commodifying Everything: Relationships of the Market*. Oxford: Routledge.

Strauss, A. (1985) 'Work and the Division of Labour'. *The Sociological Quarterly* 26(1), 1–19.

Strickland, P., Smith Maguire, J., and Frost, W. (2013) 'Using Family Heritage to Market Wines: A Case Study of Three "New World" Wineries in Victoria, Australia'. *International Journal of Wine Business Research* 25(2), 125–37.

Sturdy, A. and Fineman, S. (2001) 'Struggles for the Control of Affect – Resistance as Politics and Emotion'. In Sturdy, A., Grugulis, I. and Willmott, H. (eds.), *Customer Service: Empowerment and Entrapment*. Basingstoke: Palgrave.

Svendsen, L. (2008) *Work*. Stocksfield: Acumen.

Swedberg, R. (2003) *Principles of Economic Sociology*. Princeton, NJ: Princeton University Press.

Talbot, J. M. (2004) *Grounds for Agreement: The Political Economy of the Coffee Commodity Chain*. Lanham, MD: Rowman and Littlefield Publishers.

Taylor, R. F. (2004) 'Extending Conceptual Boundaries: Work, Voluntary Work and Employment'. *Work, Employment and Society* 18(1), 29–49.

Tennant, L. (2012) 'Finding Work in the New Zealand Film Industry. The Creative Industries Volunteer Ten Years on: Emancipated or Exploited?'. Unpublished Master Thesis, Auckland University of Technology.

Thomas, A. and Garland, R. (1993) 'Supermarket Shopping Lists: Their Effect on Consumer Expenditure'. *International Journal of Retail and Distribution Management* 21(2) 8–15.

Thompson, C. J. and Arsel, Z. (2004) 'The Starbucks Brandscape and Consumers' (Anticorporate) Experiences of Glocalization'. *Journal of Consumer Research* 31(3), 631–42.

Thompson, P. and Smith, C. (2009) 'Labour Power and Labour Process: Contesting the Marginality of the Sociology of Work'. *Sociology*, 43(5), 913–30.

Thomson, K. (1998) *Emotional Capital: Capturing Hearts and Minds to Create Lasting Business Success*. Oxford: Capstone.

Thrift, N. (2005) *Knowing Capitalism*. London: Sage.

Todd, A. M. (2004) 'The Aesthetic Turn in Green Marketing: Environmental Consumer Ethics of Natural Personal Care Products'. *Ethics and the Environment* 9(2), 86–102.

Tokatli, N. (2003) 'Globalization and the Changing Clothing Industry in Turkey'. *Environment and Planning A*, 35(10), 1877–94.

Tomkins, S. S. (1995) *Exploring Affect: The Selected Writings of Silvan S. Tomkins*, edited by E. Virginia Demos. Cambridge: Cambridge University Press.

Tomlinson, J. (2013) *Globalization and Culture*. Hoboken, NJ: Wiley.

Tréguer, J. (2002) *50+ Marketing: Marketing, Communicating and Selling to the over 50s Generations*. Basingstoke: Palgrave Macmillan.

Trentmann, F. (2004) 'Beyond Consumerism: New Historical Perspectives on Consumption'. *Journal of Contemporary History* 39(3), 373–401.

Trentmann, F. (2007) 'Before "Fair Trade": Empire, Free Trade, and the Moral Economies of Food in the Modern World'. *Environment and Planning D: Society and Space* 25(6), 1079–102.

Trentmann, F. (2009) 'Crossing Divides: Consumption and Globalization in History'. *Journal of Consumer Culture* 9(2), 187–220.

Turner, B. (2008) *The Body and Society: Explorations in Social Theory*. 3rd Edition. London: Sage.

Twigg, J., Wolkowitz, C., Cohen, R. L., and Nettleton, S. (eds.) (2011) *Body Work in Health and Social Care*. Chichester: Wiley-Blackwell.

Tyler, M. and Taylor, S. (1998) 'The Exchange of Aesthetics: Women's Work and "the Gift"'. *Gender, Work and Organization* 5(3), 165–71.

Ulver-Sneistrup, S., Askegaard, S. and Kristensen, D. B. (2011) 'The New Work Ethics of Consumption and the Paradox of Mundane Brand Resistance'. *Journal of Consumer Culture* 11(2), 215–38.

Underhill, P. (2000) *Why We Buy : The Science of Shopping*. New York: Touchstone.

Ursell, G. (2000) 'Television Production: Issues of Exploitation, Commodification and Subjectivity in UK Television Labour Markets'. *Media, Culture and Society* 22(6), 805–25.

Vaggi, G. and Groenewegen, P. D. (2003) *A Concise History of Economic Thought: From Mercantilism to Monetarism*. New York: Palgrave Macmillan.

Van Maanen, J. (1991) 'The Smile Factory: Work at Disneyland'. In P. Frost, L. Moore, M. Lewis, C. Lumberg, and J. Martin (eds.), *Reframing Organizational Culture*. Newbury Park, CA: Sage.

Veblen, T. (1964 [1914]) *The Instinct of Workmanship: And the State of the Industrial Arts*. New York: Augustus M. Kelly and the Sentry Press.

Veblen, T. (1965 [1899]) *The Theory of the Leisure Class*. New York: A. M. Kelley, Bookseller.

Venkatesh, A., Joy, A., Sherry Jr, J. F., and Deschenes, J. (2010) 'The Aesthetics of Luxury Fashion, Body and Identify Formation'. *Journal of Consumer Psychology* 20(4), 459–70.

Venkatesh, A. and Meamber, L. A. (2008) 'The Aesthetics of Consumption and the Consumer as an Aesthetic Subject'. *Consumption Markets and Culture* 11(1), 45–70.

Venn, C. (2009) 'Identity, Diasporas and Subjective Change: The Role of Affect, the Relation to the Other, and the Aesthetic'. *Subjectivity*, 26(1), 3–28.

Villarreal, A. T. (2010) 'The Bus Owner, the Bus Driver, and His Lover: Gendered Class Struggle in the Service Work Triangle'. *Work and Occupations*, 37(3), 272–94.

Vinodrai, T. (2013) 'Design in a Downturn? Creative Work, Labour Market Dynamics and Institutions in Comparative Perspective'. *Cambridge Journal of Regions, Economy and Society* 6(1), 159–76.

Votolato, G. (1998) *American Design in the Twentieth Century: Personality and Performance*. Manchester: Manchester University Press.

Walby, S. (2007) 'Introduction: Theorising the Gender Ring of the Knowledge Economy: Comparative Approaches'. In Walby, S., Gottfried, H., Gottschall, K. and Osawa, M. (eds.), *Gendering the Knowledge Economy: Comparative Perspectives*. Basingstoke, Hampshire and New York: Palgrave Macmillan.

Wallerstein, I. (1974) *The Modern World-System*. New York: Academic Press.

Wallerstein, I. (2004) *World-Systems Analysis: An Introduction*. Durham, NC: Duke University Press.

Wallerstein, I. (2011) *The Modern World-System, vol. IV: Centrist Liberalism Triumphant, 1789–1914*. Berkeley: University of California Press.

Warde, A. (2005) 'Consumption and Theories of Practice.' *Journal of Consumer Culture* 7(5): 131–53.

Warde, A. and Martens, L. (2000) *Eating Out: Social Differentiation, Consumption and Pleasure*. Cambridge: Cambridge University Press.

Warf, B. (2007) 'Embodied Information, Actor Networks and Global Value-Added Services'. In Bryson, J. R. and Daniels, P. W. (eds.), *The Handbook of Service Industries*. Cambridge: Edward Elgar.

Warhurst, C. and Nickson, D. (2001) *Looking Good, Sounding Right: Style Counselling in the New Economy*. London: The Industrial Society.

Warren, R. C. (2005) 'Ethics and Service Work'. *The Service Industries Journal*, 25(8), 999–1014.

Webb, J. (2009) 'Gender and Occupation in Market Economies: Change and Restructuring since the 1980s'. *Social Politics: International Studies in Gender, State and Society* 16(1), 82–110.

Weber, M. (1949) 'The Meaning of "Ethical Neutrality" in Sociology and Economics'. In Shils, A. and Finch, H. A. (eds.), *The Methodology of the Social Sciences*. New York: The Free Press.

Weber, M. (1976) *The Protestant Ethic and the Spirit of Capitalism*. London: Allen and Unwin.

Webster, E., Benya, A., Dilata, X., Joynt, K., Ngoepe, K., and Tsoeu, M. (2008) *Making Visible the Invisible: Confronting South Africa's Decent Work Deficit*. Report Commissioned by the Department of Labour, Pretoria.

Weeks, K. (2007) 'Life Within and Against Work: Affective Labor, Feminist Critique, and Post-Fordist Politics'. *Ephemera: Theory and Politics in Organization* 7(1), 233–49.

Weeks, K. (2011) *The Problem with Work. Feminism, Marxism, Antiwork Politics and Postwork Imaginaries*. Durham, NC: Duke University Press.

Welsch, W. (1997) *Undoing Aesthetics*. London: Sage.

Wernick, A. (1991) *Promotional Culture: Advertising, Ideology and Symbolic Expression*. London, Sage.

Wetherell, M. (2012) *Affect and Emotion: A New Social Science Understanding*. Sage: London.

Whalen, J., Whalen, M., and Henderson, K. (2002) 'Improvisational Choreography in Teleservice Work'. *British Journal of Sociology* 53(2), 239–58.

Wharton, A. S. (1993) 'The Affective Consequences of Service Work: Managing Emotions on the Job'. *Work and Occupations*, 20, 205–32.

Wheeler, K. and Glucksmann, M. (2013) 'Economies of Recycling, "Consumption Work" and Divisions of Labour in Sweden and England'. *Sociological Research Online* 18(1), 9. http://www.socresonline.org.uk/18/1/9.html

White, H. C. (2002) *Markets from Networks: Socioeconomic Models of Production*. Princeton, NJ: Princeton University Press.

Whyte, W. (1946) 'When Workers and Customers Meet'. In Whyte, W. (ed.), *Industry and Society*. New York: McGraw-Hill.

Williams, C. C. (2005) *A Commodified World?: Mapping the Limits of Capitalism*. London: Zed Books.

Williams, C.C. and Windebank J. (2003) 'The Slow Advance and Uneven Penetration of Commodification'. *International Journal of Urban and Regional Research* 27 (2) 250-264.

Williams, C. L. and Connell, C. (2010) '"Looking Good and Sounding Right": Aesthetic Labor and Social Inequality in the Retail Industry'. *Work and Occupations* 37(3), 349–77.

Williams, R. (1989 [1958]) 'Culture Is Ordinary'. In *Resources of Hope: Culture, Democracy, Socialism*. London: Verso.

Willis, P. (1990) *Common Culture*. Buckingham: Open University Press.

Wilson, A. (1998) 'Decentralization and the Avon Lady in Bangkok, Thailand'. *PoLAR: Political and Legal Anthropology Review* 21(1), 77–83.

Wilson, E. (2003) *Adorned in Dreams: Fashion and Modernity*. London: I.B. Tauris.

Windels, K., Mallia, K., and Broyles, S. (2013) 'Soft Skills: The Difference Between Leading and Leaving the Advertising Industry?'. *Journal of Advertising Education* 17(2), 17–27.

Wissinger, E. (2007) 'Modelling a Way of Life: Immaterial and Affective Labour in the Fashion Modelling Industry'. *Ephemera: Theory and Politics in Organization* 7, 250–69.

Wissinger, E. (2012) 'Managing the Semiotics of Skin Tone: Race and Aesthetic Labor in the Fashion Modeling Industry'. *Economic and Industrial Democracy* 33(1), 125–43.

Witz, A., Warhurst, C., and Nickson, D. (2003) 'The Labour of Aesthetics and the Aesthetic of Organization'. *Organization* 10(1): 33–54.

Wolkowitz, C. (2006) *Bodies at Work*. London, Thousand Oaks, CA and New Delhi: Sage.

Wong, M. W. (2012) 'Negotiating Class, Taste, and Culture via the Arts Scene in Singapore: Postcolonial or Cosmopolitan Global?'. *Asian Theatre Journal* 29(1), 233–54.

Wouters, C. (2007) *Informalization: Manners and Emotions since 1890*. Los Angeles, CA: Sage Publications.

Wright, D. (2005) 'Mediating Production and Consumption: Cultural Capital and "Cultural Workers"'. *British Journal of Sociology* 56: 105–21.

Xu, B. Y. (1991) *Marketing to China: One Billion New Customers*. Lincolnwood: NTC Business Books.

Xu, G. and Feiner, S. (2007) '*Meinü Jingji*/China's Beauty Economy: Buying Looks, Shifting Value, and Changing Place'. *Feminist Economics* 13(3–4), 307–23.

Yano, C. R. (2009) 'Wink on Pink: Interpreting Japanese Cute as It Grabs the Global Headlines'. *The Journal of Asian Studies* 68(03), 681.

Yue, A. (2006) 'Cultural Governance and Creative Industries in Singapore'. *International Journal of Cultural Policy* 12(1), 17–33.

Zelizer, V. A. (1985) *Pricing the Priceless Child: The Changing Social Value of Children*. New York: Basic Books.

Zelizer, V. A. (2005) *The Purchase of Intimacy*. Princeton, NJ: Princeton University Press.

Zhang, L. (2010) *In Search of Paradise: Middle-Class Living in a Chinese Metropolis*. Ithaca NY: Cornell University Press.

Zukin, S. and Smith Maguire, J. (2004) 'Consumers and Consumption'. *Annual Review of Sociology* 30(1), 173–97.

Zwick, D., Bonsu, S. K., and Darmody, A. (2008) 'Putting Consumers to Work: "Co-creation" and New Marketing governmentality'. *Journal of Consumer Culture* 8(2), 163–96.

Zwick, D. and Denegri Knott, J. (2009) 'Manufacturing Customers: The Database as New Means of Production'. *Journal of Consumer Culture* 9(2), 221–47.

Index

Ritzer, George, 22, 55–6, 102
Rival views of market society, 30, 140, 193
Routine work, 66, 84, 91–2, 95, 98, 106–7, 112, 117, 119, 120, 150–1

sales assistant, 6–7, 48, 90, 91
science and technology studies (STS), 38–40, 190
secularisation, 53
seduction, 48, 54–6, 66, 67, 70, 134, 141–5, 149, 154, 168, 193, 199, 202, 203, 213, 218
Self, 53
  self management, 141, 211
self assembly, 167
Self destruction/destructive markets thesis, 33–6, 193, 194–5
self service, 50
Selling spaces
  and feeling in Puerto Rico, 144
  branded spaces, 175, 176, 205
  flagships, 172
  ordinary spaces, 172
  streets and shops, 48, 55
  themed spaces, 145, 175
Sensory, 3, 10, 12, 61
  experience of work, 129
  dimensions of feeling, 138
  and aesthetics, 166, 169, 171, 176–7
service triangle, 153–4
Services, 2 11, 71, 75, 77
  limits of concept, 81
  local cultures of, 155–7
  specialisation, 80
shoplifting, 202
shopping trolleys, 38–40, 50
shopping, 43, 45–6, 48–9
sign value, 64–5, 170, 215
Silk Road, 18
Simmel, George, 54, 181
Singapore, 10, 43, 85
Skill, 12, 76
  aesthetic labour and, 185–6
  collective, 115–6
  emotional labour and, 115, 151, 212–3
  folding jeans, 115–6
  formation of, 12
  low 91, 110–18

national differences in definition, 114
soft skills, 116–7
tacit and social, 12, 96, 114–6
training, 90
skin tone, 185–6, 218
Skov, Lise, 82, 88, 89, 199
Smith Maguire, Jennifer, 90, 93, 143
Smith, Adam, 30–1
snapshot aesthetics, 171–2
social media, 65, 102, 174
  and brands, 146, 184, 204–5
socialisation, 136
sociology, 8, 38, 45, 136, 181
Sombart, Werner, 18, 46
sonic branding, 176
spectacular consumption, 49, 66, 69, 71, 172, 176, 186, 190, 191, 205, 213, 215, 217
Spirit of capitalism, 36–7, 47
sport, 69, 76, 88, 103, 172, 173
staging value, 170–1, 215
Starbucks, 22, 27, 57, 174, 175, 176, 205
subculture, 5, 63–4
Subjectivity, 54, 57
  and aesthetics, 165, 167
  consumers moral dispositions, 202
  personal meaning of brand, 174
  working and consuming, 220
supermarket, 38–40, 50, 141
  aesthetics of rationality, 172–3
supply chain, 7–8, 11, 32, 50–1, 194
sustainability, 197–9
Sweden, 22
symbolic value, 2, 4, 11–12, 84–5, 89, 103, 215, 217
  content of cultural products, 64, 68, 83, 85
symbolic violence, 63

tabbies, 48
Taste
  and aesthetics, 164
  and class, 62–3, 87, 181
  and cocktails, 115
  changes in, 182
  differences between social groups, 165